G000244622

RONALD HEARN: MEDIUM

By the same author:

The Little Dutch Boy (Book Guild, 1993)
The Little Boy Who Listened (Book Guild, 2008)

Books that feature the work of Ronald Hearn

The Enfield Poltergeist by Guy Lyon Playfair
Belle of Two Worlds by Pamela Mills
Inevitable Journey by Donald Galloway
Window to the Past by Hanz Holzer

RONALD HEARN: MEDIUM

A Yeoman of England

Ronald Hearn

Book Guild Publishing
Sussex, England

First published in Great Britain in 2010 by
The Book Guild Ltd
Pavilion View
19 New Road
Brighton, BN1 1UF

Copyright © Ronald Hearn 2010

The right of Ronald Hearn to be identified as the author of this
work has been asserted by him in accordance with the
Copyright, Designs and Patents Act 1988.

All rights reserved. No part of this publication may be reproduced,
transmitted, or stored in a retrieval system, in any form or by any
means, without permission in writing from the publisher, nor be
otherwise circulated in any form of binding or cover other than
that in which it is published and without a similar condition being
imposed on the subsequent purchaser.

Typesetting in Times by
Keyboard Services, Luton, Bedfordshire

Printed and bound in Great Britain by
CPI Antony Rowe

A catalogue record for this book is available from
The British Library

ISBN 978 1 84624 516 9

With special thanks to Peter Ingold, the best friend one could wish for and without whose great help and support throughout the years I would not have been able to write this book.

Contents

Acknowledgements

Donna Suwall, Edith Roman, Mary Sharp, George Burns, Rudolf Schneider, Pamela Mills, Maurice Barbanell, Beryl Padgem, Betty Lawrence, whose music lingers on in the heart, and Robert Anderson, for his excellent help in editing the manuscript.

1

My Family

'Where are the Yeomen, the Yeomen of England?'

These are the words of an old song which I remember being sung when I was a young lad. It was a very rousing song and one which I always enjoyed hearing then and which I often still hear in my mind. More recently, however, those words have become important to me in a way that I could not have, for most of my life, imagined, and therein lies an interesting story of discovery that ultimately proves that there were 'Yeomen of England' and that there still are! To explain this curious statement, I should begin at the very beginning...

I was born in Stonebridge Park in the London Borough of Willesden. My parents had by then managed to rent a flat in a one-up, one-down terrace after having had a very hard time. Mother had been in service and Father, after his discharge from the army in the First World War, undertook all sorts of jobs but also had long periods of unemployment. Life was far from easy and, apart from being considered as working class, we were very poor and often relied on what were called meal tickets, better known as 'pink tickets', which you handed in to get food. Fortunately, my parents were very proud people and independent so they would accept such a situation only as long as it was absolutely necessary and luckily that was not for too long. In due course things got better, though we remained a family who had to work hard. Fortunately none of us was ever afraid of hard work, although that alone never afforded us much status.

Our family comprised of my brother, Bill, who was seven years older than me, and my sister, Winifred, who was three years older. There was a half-sister, Marjorie, who never lived with us as she was adopted by my father's parents, but with whom we did have contact from time to time. Being the youngest family member had its advantages but I was never really spoilt. There would have been a younger brother but unfortunately he was stillborn. I must confess that I wished he *had* lived, as he would have been only a year younger than me and I felt we would have been close. Bill was a fine brother and was good to me when I was a child as he would push me around in my pram and enjoy doing it. However, as we grew older we drew apart to a great degree and, although I am sure we loved each other, I could not somehow get close to him.

Winifred, who hated to be called by that name and insisted it should be Winnie, was very much closer to me and it seemed that Father wanted us to be together always. As our home backed on to a recreation ground, there was little chance of disobeying him as we could be easily seen from our living-room window, and at that time neighbours were apt to report if children were doing things they oughtn't. So for a few years we were known as the twins. We both had curly hair, the only difference being hers was fair and mine dark brown just like Mother's. She was a little taller than me at the time but there are photos of us wearing clothes that Father's mother had made for us out of pieces of left-over material. This was a great help to my parents as they could not afford to dress us like many other children. For all that, we were happy enough, as the photos show. I often smile when looking at a photo of me sitting on a cushion and looking like Little Lord Fauntleroy in the 1930s film. I am dressed in a little outfit made by Grandmother and look rather serious. It was the first photo taken of me as I was born a blue baby and had to be smacked into life, and then, until the age of four, was too ill to have a photo taken.

Mother was an incredible lady whom I loved dearly. When old enough to know and understand, I realised she had been through a great deal of hard work and worry, but she was never one to be beaten. She was not afraid of anyone or anything, though I feel she would have had good reason to be, and she loved us children, sometimes perhaps a little too much. She was born in Stockport, although her parents were Devonshire born and bred. She was one of identical twins and, although I never knew her sister Mabel, I cannot tell one from the other in the photos I have. They were extremely beautiful ladies, very fashionable as far as times and lack of means would allow, and had very similar personalities, which is not always the case with twins. I have learned more recently they were Suffragettes and I think that at some point they must have chained themselves to the railings in a demonstration, as I now recall my father saying to Mother when she got angry about anything: 'Well, you'd better chain yourself to the railings then.' I feel very proud to know this now but even when I was younger I realised that, although she was kind and caring, she would always fight for what she believed in. Luckily I inherited this characteristic from her, although I am sure she must have inherited it from *her* forebears, as we shall later see.

Mother told me her parents had moved up to Stockport from a little village in Devon called Landkey, near Barnstaple, in order for her father, Henry Yeo, to take up journalism for a better living. Sadly her mother died from typhoid fever at the age of thirty-three; Henry also had it but survived. Mother said he married his nurse, a lady named Edith Lawson who had been a hospital matron, and they had one son, but there seems to be no record of this. She said that she and Mabel were unable to stand the strict discipline of their stepmother and so, at the age of eighteen, they ran away to London where Mother went into service and Mabel became a respectable barmaid. It could not have been easy living in the big city but the young ladies had no regrets since they felt they had escaped from what would have been a difficult life. Sadly Mabel died from influenza in the First World War epidemic without ever getting married, although according to Mother she had a lot of gentlemen friends. She was fiercely independent and a very popular barmaid; many of the regulars of The Greyhound public house in Dulwich where she worked turned out for her funeral.

Mother was working for a family who took her to their hearts and she was happy there. She had agreed with the lady of the house that she would do all the hard work of cleaning but did not want to do any cooking. This suited the lady as she liked cooking and Mother only had to do a little if the lady was away. I could never quite believe Mother wasn't interested in cooking as I still have memories of some lovely dishes she cooked – plain, honest dishes that one never sees now as the 'fancy stuff' has taken over. Having said that, I can understand her reluctance: I myself am a very good cook, both of the fancy stuff and the plain, but I do not *like* cooking. To me it is one of those things which, if it has to be done, then it might as well be done well. In a way it is a discipline like any other and I am one of the most disciplined people you will find. It was while working with this family that

Mother had a child called Marjorie. The details are somewhat mysterious and Mother would never say much about it, however often I asked her. It was at this time she met my father who was a few years younger and whose parents adopted Marjorie. He was absolutely mad about Mother and so they were married, set up home and raised a family.

Mother was remarkable indeed. At the age of seventeen she had contracted glandular fever and had been told by a Harley Street specialist she should not marry, and, if she did, she should not have children. Apart from those I have mentioned she had three miscarriages, making eight pregnancies in all. I remember when she had a collapse in her early sixties she saw the same specialist who recognised her and remembered what he had told her. He proceeded to scold her soundly: 'You are one of the miracles of modern nature as you have no right to still be here. However, I am delighted to see you, although I must warn you that you have gone as far as you can go now and work is out for you in future.' As he was being shown out, Mother whispered to me, 'We'll see about that!' and well she meant it. However, it was not to be, and eventually she suffered a stroke and was an invalid for six years, always complaining she was not allowed to work. Finally, after several more strokes, she went into a coma and passed on at the age of seventy-one. Never have I seen a greater fighter, nor anyone who bore her suffering so well. With her, there were always things that had to be done. I remember her cleaning the windows once and falling down in a faint due to a weak heart (she carried a heart twice its normal size as a result of the fever). We brought her indoors and gave her some brandy and tried to make her rest, but her eyes were already on the clock and she got up to finish the windows, saying, 'It's got to be done! Your father will be home at five and want his tea on the table.'

At the age of thirty she had a nervous illness called St Vitus' dance (chorea) and at the same time her hair turned pure white overnight. Actually it was lovely and suited her well and she was known for years around the district as 'the lady with white hair'. She also had terribly ulcerated legs, which had to be bound, and for much of the time she was in great pain. Many is the time I saw her kneeling at the washtub, scrubbing away with tears in her eyes. When we would tell her to leave it, her reply was the perennial 'it had to be done'. Things were much harder in those days and there were no washing machines and labour-saving appliances; it all had to be done by hand the hard way and Mother was only one of many women who had little or no choice but to do it. It is no wonder that, when she passed away, the doctors said she had completely collapsed as she had no more to give. She was always a giver rather than a taker and her joy was in giving and doing for others, another thing which maybe I inherit from her as I try to do the same.

She was passionately fond of animals and we always had a cat. Mother worked for animals when she could and the animal societies wanted her to become an official but this she couldn't do. I remember two incidents where she just 'sailed' into situations when I would beg her not to get involved. In one she saw a man beating his dog very badly and the man had just bought an ice cream. She grabbed hold of the dog's leash and started to beat the man who dropped his ice cream and Mother trod on it. She told him she was an RSPCA official and that, if she ever caught him doing this again, she would take action. He was a big burly man and I was afraid for Mother, but need not have been as he walked away very meekly while making a fuss of the dog. One felt he would not ill treat it again.

The second incident took place in a side road near to where we lived. A horse and cart came along going at great speed and the driver was whipping the horse and treating it very badly. Mother called out to him to stop and, if he didn't, she would get the police on to him. He turned out to be the son of a local greengrocer and was something of a rough character. I feared for Mother as he looked a real brute. He stopped and started cursing and threatening Mother whereupon she demanded he get down off the cart, which surprisingly he did. She asked how would he like to be put between the shafts of the cart and whipped mercilessly. She further told him that if she ever caught him doing it again she would take action but in the meantime she would have words with his father. He did not utter another word but, like the dog owner, went meekly off and made a show of treating the horse kindly. Whenever we saw him in the future he appeared to have great respect for the horse. Mother did have words with his father, who was a really tough man and what was generally called a rough diamond. Once again I was afraid for Mother, but evidently she tamed him too because we later learned that he boxed his son's ears and gave him a strong warning. Mother was fearless all right!

Despite the fact that she suffered so much during her life, she never lost her looks. Naturally she was not the young beauty she once was but one could always see a hint of someone who had been beautiful and who still had great dignity and charm. I was always very proud of her and, despite our poverty, she always managed to dress beautifully. She was helped in this in later years when she went to help out an old friend who had been ill and needed someone to clean for her. As this was the daughter of the people with whom she had been in service, it was not surprising that her good work and loyalty was not forgotten. The lady she went to was quite well off and happily the same size as Mother, and she would often give Mother clothes and shoes that she didn't want any more. Sometimes these things had not even been worn and were always of high quality. Fortunately everything suited Mother so well and seemed to set off her lovely white hair. I have an abiding memory of her walking along the street in a beautiful green velvet dress with a brown corduroy coat and a velvet hat to match, the whole outfit topped by a silver fox fur. I always used to put her hat on for her as she could never get the right angle, and before she left home I would make sure her make-up was right, one thing she always seemed to get wrong. It made me so proud to walk beside such an elegant lady. To me she was like a queen, even to her walk, and I would notice curtains being drawn back as she passed and a bit of jealous tut-tutting coming from 'nosey neighbours'.

Despite illness throughout her life, my mother hung on until the last and always tried to do what she felt was her duty. I loved my mother dearly and she often said I was the only one who understood what she was going through and that I made her feel better because I was so calm and never got into a panic. If I did, I never let her see it as I felt for her and the pain she was suffering. When she had a stroke at the age of sixty-five life was tough for all of the family because she needed constant attention. Mother was a fighter and often would try to do things she was not supposed to and then get into a muddle. Father, who nursed her most often, got annoyed and when he was out of the room she would say to me, 'Let me do it before he comes back!' but I had to restrain her as she really could not cope. She passed on six years later after she had gone into a coma for a few days. The evening before she passed I was booked to take a meeting and I wondered whether I should go or not, so I sat by her bedside for a while and hoped she would somehow know I was with her. After a time she suddenly opened her eyes, sat up in the bed, reached over to put her arms around me and said, 'You go to your meeting, Ron, I will be all right,' after which she kissed me and lay down again and went back into her coma. She never regained consciousness, at least not in this world. It was an extraordinary event, to say the least, but it gave me an enormous sense of peace knowing she would be free of all her pains and so I went to my meeting knowing it was what she wished.

If one person in the family was religious it was certainly not my father as he did not seem to believe in anything on the spiritual or religious side, although he had very strong opinions on politics and as to how everything should generally be done. However, my godfather was minister of the little mission church which was just over the road from our home and we children had to attend his services regularly. Because we would be watched until we had entered the church, there was no way we could play truant. For me it was rather too much as I had to attend three times on a Sunday, and being in the choir there was choir practice on a Tuesday and yet another service on a Thursday as well. This lasted until I was fifteen when I rebelled and refused to go any more. Mother was a little disappointed, even though she rarely went to church herself; she felt it was the right thing to do and that, being in the hands of the minister, my godfather, I would be well guided. If he had been allowed to have his way I would have become a minister, but that honour I fiercely declined. When he climbed into his pulpit he truly put the fear of God into everyone, me included, but I could never believe all he said. I suppose I must already have had strong feelings then about what I believed and what I wanted to be, and also about what I *did not* want to be. I believe our lives are mapped out before we come here, at least to a very great extent, and so whatever will be will be.

The one thing I did enjoy about church was the hymn singing. Having a reasonably good voice I sometimes had to do solos, which was somewhat difficult as the other choirboys would try to make me giggle. I always just about managed to make it through. I did not always like the things I had to sing but there was something stirring about it all once the congregation joined in. I still remember the words of most hymns and anthems even to this day. Mother would often sing some of the hymns at home and I once asked her why she didn't come to the church herself. She told me that Father would not allow it as he wanted her to be with him so they could have some peace and quiet without us children. That, I discovered, was the reason he insisted we went to church – merely to get us out of the way!

Father was a very difficult man: his background and upbringing was anything but easy. He had been in the army in the First World War, which for him was a ghastly experience that left him forbidding us boys to have toy guns or soldiers. He did not even want us to see war films and whenever he could he would steer our minds away from such things. He was not a man one could get really near to, and I often longed to be able to tell him my troubles. He had a strong temper and yet he never really hit any of us; his punishment was to lecture us on not only the wrongs we had done, but on how much he had sacrificed and worked for us. He would sometimes go on for an hour, and often, if we had gone to bed, he would get us up and start all over again. Many times I asked him to hit me and let me go back to bed but he would not be moved.

Yet for all that he had a very kind and good side. However hard times were, whether he was in work or not, we would always be fed and clothed to the best he could afford. He always said that if he had it we could have it, but if he didn't we would have to do the best we could. I have a lot to thank him for: though sometimes I did not want to do what he wanted me to, now I am more than glad he made me. He often used to take Mother, my sister and me to the local cinema called the Hippodrome where we would sit 'up in the gods', from where we had a very good view and where we would see all the old films for four old pence (adults) and twopence (children). It was where I discovered how much I love films and cinema. Sometimes he would also take us to the music halls, mostly the Shepherd's Bush Empire or The Metropolitan in the Edgware Road in London. I just loved seeing and hearing all those good old artists and the 'spit and sawdust' atmosphere; perhaps a bit of their talent rubbed off as I can sing and do a very convincing music-hall act myself. It was all great fun and we would have a bag of peanuts to chew, and after the entertainment we took home supper from the cooked meat shop. My parents would have faggots and pease pudding while my sister and I would have saveloys, which we were often allowed to eat on the bus home while they were still hot.

One of the things that I will always remember on one of our visits to the Shepherd's Bush Empire occurred when we were waiting in the queue to see the show. It was quite the usual thing for people such as jugglers, tap dancers and singers to come along to entertain those waiting. and on this particular occasion an elderly lady with long grey hair, and who was rather shabbily dressed, stopped at the side of the queue and began to sing. With her was a man whom I assumed to be her husband. She had the most beautiful voice I had ever heard and I felt she must have been an opera singer or at least have a trained voice. I can still remember the first two lines of her song – 'We will meet again by the roses / In the valley of the moon' – but it was not one I had heard before. The tune was absolutely beautiful and lingered in my memory. It was not until a long time later, after I became interested in classical music, that I listened to Mendelsohn's Violin Concerto and suddenly recognised this beautiful melody in one of the movements.

Brother Bill, being seven years older than me, never took part in these outings and he was not especially interested anyway. His interests were so different and he would always be off with his mates. I never knew what they got up to as Bill could be very secretive. Actually I think he was more shy than anything but I wish it were possible to be able to tell of more things that we shared. Nonetheless I have good memories of Bill and, although he did not share my interests, I feel sure he was as proud of me as I was of him. One characteristic we both shared was perfectionism. He worked as a chromium plater and would not be satisfied until his work was perfect, no matter how many times he might have to redo a thing. It is the same with me. However, I don't think I possess his absolute charm and good manners, for he was one of nature's gentlemen. He had a great sense of humour and in later years could be a tease. On the other hand, he could sometimes be a very different character. When he was seventeen he suffered a fractured skull in a cycling accident, and this injury was compounded when he later ruptured a blood vessel in his head while on army exercises. Both accidents left him with a form of schizophrenia that on rare occasions resulted in a very different side to his personality coming to the fore.

Winnie, to whom I always stayed close, was a mixture in temperament of both Mother and Father. She had the charm and kindliness of Mother and could be quite ladylike when she wanted to be, but could also often display some of Father's temper and strong determination to have her way. Yet she too had a great sense of humour in most things and could be fiercely independent. She never married despite having two or three men who would have been only too pleased to have the chance. Winnie always said that she never wanted to be anyone's servant and she did not like housework. However, she did like cooking and was excellent at needlework and knitting. She could have won competitions and prizes for her beautiful work, which included tapestry, but declared that she just loved doing it. With all that she was endlessly patient but in other things could be extremely *im*patient. Like Mother, she was passionately fond of animals and especially cats, and like Mother, too, she would have the same reply to anyone who dared criticise her for making so much fuss over them, saying 'Well, they can't answer back like you and they are grateful for what they get.' Not something everyone would agree with, but she, like most of us in the family, never cared what people thought or said as long as we felt within ourselves that what we were doing was right.

As children Winnie and I spent a lot of time together, partly because we liked being together but also, as I've said, on Father's insistence. In doing so, I rather missed out on a lot of the things I would have liked to do. That's not to say there weren't times when I was able to escape Father's watchful eye and get up to some mischief with the boys, just as my sister did with the girls, but usually such escapades ended with us getting into trouble. If the neighbours didn't report us then we would probably come home with the evidence of our misdeeds on our person. Once I went paddling in the local river and I slipped in getting myself soaking wet. There was no way of drying off and Mother was very cross when we got home but kindly sent us to bed early so that Father wouldn't know. Somehow, though, he found out and I was hauled out of bed for the usual lecture.

I used to go to the cinema five times a week in my teens and my frequent companion was Winnie, who loved films and the theatre as much as I did. We often went to the theatre on a Saturday evening when we would queue to get into the gallery, which was all we could afford. After I came out of the army, Saturday night and Sunday afternoon at the flicks was a regular fixture. Not having to go to church any more was a relief and I certainly felt no guilt about going to the cinema on a Sunday. By then I was not so attached to Winnie and usually went with some pals.

It would not be true to say that I had an unhappy childhood, although like most children we could not really understand why we could not have everything we wanted. While others were getting bicycles and more expensive gifts for Christmas, we had to be content with a brown paper bag containing a few little items bought at the local Woolworths. There would be things like a torch, little games and maybe a jigsaw puzzle, plus an orange and a few nuts. Sometimes Father would make something for us as he was quite good at woodwork. Once my sister got a little doll's house, which gave her great delight, while I got a wooden soldier, which I quite liked but could never understand why he made this as he was always so against war. One time the lady for whom Mother worked gave me a fort with toy soldiers and I enjoyed it for two days before Father gave it away as he did not want me to become military minded. Little did he know that when out with my friends I played with toy guns and water pistols that, because I could not take them home, a friend hid for me. Similarly I was not allowed to play football with the boys as my parents could not afford to keep having my boots repaired. To me as a child this was hard to understand but as one grew older it made a lot of sense, especially when we all finally went out to work and had to learn the true value of money for ourselves.

Our childhood is a time when our character is formed. In retrospect, however, it seems to me that as a child I never quite got round to forming one, as there were so many things I could do that I could never decide which to concentrate on. Like most children I had a vivid imagination and would spend hours dreaming of how I would like to be, yet knowing it couldn't happen. Coming down to earth, it left me frustrated as I just could not make up my mind. Everything in my life so far seems to have been chosen *for* me, which leaves me looking back as I did then and wishing I had tried harder in achieving some of those other things. Despite what I do now, which is something that has proved to be highly successful, I wish I could have pursued other options that would have been more in keeping with the artistic and creative side of my nature. I sometimes think I am to blame for this but the circumstances of my life made it very difficult, if not downright impossible. My only consolation is that in many ways I have at least had a taste of these things.

2

The Misery of Geometry

Being an obedient child I went to school because I had to but not because I wanted to. There were two schools very close to my home: one was the infant and junior school, and just across the road from there was the senior school. All I can remember of the infants was being taken into a classroom by a nice kind lady and then playing with different-coloured bricks all day. This was followed by learning to count and recite the alphabet. With the junior school upstairs began the more rough-and-tumble life, as it was for boys only and the girls had their own department. There seemed to be innumerable teachers and each time we moved up a year there would be a different form master. This was a problem for me because I felt that, as soon as I got used to and felt at ease with one, then another one was foisted on me and the process would begin all over again.

I did not relish the thought of having to face someone who I instinctively knew would make me very unhappy. The top and final class of junior school was taken by a man called Bill Williams and a bigger and more frightening bully you would never find. He insisted on cuffing one round the ear or using his little pointed stick when anyone played around or disobeyed, and delighted in calling me and some of the others a 'namby-pamby'. This was because, if a boy had been kept at home through illness or had brought in a note from his parents asking to be excused from physical training, he would accused him of being a spoilt brat and make his life a misery. It was a very common sight to see parents coming around to sort Mr Williams out and one irate mother even tipped a whole bottle of ink over him. Needless to say we boys enjoyed seeing this spectacle.

Amazingly Mr Williams managed to teach most boys quite a lot. His preferred phrase would be that he 'knocked sense into them' and most of us would agree that was his pedagogical method. I have to admit I did learn a lot there and can even remember some happy times.

At the end of junior school we had a scholarship exam to see if anyone could be sent to secondary school, which would be quite a step up the education ladder, although not too many parents wanted their children to go there as it would mean they would have to buy uniforms and other essentials. There was a small grant involved but it did not cover very much and, it being a working-class area, people could not afford it. However, I passed the scholarship with excellent marks and as it happened my parents were very proud of me and said they would manage to find the extra money somehow. My sister Winnie was already at the Willesden County Secondary school, having passed her scholarship two years earlier, which meant it would be harder still for our parents. Nonetheless they were determined to give us the best education they could afford – something which I will always remember with gratitude. At first I did not like going to the same school as my sister because she could keep an eye on me. Soon, however, it dawned upon me that I could do the same to her and we agreed not to tell tales on each other. It worked out quite well.

One of the tales that I could have told was that Winnie was sweet on a boy called John Neville, who was in the same form. They were always together and he often carried her books home for her. Les and I often used to walk behind them making fun and John used to playfully threaten us but he had a keen sense of humour and could never help laughing about it. They lost touch after school and John went on to become one of Britain's finest actors. Winnie never forgot him and followed his career with interest, but thought John would have long forgotten her. Imagine her surprise more than thirty years later when she went to see him in a play at the Mermaid Theatre and, coming out of the stage door, he saw her through the crowds and made his way through to her and said, 'Hello, Winnie, it's nice to see you after all this time,' and introduced her to his wife. Winnie's other famous friend from school was the composer and conductor Ron Goodwin but they were not so close, although she always remembered him and spoke well of him.

As I approached the school for the first time I remember being surprised to see how much bigger it was than I expected. There were playing fields and next door there was even a swimming pool. The first thing we had to do every day was to assemble in the big hall that doubled as the gymnasium, where we had to sing a hymn and say prayers after which the headmaster would make various announcements and then dismiss us to our forms. The newcomers, myself included, were designated certain rooms which became our permanent form for as long as we were there. We were also told that in Form 1a French would be the language taught, while in 1b it would be German. I was in the latter which did not fill me with pleasure as I thought then that all foreign languages were hard but German was the worst. We were also assigned to a house and mine was 'Normans'. The different house names were mainly for the competitive side of things and I could already see that that might be fun. At first I was not too keen about mixed classes but as maturity approached I rather liked the idea.

What, or rather I should say who, impressed me most at first was the headmaster, Mr Wallis, because he seemed to be a very kindly man yet he could be strict, too. He always took a much more personal interest in the pupils than most and was extremely fair. Even when I was called before him for a punishment I could fully accept his judgement because it felt right. Not all the boys and girls felt the same way, I'm sure, but that is only natural.

On that first day we were told about school uniforms. For the boys it was grey flannel trousers, navy-blue blazers with the school badge on the top pocket and a cap that also had a badge. For the girls it was blue check dresses with blazers like the boys' and panama hats. I always remember my sister refusing to wear the hat, but she had to work to rule; as soon as she got home, though, she would change out of anything to do with the uniform. I hated to wear a cap and only ever put it on when I was approaching the school gates. There was also another reason for this as one would get 'ragged' by other boys and have the cap thrown somewhere from which it was awkward to retrieve.

The hurly-burly of school life involved, of course, a lot more than cap removal but perhaps it is best not to go into too much detail. One had to learn to take it and, as I had a good sense of humour and could see the funny side of things, I was mostly able to laugh it off. I remember once when we were getting changed after sports some of the boys kept me behind in the changing room and took all my clothes and hid them outside before running off. There I was, all alone and naked, just as the Biology mistress, who was doing the rounds to make sure everything was as it should be, opened the door and froze in her tracks. She asked me the silly question as to what was I doing there and why? What else could I say but that some of the boys had played a trick on me, but she did not believe it and said I was to get dressed, go home and report to her in the morning. By then she seemed to have changed her mind which was surprising but I was happy just to be warned not to let it happen again.

The innocent always seem to come off worst in such instances, victims of both the bullying and the disbelief of teachers. Another time I was set upon by a gang of classmates who tried to unbutton me and then piled desks on top of me just before the next mistress came in for a lesson; nonetheless, in the eyes of that teacher I had instigated the whole thing myself and was sent out of the room into the corridor to await the possible wrath of the headmaster, if he happened to pass. I would mostly never tell on the others, although sometimes I wish I had. We would all have a good laugh about it and I would be told by the others I was a good sport.

Something surprising happened shortly after the changing room business. One day the boys in my class were supposed to be taking a Physics lesson but the teacher was ill and so we were told it would be 'a general lesson', whatever that was. We soon found out when who should walk in but the aforesaid Biology mistress. She took one look at us and said, 'What am I going to do with you lot? Of course none of us answered but there were a few whispers from the back as she was very attractive and we were boys fast approaching manhood. She either did not hear or was secretly flattered but any dreams were shattered when she decided we had to write an essay on 'washing up', which most of my peers thought was having a bath. I was secretly elated as I actually knew all about it. Once our papers were handed in and she had read them she said, 'I am disgusted that so few of you know about the subject, but thank goodness there is one of you who knows how it is done and so I am going to ask Hearn to read out what he has written.' My elation turned to horror when I realised I would be in for a lot of ribbing and unkind remarks, but what was done was done and so I read out my piece. The mistress then asked me how I knew so much about the subject and I had to tell her that my mother was often ill and, being the youngest in the family (my brother and sister were out at work then), once I got home from school she would give her orders from her bed, so there would be a meal for the workers when they got home. And so I learned to cook and wash up, which maybe did not please me so much then, but which in the long run has proved an invaluable life skill. Looking back, I often wonder what the Biology mistress thought of the naked young man who knew how to cook and wash up! I must admit after all that, whenever she saw me she always had a nice smile and hello for me! Needless to say it made the other boys rather jealous but, as I told them, you should learn to wash up and you may be smiled upon.

I was not good at, nor fond of, sports such as football or cricket; in fact I was probably useless at them but had to play whether I liked it or not. It meant my parents buying football boots and white cricket flannels, which I thought unnecessary because I just hated being forced to play. On one occasion on the football pitch the other boys decided I should be goalkeeper as a way of getting me involved but I stubbornly refused to try to save anything. The same with cricket where I was useless as a batsman and more so as a fielder, not being able to catch a ball. I just hated it and used to disappear from the field and would be found playing tennis with the girls or sometimes having a swim. They could never report me as I had too much on them and some were jealous of my being with the girls, but it was nice for me to have them all to myself. There was one occasion when the boys thought they would teach me a lesson by hauling me to the practice nets and forcing me to face an onslaught of bowling. Being me I usually get mad at being forced to do something I don't want to and so I hit every one of the balls for six and went on doing so despite their protests. I said, 'You made me do this so you get me out!' Which they couldn't and I stayed in until the end of the lesson. No wonder they never forced me to play cricket again! This was the kind of the thing that at the time made me aware of the fiercely independent spirit growing inside me, the right to do what I believed in and what was the right thing for me.

The boy who used to sit next to me in form was called Leslie Goody. He lived but a few doors away from me and so we had known each other before but never closely. We both rode cycles and so we met to go to school as well as riding home together.

The more I knew of him the more I envied him because he was always much better than me and often told me so! We had a lot of fun one way or another and shared a great love of the singer Peggy Lee, who was very popular at the time and still is. We once wrote a school newspaper which made fun of the teachers but was really harmless, but were severely ticked off when it was reported to the headmaster. It was then that I realised that I could write. My English results were always good and I was accomplished at writing essays and so on.

We also had to do play reading at school, which I loved though I never seemed to get the really good parts. Les always got a leading role and used to boast about it, but I never minded as at that time I doubted my abilities. I had not yet generated enough belief in myself and what I could do, but it was coming along and would grow and take me to where I wanted to be. One of my real disappointments at this time, however, was a missed opportunity to have a real go at acting. The Second World War was on at the time and when there was an air raid we would have to go down to the safety trenches on the playing field. While there one day a man who must have been a talent scout was allowed to come around and ask if any of us would like to play a part in a film called *The Ghost of St Michael's*, starring Will Hay. They needed a lot of schoolboys and would pay the then princely sum of four pounds a week. It would have meant giving up school but, as I was of leaving age then, I rushed home to my parents and told them it was something I would like to do. My father was angry and said no; he and Mother had worked hard to give me a good education and I was going to finish it! Sadly I had to accept as I always knew what they were doing for me must have meant a lot of sacrifice.

A second disappointment happened shortly after that when the husband of the local hairdresser, who was one of the heads of a large and very well-known printing firm, asked me if I would like a job with him as a reader, under his personal supervision. Apparently he had watched me grow up and was impressed by what he saw. My parents had told him about me and I thought I would like a chance to try this. Again I was still at school and the answer given to me was just the same: I had to finish my education. I thought that Les would have liked the acting and possibly the reading job but he seemed indifferent to it and I somehow think he liked school far more than me. Strangely enough, in later years Les was to be instrumental in pointing me to the thing which would more or less be my life's work.

There were lots of things I didn't like about school but naturally when one is young it always seems as though we have to do a lot that seems a waste of time when in fact it helps us to understand and respect other people. I have never liked wasting time but these apparently pointless lessons eventually helped me to understand other people better and to help them, too, which has been a large part of my life's work. We have to be taught but like so many people I never realised at the time how important it is to look, listen and learn. In the end, experience is the best and possibly the only teacher.

Out of all the subjects I took at school, the two I hated most were Physics and Chemistry. I did not need to attend these lessons to discover my dislike as for some time I had realised I was simply not interested in those things. I have always seen myself as an artistic person and anything to do with electrics or mechanics is very mysterious and boring as far as I am concerned, and nothing on earth can make me have any feeling for them or a desire to understand anything connected with them. Although I can type with two fingers, and indeed have used a computer to write this story, I can only succeed at it by being told exactly what to do! The Physics master was a very pleasant man who often joked with us boys and, if he found anyone not doing what they should, he would simply tell us that it would be our loss if we didn't listen or do as we were told. I struggled on for a time, getting the most appalling marks in exams, until our last year where out of all the subjects we were taking we had to drop two, as only seven were required for the Matriculation examination we would take before leaving. I told the master I would drop Physics to which he replied, 'I would jolly well think so, as you are useless.' All the same he wished me good luck in whatever else I would do. The Chemistry master was more or less the same and he said he was relieved I and some of the other boys were dropping out as we were nothing but a useless bunch of idiots who only saw his lessons as a game and were not really interested in anything except ruining experiments. I must admit he was right, but on the other hand he was rather a foolish figure and for some reason had the irritating habit of giggling at everything, which made it hard to take him seriously. So it was a welcome farewell to those two subjects, though that also meant more hard work on others.

There was a war on during the whole of my school years and at the beginning I was evacuated with the school to Northampton, which I did not much care for except that it was a safer place than London. After a short time my father decided that he wanted me and my sister, who was also there, to come back to London where we could be together as a family. We were both happy to be 'home' again but it was not a good time as London bore the brunt of bombing and our nights were spent in air raid shelters, which was not exactly conducive to sleep. We lived in a particularly bad area, because with the recreation ground at the back of our house and a railway with what were then the largest sidings in Europe, plus a large factory area, it was a nightly target for German bombers. So apart from the Anderson shelter, which was often damp and flooded, we were subject to falling bombs, landmines and 'doodlebugs', plus anti-aircraft fire and falling shrapnel. At a later stage we were offered the chance to stay in Wembley in the home of the lady Mother worked for. She had gone away and thought we could take care of her home and use the brick-built shelter in her garden. It was much better than the Anderson but no safer and we were made to sleep there every night. This meant sitting in a chair, which often resulted in our ankles being so swollen in the morning that we could not get our shoes on. We tried to use this as an excuse not to go to school, but Father would not allow us to get out of it except on the odd occasion.

I especially tried to get out of going to school when I had Maths that day. Maths was a compulsory subject and generally I was good at it except for geometry, which falls in with my other 'technical' failings. It wasn't that I feared geometry; it was the master, Mr O'Brian, who we all knew as 'Obbo'. He was a tough-looking man, very bad tempered and quite a bully. He was also the sports master then and I hated to be on the field with him. Sometimes he would take a shower with us after sports when he would make fun of anyone slightly different. I was rather fat at the time, so I was often a victim of his bullying. When it came to Maths he rarely picked on me, but I always sat wondering when my turn would come.

I was never more glad when 'Obbo' left and we got a new teacher, the formidable Miss Thompkins. The said lady was somewhat sour-faced with penetrating eyes that dared one to misbehave. It was easy for some of us to realise why she wasn't married, though on reflection I am sure that underneath the hard steely exterior was a kind and caring person who, because of her experiences, had to do it her way. It would be wrong to say she was a bully in the regular sense of the word but I always felt threatened by her. My friend Les sitting next to me had rather the same thoughts but, being someone I would call a clever dick and too brainy by half, he never provoked the good lady to trouble him. It was me that suffered! I was good in the adding-up and algebra departments, but oh the geometry! As soon as 'Tommo', as she was inevitably known, realised my hopelessness in the subject, she seemed to take endless delight in calling me out in front of class, giving me a stick of chalk, and demanding I solve some geometric conundrum on the blackboard for all to see. Needless to say, I never could but she never gave up trying. For me it was a minor nightmare and so Tommo's lessons were to be avoided. Right to the end I was not able to master geometry: in the final exams we had to do a paper which demanded we answer seven questions on spheres, cones and the like, and by the end I had got through only two and a half of them and most of that was wrong. The amazing thing was that my marks in arithmetic and algebra were so good that I managed to get a 'pass'. Even Tommo said I had done well though she hoped I would never have to solve anything geometrical.

There was just one time that Tommo showed a slight sense of humour. Towards the end of the lesson she said she had to give us our homework and, as she was walking in the aisle between the desks, she happened to stop at mine and asked me to get out the book she would require. Imagine my embarrassment when, on my raising the lid, she could see what I had stuck on the inside for only me to see: a lovely picture of Peggy Lee, and one of a pair of lady's legs. They had been cut out of an advert for Kayser Bond stockings and were really beautiful. I waited for a blast but noticed her trying to stifle a smile. Regaining her composure, she said, 'You had better take those down and don't do it again,' which caused the whole class to laugh as they all knew what was happening and were interpreting the order in another, less polite way. Tommo's final statement was: 'If you could pay attention to your lessons as well as you do to that, then you might get somewhere.'

I did in the end and I have never forgotten this lady who

unwittingly may have taught me something about teaching. I wanted to be a schoolteacher at one time, though it seems it was not meant to be. I have done a lot of teaching in other ways instead and it is something I greatly enjoy. I often wonder what all my teachers at school would think of the way I do it now. There have been teachers in my family some way back in past generations and I feel sure I must have inherited that gift from them. More of that later.

Among the other teachers I would like to mention was one known as Daisy Carr, who was slightly plump and short with hair tied back in a fierce bun. She was our form mistress and for some time an English teacher, and it was she who made me more aware of acting and the theatre. The one thing Daisy could not teach me or force me to enjoy was country dancing. It was probably all right for the girls but I was not alone in thinking it was a 'sissy' thing for boys to do. Daisy did not give up trying and we boys were often reported for refusing to take part. It was another teacher called Tilly Edghill who was actually the girls' games mistress who was successful in getting the boys to participate.

One afternoon we were sent to the big hall where Tilly was going to supervise the dancing. It happened to be an afternoon when we should have been doing something else and the teacher was unavailable. Someone had this bright idea of spending two and a half hours learning 'Sir Roger de Coverley' and other such dances. At first most of the boys refused except for two who were known to be 'pansies', or so it was alleged. We would say anything to try to get out of doing it, and for a long time the rest of the boys sat watching and making rude remarks. It was surprising that Tilly said nothing until it was almost going-home time, when she stopped the music, raised herself to her full height and looked the boys straight in their faces and said, 'You no doubt think you are being clever and disobedient, but I have news for you: until you get off your bottoms and join in you will stay here all night if needs be. I have no other arrangements but I'm sure you do, so make up you minds quickly.'

A motley bunch of boys reluctantly got off their bottoms and went onto the dance floor. They thought if they just sort of messed around it would be OK but Tilly made it clear they would do it properly or else. To this day I am not keen on country dancing but I do like most other kinds and am quite good at it. I will not forget Tilly. She was a very strange sort of lady but the girls all loved her because she was enthusiastic about netball and other games. She had a determination to do what was right and had to be done to maintain discipline, something which I admire and still try to do myself.

Teachers need to believe in what they are doing and Verbena Barge was no exception. She was a very funny lady and had a comical appearance with a dress sense that did not help matters much. She was the butt of many a joke and seemed to have little or no control over her pupils. She was the Geography mistress and actually had a very good way of teaching it. It wasn't one of my most favourite subjects but strangely enough she made it all sound interesting – when, that is, the boys were not calling out funny remarks. She never seemed to get angry; she would just tell the boys not to be naughty and spoil it for others.

The one subject I really loved was art and in the sixth and last form I discovered just how much it would mean to me. By then I had come to realise how sensitive I was, much more suited to the creative world than the scientific. I had deep feelings then which I could not fully understand but which made that last year more special. Art was one of my chosen subjects for the final exams and it was divided into three parts, one of which was compulsory. That was perspective – something which I could never get right, probably because I thought it was boring. The other two parts, which I chose, were design and flower drawing – unsurprisingly perhaps I was the only boy who chose the latter. Once again it put me amongst the girls who had all decided on flower drawing, much to the chagrin of the other boys. Of course, once again I was the butt of all sorts of rude remarks, but I used to tell them they were only jealous, and at least one or two admitted they were.

The Art mistress, whose first name I never knew, was called Miss Sparks and proved to be a very interesting lady who made everything sound possible if we would only pay attention to her. This was not at all difficult since she was very attractive; at the same time, however, she would not have any nonsense and so it was truly art for art's sake. She seemed to favour me a lot but only in respect of my ability to produce some excellent design work, especially posters. Most of what I did was hung on the wall of the art room. She said I had some unusual ideas but not too complicated, and they were ones which people could understand.

When she saw my flower drawings she was even more attentive as she said I had the feeling and the right touch to produce almost perfect pictures. I must admit that I loved doing this because I felt it to be something of deep beauty. At that time I was struggling to find what it was within myself that often made me feel different from others and very individual. A lot more experience was needed before I would really understand and accept something which would lead me into uncharted territory and express my true character and ability.

When I look back I realise it was Miss Sparks who gave me some of the best advice I had at school and I will never forget her. She helped instil confidence and self-awareness in me, yet at the same time she was honest not only in her appraisal of my work, but in outlining the possibilities for using my gift after leaving school. In the final exam, the first part was the dreaded perspective, in which we were required to draw a garden wheelbarrow, which was wheeled in and set before us. We were sat in a circle around it so each of us would have a different perspective. I had a terrible angle but I doubt it would have been any different wherever I sat. After the exam was over and the papers collected, Miss Sparks took me aside and said she was not supposed to say anything to anyone but she thought I ought to know how bad my drawing was and that, if I was to pass the whole exam, I would have to do much better on the other two parts. She had been hoping I would get an 'honour' but the best I could produce now would get me through with a 'pass'.

After the design exam, thank heavens, she was pleased with me and when it was the day for the flower drawing she sent me to the florist to collect the flowers to be drawn. To my horror these turned out to be blue scabious, a lovely flower but with delicate, feathery petals. She told me I would have a chance to study them on the way back, which I most certainly did. It had to be our secret and I felt very honoured that she would help me in this way. After the exam she took me aside and was absolutely ecstatic about my effort and was certain I would get a pass, which I subsequently did. She then asked me what I hoped to do after I left school, which by then was just a few days away. I told her I would like to be a designer as I was already designing dresses for my mother and sister as well as most ladies I knew. Of course they were never made but everyone felt I could make a good career doing this. She then asked me if my parents could afford to send me to university because I would need to do this before I could get work. Her guess was that my parents couldn't. I admitted sadly that this was true and in no way would I cause them any more expense – they had already sacrificed so much for my education. She then said that I could get a ten-pound-a-week job as a material designer and hope that I would be discovered for greater things. Otherwise all I could do was to get into any other job I liked and earn money while keeping my artistic abilities in view. Her advice was hard to accept but I knew she was right, so I left school with a heavy heart and wishing I could still have her teach me more. I had no earthly idea of what else I wanted to do, but then consoled myself with the idea I could at least have a holiday before having to decide, which made me hope something would turn up in the meantime.

Miss Sparks and the art exam left me with an abiding love of blue scabious and I always plant them in my garden wherever I may be, and what is more they always seem to grow bigger and better than they normally would. This makes me feel that maybe Miss Sparks remembers me as much as I do her. She certainly helped me to realise a great potential and most importantly a love of the beautiful things in life.

3

From Tea Boy to Intelligence Officer

Unfortunately even after the holiday nothing had turned up and I got myself into a very worried and even tearful state. My parents said I must decide and so I said I would just have to go into office work, but it was not what I wanted. Upon reflection now, I feel perhaps something greater was meant to materialise but it would not happen until the time was right and then was not the right time. So I found myself being employed as a junior in the office of a long-distance haulage firm called Coulsen & Co. It was a very small office with four men and the boss in one room, a cashier in another and me in an outer room where I had to man a switchboard, make tea and do any odd jobs required. Through my window I could watch the long-distance lorries going in and out, but it was not exciting. The office was not far from home and I was paid the sum of twenty-five shillings a week. After I had given some to Mother for my keep I actually had money in my pocket, which was some consolation. I have always been strongly independent, not for any other reason than I feel it is fair to try to be responsible for oneself.

Every morning at a certain time I had to take a large teapot over to the blacksmith's where he had a huge kettle on the boil knowing I would be coming. Although it was a very hot place it was a welcome relief to be able to talk to someone as everyone in the office rarely had anything to say to me except to give orders. The blacksmith and his assistant seemed to like me and so we had some good chats and they were very encouraging, saying I deserved something better than this job, but that it would come in time. After a while a young lad of my own age came into the forge in order to make tea and he was instantly friendly. He was working as a storekeeper for the haulage section and his father was one of the long-distance drivers. We found we had a shared love of music and other interests in common and a good friendship started, for which I was so grateful. He suggested we went to a promenade concert at the Albert Hall and it was great fun. Sadly our friendship wasn't to be, as shortly after that he told me his father had forbidden him to talk to me any more as we were of a different class. Being only seventeen we had to obey our parents but it was something that upset me. I then considered myself working class and could not see why his father thought I was any different. It was one of the things that would eventually make me ponder a lot, as later on a few people seemed to think I had been born with a silver spoon in my mouth. One man in particular refused to believe I lived in a terraced flat in a working-class neighbourhood and was sure it would be in a very large house with servants. I never consciously gave that impression but presumed there must be something I didn't know about and just got on with being me, whatever that was.

After a year in that job I felt I had to get away from there and as it happened someone told me they were looking for juniors at the local town hall where the money was better. It was still an office job but, as the possibility of being called up for National Service when I was eighteen was looming (the war had not yet been won), I felt it would be worth trying for. I got an interview and was accepted without any trouble and so a new phase in my life began and a very different one in many ways. The town hall was further away from home but that did not matter as more money meant more things I could enjoy. I also had a little job in the newsagent's opposite to my home some evenings and Saturdays, although eventually I gave this up as I started to make more friends and had more of a social life.

Working in the newsagents was quite an experience, although I had to do some menial tasks as well as serving in the shop. I used to take their dog out for walks and in a way I became a good friend of the family. I remember that one of the daughters there was very impressed with me and my speaking voice and thought I might be able to get a job with the BBC. As she knew somebody there with influence she persuaded me to apply. After filling in a huge questionnaire I received a negative reply as I had not been to public school. I was rather sad but felt it would not be for me anyway, even if such conditions had not existed. Not to be beaten she suggested that I go to work at an insurance firm in London but there the condition would be that as a junior I would have to wear a top hat and begin as a sort of errand boy. I felt that, too, was not for me and on reflection if either of these jobs had been successful then it would have changed the course of my life; my road was definitely leading elsewhere.

On my first working day at the town hall, a somewhat gloomy-looking building, I was directed to the General Office. This was quite a large room with a very long sturdy table down the middle, which was where I had to sit with three other juniors. Our main task was to sort out the mail, which was very heavy, and to run between the offices delivering it as well as fetching things at the command of the man in charge. He was called Mr Edridge but was better known by his nickname, Ghandi, which he earned because he was almost a double of the Indian leader. Mr Edridge, however, had a somewhat acid tongue and would sit at his desk which overlooked the long table and constantly criticise our work and behaviour. He was considered to be a very mean man and one who took delight in telling us what cowards we were when we would all dive under the desk when there was an air raid warning or the sound of an approaching doodlebug. He would remain at his desk saying that if we were going to 'get it', meaning if we were hit by bombs, it was just too bad – work had to go on.

What he didn't know was that while under the table a lot *was* going on. There was only one girl to three boys and poor Georgina, a lovely redhead, was the target of our affections. The chance to kiss her was too good to be missed. She always protested and pretended to put up a struggle but I am sure she loved it. We had a lot of fun especially when Ghandi was out of the room, though we also had to be careful in case the big chief walked in. We were lucky on the whole but our routine was boring and at times very annoying as every day at the end of work we had to help carry all the heavy ledgers down to the safety of the basement. It also meant bringing them up in the morning and we were put on a rota where we were supposed to get in a little earlier to deal with the task. Mostly we didn't and used the excuse of air raids or transport stoppages for being late.

Even then I realised that local government was not an exciting job and most of those who worked there were pompous bureaucrats. After a time I was posted to the audit section and it all seemed worse. I was and still am good at figures and to some extent the work there was more interesting but the backbiting and jealousy that went on between the staff was very unpleasant. I was more or less ignored and left to get on with my work, but the atmosphere was tense. However, there was no chance of escape until my eighteenth birthday, when my call-up papers arrived and the army claimed my services. I could not refuse even if I had wanted to. I said my goodbyes and walked out of the town hall swearing that I would never come back and, if I survived the army, then I would get a different job. In a way it felt like escaping from a sort of prison but my new-found sense of freedom proved short-lived. In the army I quickly learned that no one stood a chance of expressing individual gifts; our lot was to obey and do or die.

I had to report to the depot of 'The Buffs', an infantry regiment in Canterbury. Strangely enough it was the same depot my father had been in during the First World War, and I was put in the very same barrack room as him. It was sheer coincidence but for me the thought of being in the infantry was frightening: marching for miles on end simply did not appeal to me. However, I knew that I was to be there for just six weeks' general training and then every man would be assessed and put wherever he could best serve. A ray of hope dawned upon me but it did not help much on that first fateful day. It would all take a lot of getting used to. I was surrounded by a lot of men in the same boat and probably feeling and thinking the same way as I did. We were soon to learn about *esprit de corps*, which meant working as a team and for the glory of it. I wanted no glory but to be able to get through it all and to let it end soon.

Once through the checking in and getting sorted out, not to mention being introduced to the gleaming-white parade ground where we would later be put through drill, we were allowed to go to bed on awful wooden bunks in the sparsely furnished barrack room. One could actually hear some of the men sobbing but I didn't succumb to that, although I must have looked sad as one of the men nearby smiled and said to me, 'Don't worry! You'll be all right.' I dropped off to sleep thinking, 'Please, God, let it be so!' After what seemed hardly any time, I was awoken at the ungodly hour of 6.30 a.m. by the sound of *reveille* being blown by the bugler and the raucous voice of the corporal telling us to get up and get cracking. There was no tea or breakfast in bed. This was 'it'.

Fortunately, perhaps, there was no time to worry about the misery of it all, as we were told there would not be much time between now and being on parade. In the meantime we had to do our ablutions, with icy-cold water, roll up our mattresses and arrange everything in a certain order ready for inspection. Discipline started with the crack of dawn and I will never forget those first six weeks in which I had to learn, along with the others, to accept the bullying the ridicule and being made to feel small. At the time I didn't realise it would make a man out of me, but it seemed I was forever being told that was what being in the army did. It took a long time for me, but the lesson to be learned was that it was no use banging your head against a brick wall. Independence was not what the army wanted from any man as fighting war means standing together. I hated war and the idea of having to kill. I never wanted to be in the position of having to and, even when forced to do bayonet practice by lunging at sacks with Japanese faces painted on them, I could do so only in a half-hearted fashion.

I can honestly say I am not a coward and would do whatever I had to do. But like most of the men all I wanted was to get it all over with and be home again with my family. However, it would be three years before that happened – time enough in which to learn yet more about myself while doing my duty. There was a certain amount of fun to be had, but mostly it was in laughing at others and feeling happy it was not you in that situation. Fortunately it was my well-developed sense of humour which helped get through each and every day. The drilling and route marching were exhausting, the boots were tough to get used to, and handling weapons was, for me, far from exciting. It was necessary to pass tests on everything and this I somehow managed to do. There was a lot of banter between the men and often tricks would be played. One would have to be sharp enough to get out of them before being discovered by the sergeant and blamed for what you hadn't done and then put on 'jankers'. This was also called fatigues and meant polishing the sergeant's brasses, scrubbing the cookhouse floor or any other nasty menial task that could be thought of. We were told it was all part of the game but, if it was, it was one I did not like playing.

I made some friends in that time but there was not much chance for socialising as after a day of training most men were too tired to do anything but clean their equipment for tomorrow and get to bed early. I sometimes used to go into Canterbury for a look around but inevitably found myself in the cathedral, which is a magnificent and very old building. Sometimes a friend would come with me but I preferred to be alone. By then I had broken away from religion, or so I thought. I cannot adequately describe the overpowering yet beautifully peaceful feeling I always experienced there. I felt in some way I belonged there and yet until then I had had no connection with it. I certainly did not realise it would have a very special meaning later in my life and that it would, in effect, call me back again.

At the end of the six weeks we all had to be interviewed by an officer as to our future in the army. While waiting to be called we had to sit in a corridor outside the interview rooms. I had become friendly with a boy called Basil Hoskins who had been training as an actor at RADA before he was called up, and who went on to become well-known. Both of us desperately wanted to avoid joining the infantry for good. Suddenly Basil arrived all breathless and excited and told me about a conversation he had just overheard between two soldiers. Apparently there had recently been a military parade in Canterbury in which the Intelligence Corps had taken part. As this part of the parade approached one of the soldiers had heard two girls laughing and saying, 'Look at those nancy boys! They're just a load of pen-pushers!' I wondered where Basil was going with this until he added, 'So let's say we want to get into that lot. We'll have an easy time.' I enthusiastically agreed: it sounded good apart from the 'nancy boys' jibe.

Soon after, I was called into a room and confronted by a burly-looking officer. When he saw me he immediately slapped me on the chest and said he thought I would make a fine guardsman. I said I did not want to be one and he then suggested we have a look at what else I could do. First we would have to consider infantry and I quickly told him I did not like that idea. He said that I might *have* to go into the infantry and, if that was the case, what infantry regiment did I think I would like. I replied that I had no idea whereupon he asked me if my father had served in the First World War. My heart sank when I had to tell him that Father had been in The Buffs and in that very depot. I was not surprised when he said he would put me down for the same so I could honour tradition. A silly remark as I could not see anything traditional about it, so told him again that I hoped not to go into the infantry.

He then asked what I would like to get into if I could choose. I took a deep breath and said, 'the Intelligence Corps'. He looked very surprised and asked me if I was sure. He said that in the last six weeks of training all the men had been individually watched and noted as to their behaviour and abilities and what they might be suitable for. He explained that if I was to get into that corps I would have to mix with people of high and low rank and go through a very tough and rigorous training, and that my work would be of a highly specialised nature. In observing me they had come to the conclusion I was a very shy person who would not say boo to a goose, and that I had not made many friends although I had responded well to discipline. So did I want to change my mind as this would be a very important decision? Feeling I had let myself in for something I hadn't expected but from which I couldn't lose face by turning it down, I said, 'No, Sir, I can do it.' His reply was: 'By God, I think you can and I am going to recommend you.' I could not feel happy about it but the die was cast and there was no turning back. The officer did say it would be very adventurous though he did not say exactly what *kind* of adventure he meant.

Basil also got into the same corps but I wondered how he did it because I could not at all see him doing all we had been told about it. When I expressed my feelings on this, he laughed and said he had no intention of staying in the corps and that he was going to get into the Army Theatre Unit one way or another. This he eventually did and I suppose it all turned out best for him. I, however, had no idea what would be best for me. All I could do was hope I could get through this period of my life and in the end gain something out of it.

Just before the end of the six weeks the war in Japan was over and it was said peace would reign. Although we would eventually be given demobilisation numbers, it would be some time before they would come up and meanwhile we would be the clearing-up mob. On VJ Day as it was called I went with several of the boys into town to witness the so-called celebrations. I was disgusted by what was happening as mobs were overturning cars and burning them, and running riot in a drunken frenzy. I returned to barracks and for a while sat on my bed pondering my future. After a time my platoon sergeant came into the room and sat beside me, saying, 'Hello, what are you doing back here and why aren't you celebrating?'

I told him why and he said he was not surprised as he did not think I was like the rest of the boys. This was a very different man to the one on the parade ground who could be tough, sarcastic and bullying, yet I always felt he was human. He told me he lived very close to where I lived in London and often had a drink in the local pub, so if ever I saw him there he would be happy to drink with me. He asked what I was going to do and, when I explained about the Intelligence Corps, he said it was what he would expect me to do and he knew I would be successful. Finally he said that I was totally different from all the others and he was proud to know me and I would go a long way. I must confess I had tears in my eyes after he left as I felt that at last someone believed in me and had encouraged me to believe in myself. There is so much to learn in life and it was then that I realised I was on the verge of becoming a man.

After Canterbury there was a short period of home leave during which I was required to attend the War Office. After a few questions by a top officer I was required to say which language I could speak so as to determine where I would eventually be posted abroad. I had learned German at school but naturally it was only schoolbook German. The officer handed me a sheet of paper on which was printed something in German which at one glance I realised was beyond my learning. I could only tell him that it was something to do with factories and very technical things which he agreed was true but was not good enough for me to be sent to any German-speaking countries. My hopes were dashed as I had pinned my hopes on Austria. I had made a friend called Ted who spoke fluent German and who had been told he would go there; it would have been good to have stayed together, but it wasn't to be. All I knew then was after the leave I had to report to Beaumaris in Anglesey for further training.

I arrived there late in the evening with some other lads I had met on the train and was shown to a Nissen hut and given a palliasse (a straw mattress) and a blanket, and told to settle down for the night. I was awakened in the morning by the usual bugle and the same routine as before. In daylight it did not seem so bad as there was a row of huts between a line of trees and further beyond one could see some of the rolling Welsh countryside. Anglesey was indeed a beautiful spot, very peaceful with interesting things to see whenever one had time to explore. This was secondary to the intense training which now began in earnest with daily drill parades and a turn around the assault course, which was frightening to say the least. It was always accompanied by the sergeant and corporal in charge throwing thunder flashes either in front or behind. When crossing rope bridges or climbing rope ladders it was not funny to be threatened with a thunder flash up one's posterior, or to have one thrown in behind you when you got stuck in a tiny tunnel with you backpack on and were unable to move. I remember once one of the lads ahead of me got completely wedged and was in a fit of blind panic. I eventually managed to get him free. Out in the open we were greeted by the sergeant saying, 'Now then, you two, this is neither the time nor the place to make love, so don't let me catch you at it again!' It was supposed to be funny but neither of us enjoyed the joke. I gradually came to accept this so-called army humour as par for the course, but the man in front who was called Sam never could. Every morning, while waiting for the command to go round the course, he trembled like a jelly and asked me if I would stay close and help him. I tried but eventually Sam had to be taken off the course and posted to another regiment as he was deemed unfit for Intelligence training. In a way I envied him but by then I was beginning to find my real self and I refused to be beaten, developing an obstinate determination for which I have been always been thankful.

There were other dreadful things to conquer, like the night-time field exercises which mostly took place on the local golf course. Although I am not a keen golfer I would have much preferred a game of golf to crawling through cowpats and rolling down craggy slopes, to mention only a few of the delights on offer. Route marches were bad enough when one's feet are not used to such things, but for what it is worth the marching songs were useful in letting off steam. Some were absolutely vulgar but at least it was possible to use them to show one's dislike of sergeants and corporals. The main thing it seemed to do was to draw the men together and a real *esprit de corps* began to show.

Strangely enough most of the men looked forward to weapon training though I did not. There were ranges in the wilds of Angelsey where we were trained to fire pistols, rifles, Bren guns, mortars and bazookas. I wasn't especially good at this aspect of the training but I managed to scrape through without difficulty. Again I was put in a tight spot when having to pair with a pal called Mark to fire a bazooka. We had to take turns from behind a barricade of firing at a target. The gun was very heavy. It had to be pulled into the shoulder when loaded with a small bomb and then held very still until fired, when it would have a tremendous rebound that could knock the firer backwards. I was not too happy about having to do this but managed to conquer my nerves and actually hit the target. Then it was Mark's turn and he was a trembling jelly, shaking and almost crying because he was so afraid. I calmed him down as best I could and he said he was glad I was with him and could I fire the gun for him? Of course I could not, and when he came to fire he almost collapsed and the bomb just trickled over the barricade and fell no more than two feet away. I pulled him down and we lay flat on the ground; there was nothing else I could do except wait there, possibly to be blown to smithereens. Fortunately, the bomb didn't explode. Suddenly the captain in charge who was looking on from his safe hut some way back came running out, all red-faced and in a panic, screaming at poor Mark and calling him a coward. I rather think it was the captain who was the coward and he was by no means setting an example to his men.

When we got back to camp after the bomb had been safely exploded, Mark thanked me for being there with him and perhaps saving his life. I felt more sorry for him than myself as he would now have to endure endless jokes from the rest of the men about having brown stains on his trousers and such like. Really the men were sorry for him too, as they realised it could have been any one of us. I began to realise that a lot of my role in life would be in helping others and having sympathy for them, though at the time I could not see exactly how this would be.

There was not much social life in those ten weeks of training but on the whole most of us men felt too tired to go into town. The NAAFI was really the place for a drink and a chat, maybe a sing-song or a game of darts, but it was not the height of excitement. Moreover, I lost my friend Basil, who, as I've said, soon found a way of achieving his wish to go into the Army Theatre Unit. He became the favourite of the entertainments manager in the camp, who was a major, and his transfer was thus easily arranged.

One important thing that happened in Beaumaris, given my later career, was that I was introduced to the subject of ghosts, which of course would have a bearing on my future. Everyone hears about ghosts one way or another but not many really believe in such things as the subject tends to be one of ridicule. Not that I wasn't frightened of them as a child but by this time I had more or less dismissed the idea until I heard that the island was reputedly haunted by several ghosts. One of these was Maggie Duffy who had been the housekeeper at the big house which was now occupied by our officers. It was reported that things were thrown around and a lot of other strange happenings occurred. I put it down to the officers' drunken parties. Then there was the White Lady and the Green Archer both of whom roamed the nearby woods. Many of the men went to see them and I am sure some of them had vivid imaginations. I even went myself but perhaps the 'ghosts' were scared of me as I did not see or feel a thing.

Again I had to help someone and this time it was 'wee Willie'. He was a short, rotund Scottish little lad who made it clear he was frightened of ghosts – the very mention of them would drive him to distraction. One evening I was going down into town with some of the lads. Willie was asked if he would care to join us but he declined. Someone then said he should not stay in the hut alone as the Green Archer would get him whereupon Willie dived into his bunk and pulled the blankets right over his head and screamed, 'Please don't let him get me.' The rest of the men went off and I said I would catch them up. This was to allow me to talk to Willie, who was by then an absolute shaking and crying mess. I explained that the others were having a joke with him and there was no such ghost as the Green Archer. I suggested that rather than stay in the hut on his own he should go to the canteen where he would find plenty of company and protection. Once he was calm and on his way to the canteen I made my way down a long unlit path through the trees to join the others.

Suddenly I knew they would no doubt be playing a joke on me, so I prepared myself for any eventuality. When I almost reached a tunnel that led into town, I saw a huge black shape before me. It was so dark all around and I felt a very eerie sensation. I knew I would have to pass this object before I could get into town and decided it must be the men playing about. So I put my hand out in front of me and approached. My hand made contact with something cold and clammy and I was rather petrified until, that is, I heard a distinctive moo and realised it was a cow that had strayed onto the path. I got past this fearsome creature and found the gang waiting for me. They asked me what had kept me and I just said I got a bit delayed but I did not tell them about Willie or the cow. For me it was enough experience for one night – so strange that I should have helped Willie to stay calm but could not do the same myself. That was enough of ghosts for me – at least for some time.

During my time in Beaumaris I also found out something that would become extremely important to me in later life, something I would probably never have discovered unless I had been made to. While there, we were given various lectures which were mostly boring but to which one had to listen because it was all to do with future work. One day we were taken to a very large hall with a stage. We all thought we were going to have a concert or show of some sort, and there were at least five hundred men seated and waiting to be surprised. It proved not to be a very pleasant surprise. The sergeant in charge announced that today we are going to have mini lectures and that some of us would be chosen to give them. They would be ten minutes long and on a subject chosen by the sergeant. The very first man he pointed at was me and I was told I had to talk on cinematography. Although I was fond of the cinema, at that time I had not thought as to how it actually worked and I felt as if I would collapse with fear. A man sitting two or three seats away from me leant across and whispered, 'If it is any use to you the Cinematograph was invented by a man called William Friese-Greene.'

It was a start anyway and so I mounted the platform with very wobbly legs and beheld a sea of faces all looking at me and thinking they were glad it wasn't them. I was sure they would laugh at me but I opened my mouth and began to talk. I cannot remember what I said and felt even worse when I saw the camp commandant come into the hall and stand at the back. The men would not have known this and as I finished there was a huge round of applause, followed by the commandant saying, 'Well done, that man! Excellent and a jolly good show.' I cannot describe how I felt but it made me realise I had a gift for lecturing which did not go unnoticed by the platoon sergeant. After that, every time we were out on exercises and were given a break, he would tell the other men to sit down and listen to Private Hearn who would give us a talk. When I asked him what I should talk about he suggested I tell them about my job and what I did before I was called up. I thought the men would be bored and inattentive but they seemed to enjoy it and there were no jokes made; in fact they seemed to respect me in some way.

Once we had completed the course at Beaumaris, we had to move on to Rotherham in Yorkshire where we would have to face more gruelling tests and trials, but as it included motor cycling most of the men were excited at the prospect. I wasn't, as I never had any interest in riding motorbikes, but in the army if they say you will do something then you will. I would not say I was afraid but I will confess that I had never more wished to be out of all this than when we were marched up to the cycle sheds. Each man was allotted a machine, which, he was told, he must learn to respect, love and look after. Next we had to wheel our machines up to a cinder track where a transport sergeant showed us how to start it and put it into first gear. Then we were told to do just that and ride around the track. Strangely enough I seemed to manage that and even began to feel at home with the idea, although admittedly riding around a cinder track is one thing, getting out on the open road with it is another. That phase came rather quicker than I expected as the next day we were shown how to use second gear and so on, and to ride the reverse way round the track. By now we were being watched by a group of sergeants and, as each man became sufficiently proficient, he was called off the track and assigned to one of the sergeants who would be his squad leader from then on. I was then shocked to be told we were going out on the open road.

At first we rode around locally but eventually we made our way to Sheffield where there were still trams running on rails down the middle of the road. A motorcycle could weave and overtake but a tram had to run its course, which made things very difficult for the learner, but the army had the habit of throwing one straight into the deep end. The more difficult part was in trying to follow the leader and in keeping one cycle's length between each of us. Surprisingly it soon became quite easy but I was never happier than when we were out on the open road and not having to dodge trams and heavy traffic. The next day we were told that we would be doing rough riding and basically all we had to do was follow the leader. He led us into fields and across undulating ground, which was bad enough for a start, but when we stopped at a quarry, it seemed as if my worst nightmares were coming true.

The leader told us to watch and listen as we would be shown

only once and then we would have to negotiate the quarry. He then demonstrated by letting his machine just roll over the edge and as it neared the U-bend of the bottom he opened the machine full throttle and climbed up and over to the other side. I think every man was afraid of having to do this but we were lined up and with the usual threats and bullying we had no choice but to do or die. When my turn came I was praying hard but I followed instructions and, by a major miracle, found myself up and over and heard the leader saying 'Well done!' I felt confidence welling up within me and that was just as well since the other things we had to master during the course were just as frightening, such as having to steer our machine along a ploughed furrow without getting stuck! This meant putting your feet up on the handlebars, looking straight ahead and just keeping going – not as easy as it sounds. Several trainees could not do it and ended up having a mud bath, but luckily I managed it without disaster. In fact, I found every one of the tests to be easier than I thought, though for all that I never wanted to make a profession of rough-riding.

My worst experience was when we had to ride up slag heaps, which of course were quite common in Yorkshire. It was all loose coal and as I almost got to the top my machine slid over and my gear lever broke. The leader said there was nothing to be done and I would have to drive back to depot with the squad. When I said I couldn't see how, he told me I would learn. He then said: 'Supposing you were dropped behind enemy lines with your machine and it broke down, what would you do?' When I said I would just pray he told me in no uncertain terms that that wouldn't be any bloody use. Of course, what he meant was that I had to know how to mend my own bike. Of course, we had lessons on maintenance but I could never understand how engines worked and that sort of thing, except perhaps how to change a spark plug. However, what this experience did suddenly bring home to me, what with the leader mentioning that I might be dropped behind enemy lines, was that I could become a spy. This wasn't a thought that thrilled me and I was thankful that the Second World War was over and that hopefully there would be no need for me to do such things.

On the whole the course was quite enjoyable especially when we would drive to a café outside Doncaster and have tea with hot buttered teacakes and jam while on a break. Also it was a chance to see the lovely countryside. At such moments I could so easily have driven right away and forgotten about the army and dwelt in the peacefulness of it all. At the end of the course we had to pass tests on all we had been doing. For road riding I scored ninety-nine marks out of a hundred, just dropping one mark for tending to leave too much space between machines, and astonishingly I scored one hundred marks on rough riding. Alas, when it came to maintenance I scored eight out of a hundred and received quite a rollicking from the squad leader who sent me to the officer in charge. He was quite a gentleman compared with the leader and sympathised with me having such good marks on two tests only to drop so low on the last. I told him I really could not master mechanics and he said that, although this should go against me, I was so good on the first two that he would give me my certificate anyway and pass me knowing I was the sort of person who would find a way through somehow and not be put off. Inwardly I hoped he was right, but later on reflection I began to realise that this experience was proving something I have subsequently always believed: that one never knows what one can do until, or unless, one tries.

The next part of the training was a course with the Sheffield police, which included customs work as well. The police course was very interesting although it had its not so pleasant moments when we were required to see horrible crime pictures and were reminded that, however sick we felt, we must get used to it because we could be involved with such things in our work. We were taught about interrogation and shadowing suspects and all possible police procedures. The Customs officers who came to lecture us and show us how to strip-search were even more fascinating, especially when explaining where people could hide things, even to the point of actually showing us (I think it's better not to go into detail). All of this was making me wiser and more aware, even if I knew I never wanted to do these things myself. Once anything is drummed into one enough, it stays for life. At least that is the way I have found it to be because I have often been suspected of being a policemen or store detective, especially because of my build. At the end of the course the chief inspector of the Sheffield police told us that, if once we got out of the army we wanted to join the police, we would not have to go on the beat but would get into CID almost immediately. There was a great murmur of enthusiasm, though not from me, and I rather expected that most of the men would change their minds once they realised there were so much more appealing experiences to be had elsewhere.

Another enduring, though much more unpleasant, memory from my time at Rotherham was when we were sent to Wentworth Woodhouse to do three weeks' guards training. We were put in barrack rooms which had previously been the stables of this huge and lovely house and immediately given bayonets in long scabbards which had to be kept spotlessly clean. Everything had to be done on the double so once on the barrack square all the drill would be at a very fast pace and extremely tiring. Anyone who could not do it was punished by having to be on the square in the evening and drilling at the double until the sergeant in charge said they could stop. Everything had to be perfect and dirty brasses or boots would mean unmentionable fatigues. Every order and even normal conversation was edged with threats and bullying and three weeks of that seemed an eternity. There was little or no social life as every evening would be spent in polishing brasses and blanco-ing equipment. Who on earth, I wondered, would want to be a guardsman and submit to such inhuman discipline?

After that it was back to Rotherham and a truck driving course – another task I did not relish but decided to do my best at, as it was necessary for my future work. I can't remember ever having a desire to drive a car; until then the most I did and enjoyed was cycling, which I found to be good exercise, even if pedalling uphill was not much fun. So came the first day of being introduced to a truck and the sergeant who would instruct me and five others on how to drive it. Needless to say, it was just my luck to get a bully instructor. He had a long stick with a nail in the end which he would hold over one's knuckles while you were driving and threaten to hit them if you did the wrong thing. On the very first day I had to drive into Sheffield and at a given point I was told to turn left. Suddenly he started yelling at me and tried to grab the steering wheel with the result that I was just able to stop within inches of a brick wall. It was not my fault as I knew what I was doing but he blamed me and in his blind panic told me to get out and join the other men in the back of the truck, at the same time accusing me of trying to kill them all. Another man took over and we made our way back to barracks. Part way the truck stopped and the driver came to the back and told me the sergeant wanted me at the wheel. I dared not disobey and when I got in and settled down it seemed to me like he was apologising. I took a deep breath and told him he was a bully and I did not respond to his methods; neither did I think it was right to threaten me or anyone with his stick. I could not feel happy with him or truck driving but he said we should give it another go and so I drove on towards the barracks. On arriving there, it was necessary to drive through a narrow archway which would barely allow the truck to get through, so I stopped and said I could not do it. He told me I could and must, so I went for it and drove through without any trouble. He said when we parked and got out that I would make a fine driver, to which I said, not with him. In the morning I went to see the transport officer and asked to be put under another instructor. The officer was quite understanding but said he knew the sergeant was a bully with unusual methods but he got results. There was no way he could change my instructor so if I cared to leave the course and go back to general duties it would not be held against me. He agreed that if I continued it might be a danger to others, so I was relieved to get away from something I did not feel was really for me anyway.

There was more social life at Rotherham and, if one did not want to stay in camp, then it was easy to get in to Sheffield for cinemas, dances and various other things. In the camp itself there was a good canteen run by the NAAFI and some very good-looking girls who were always willing to joke with the men and even go out on a date. I was lucky as I seemed to be popular with them and one in particular named Sheila. Before this I had become very attracted to a lady from a place nearby. She was a schoolteacher and I loved dancing with her at the weekly dances held in the camp which were great fun. For some reason she seemed to get upset and did not come any more, so it was then that I started to go out with Sheila, usually in the company of others. We got to holding hands and furtive kisses but we were both overcome by guilt as she was married. Apparently it was to a soldier who was posted abroad the day after their wedding and she said she was lonely and not sure that she really loved him. There was no chance to misbehave, but for me it began to get quite serious and I felt this must be the one true love. Especially when she eventually confessed to feeling the same way and said that whatever happened we must be together. There are times when guilt flies out of the window but no doubt this sort of thing happened to many of the men, so perhaps it was a good thing that we would be moving on and have our minds occupied with being good soldiers and doing our duty.

The last course that took place in England was at the School of Military Intelligence in Farnham in Surrey. It was a very beautiful spot to be in but not the school itself, as it was here that we had to learn more about how to interrogate and all sorts of things that would be necessary once we were sent abroad. It all began to feel exciting – stressful, too – but when it came to learning about military formations and the higher echelon it was absolutely mind-boggling. We had to swear on oath that we would never divulge any of this information and I for one thought that this could be assured as I could not understand it, at least to begin with. Fortunately it did not affect our final grading, and after going through a series of tests, we were given an IQ rating. Most of the men got an 'IQ4' like me, which was the normal pass, but the odd one or two got a bit higher. I consoled myself that I was considered brainy enough to do the work which lay ahead and was quite relieved to leave the school and return to Rotherham where we would be told where we would be posted.

At the school we had been shown more ghastly photos and told the sort of things we might have to deal with in the future and I began to wonder if anything like that would ever happen, as time was passing and we were getting ever nearer to demob when all this could be left behind. One thing I will always remember is that on the walls of the lecture room there were several posters showing ladies in various states of undress with captions underneath. The one I liked best was of a very voluptuous lady with the caption 'You would no doubt like to take down her particulars but remember she might like to take down yours.' It was meant as a security warning but most men, including me, preferred the other idea and it only made one anxious for the chance. Like most, I was very impatient to get back to normal life and I can't say that all this was teaching me to be patient as it is not really one of my attributes even now. There is within me a strong desire to do things the right way, whatever that is, and I hate wasting time as there always seems to be so many things one could be doing. I am not perfect within myself but I aim for perfection in what I do and can't be happy until it is achieved, no matter how one has to go about it.

At Rotherham we were told we were going to India, which did

not please me one bit as all I could think of was the great heat and the monsoons. It was so far away from home and those I loved but since there was no choice I tried to treat it as an adventure. We were allowed home leave for a few days and then it was the time for us to march out of the barracks with all the girls waving, including Sheila, who had tears in her eyes. I might have had one or two but having to concentrate on what I was doing made it somewhat easier. I was sure I would not forget this lady I loved and we would keep in touch. I might add that I was also keeping in touch with my schoolgirl sweetheart, who was also a very beautiful girl, though somehow I felt this would not be. I am not a Romeo or mad about every girl I see, but most of us at eighteen would be the same. One did not think of marriage and settling down when there were other things to experience but nonetheless it was good to keep one eye open as they say.

4

Of Snakes and Potholes

We were taken to Southampton with all our necessary kit where we boarded a ship called SS *Corfu* and were settled in for a nineteen-day trip to Bombay. I can't say I really enjoyed the trip as I am not a good sailor and was seasick for seventeen days until I found my sea legs. By then it was time to disembark when I was promptly land sick. During the voyage we had a lot of freedom to play games and all sorts of things, and it was interesting to stop at Malta and Port Said, and to see flying fish and whales plus many more things one would not see in England. We were given lectures and some kind of drill but on the whole it was easy to understand why people go on cruises, as they say that, once you set sail and get out to sea, anything goes. Except it wasn't quite like that for us but one could get the idea.

We landed in Bombay at night and then travelled on by train to the transit camp. The onboard toilets were full of scorpions, our introduction to the many dangerous things one would find in the Subcontinent. It was a relief to be back on dry land but very quickly we were plunged back into army routine and dispatched to Karachi for yet another course to get us used to India with its many castes and customs. It was basically a barracks where we would have to undergo drill and various exercises as well as attend lectures and be shown more photos of crimes and the things we would have to deal with in India. The most difficult part was to learn Urdu, something which most men found hard except for the rude words. As there was a lot of English spoken in that country it was not absolutely necessary, and having been brought out much against their will most of the men felt like being difficult on this score; some even felt they were dealing with inferior people, something which was dealt with in the training and anyone who had this attitude was reprimanded. It was mostly a case, however, of getting used to new surroundings and the intense heat, and generally it did not take very long before one understood the actual task in hand, the 'clearing up' as it was called. At that time there were murmurs of India gaining independence but for the time being the security of the British forces had to be maintained as well as that of the Indian army, which was what we had really come for. Once again we were made to swear an oath of secrecy but I personally always wondered what it was we were actually supposed to be keeping secret, so much information was being drummed into us.

Karachi was an interesting city, although we rarely could go into it. It was strange to see a lot of camels being used and the people with their dress designed for the heat. Our olive-green lightweight uniforms were not especially cool but like everything it takes time to get used to it. I think that most of the men including me were anxious after all this time spent in training to get down to doing a real job, which we hoped would be a relief after so much drilling and route marching, not to mention the endless courses. I for one could not imagine what might lay ahead, which at that point was just as well. We had been warned to respect the different castes and their customs and never to upset anyone. If we saw men with their wives we were not to look at the ladies as we could meet with trouble – a pity as there were so many beautiful women around who in their traditional dress looked very attractive. There were some compensations. For example, dances were held for the men in the canteen, which was quite a pleasant place. There was a band and good refreshments and a lot of Anglo-Indian girls who, although they claimed to be British anyway, were all for meeting men whom they could marry in order to get to England. It was quite understandable but very few men were in the market for that, but the girls were good dancers and keen for some fun. There was the chance, too, to go swimming and boating, as on a Sunday there were trips to a nearby island where one could have lunch and sunbathe or do whatever one wanted. The local bazaars were always interesting places to see and perhaps buy things to send home to loved ones. I was more eager to buy and send back tea, as at home they were still on rationing. My mother never forgot getting these little packets as we were very much a 'tea family' and the ration of two ounces per person per week did not go very far.

After a time the men became restless as they wanted to receive postings and to see some sort of action. Eventually it happened and I was to be sent to Ranchi, a small town fairly near to Calcutta. It involved a four-day train journey across some desert-like country and, what with the wind blowing sand into the open windows of the ramshackle carriages, and very little water available, it was hardly first class. We did get a stop off at Lahore where we had a meal and were able to take showers, but mainly it was army food, which says it all, and all in all it was an uncomfortable and tiring journey. We finally disembarked at Calcutta, though I could not see much of it as I had to take another train to Ranchi. There I was met by a sergeant called Barry who took me by jeep to what would be my base for some time. By then I had reached the exalted rank of sergeant myself so I was more able to feel at ease. That was until I arrived and met the warrant officer in charge, who pretended to be very friendly while at the same time making it clear he was in charge and we would all get along if we did exactly as he said.

Life at Ranchi was not the best. There were six of us altogether in this unit, housed in a sort of bungalow with no running water, a toilet in the grounds, and some not very comfortable beds. For our meals we had to drive into Ranchi which was some distance and eat in a little hotel there, but we all had to pile into the jeep as there was no other transport which could be used for that purpose. So wherever dear Jerry went, for that was our leader's name, we all had to go. There were motorcycles which we lesser mortals used for work, but we were all pretty much held captive by Jerry, who after the evening meal would decide we were all going to the garrison cinema whether we liked it or not. We all put up with this for a time but eventually some of us decided to rebel and insist that we could go back to our billet if we wished. His reply was that he could not stop us but he would not take us, so we would have to hire a *gari*, which was a bicycle with a two-seat carriage behind, and pay our own way back. It involved a long dark journey which made one feel sorry for the driver who had to pedal so hard, but it was also very dark and eerie so one was afraid of being set upon. We had been told that a village near to our bungalow had practised cannibalism a few years back and, judging by the noises that emanated from there at times, we felt it might still be so. But anything – even being eaten! – was worth it to get back and have time to oneself and for some of us to get to know each other better, even though we knew Jerry would make us pay for it the next day by having his way in everything. We spent countless hours playing badminton on the lawn in front of the bungalow, at which Jerry always had to win and of course we let him. Anything for a quiet life!

Our work was mostly done in the mornings as it was too hot by midday, and usually we went in pairs to check security on various units around the area. It was rather boring and somewhat routine, not that I wanted too much of the cloak-and-dagger stuff. There did not appear to be much 'clearing up' to do either and in my time only two things that represented anything dangerous ever occurred. The first was when we had to cover a local meeting at which a well-known speaker was to address a crowd on the subject of getting the English out of India. All six of us went in a large covered lorry and parked amongst some trees near to the arena so that we could see and hear all that was going on but could not be seen ourselves. It was a frightening sight to see such a huge crowd of Indian men being egged on by the speaker to follow him and shouting in unison, 'Death to the British!' There seemed to be hundreds of them and the atmosphere became very tense and poor Jerry, instead of setting us an example, was trembling and saying we would all be killed if we didn't get out of there. Ours was not to reason why, but we all got out of the lorry and pushed it quietly away from where we were, and then all jumped in, started up and drove off as fast as the vehicle would go. I realised we would never get to play the hero with Jerry in charge but, as I've said, I was not looking for adventures of that sort anyway.

The second dangerous moment came when the Calcutta riots were taking place. Being fairly close to where it was all happening, a curfew had to be imposed on Ranchi and it was our job to patrol the streets to ensure it was done. One evening I had to take John, our one member who was not allowed to ride a motorcycle on his own, as my pillion rider. We had loaded pistols, one on each hip, ready to fire if necessary and I don't suppose either of us wanted to be there. As we drove along through deserted streets, we both had the eerie sensation that there were people lurking in the shadows. Suddenly John said to me, 'Ron, I am dead scared. What are we going to do if a screaming horde of Indians attack us? I'm sure they are watching us?' All I could reply was: 'Well, John, you have two loaded pistols and if such a thing happens all you can do is to fire and kill as many of them as you can before they kill us!' It did not happen, of course, but I doubted if I was any more courageous than he was. All one could do was to try to put on a brave show. This was something I would do so much more in later life, particularly as looking and acting afraid does not help much.

To balance things out a little, there is another story to do with John which suggests that one is as brave as one wants to be when the daring is more to one's liking. One day when we were out on a work call we stopped on the way back to the billet in order to have a rest. It was very hot and we parked amongst a group of trees for shade. Suddenly John disappeared but, knowing he was inclined to be 'nosey', I thought little of it until he reappeared looking flushed and excited. He begged me to go and see what he had been looking at and I decided that, if it had made him so excited, it might be good for me, too. He took me to a small clearing in the trees from where could be seen a man-made lake of sorts, some cattle being washed and, more to the point, some beautiful naked young maidens. I pulled John away and reprimanded him for being such a fool – if he had been seen casting his eyes on the women he could have got in great trouble. He was reluctant to leave as he was sure we wouldn't be seen and he was pretty annoyed with me. I did not tell him it was a sight I could appreciate but a chance I would not take. All the way back he kept on telling me I had missed a great chance and remained obviously excited. Had there been a nice cold empty lake around I would have happily thrown him in it to cool off but inwardly I had to laugh at what I felt was a lucky escape.

Finally, enough was enough – I was told I was being sent on detachment and it would be just me alone. At first I thought it would be a relief to get away from Jerry and the rest of the group, but it did not turn out to be that way. I was being sent to a place called Danbad and, having journeyed there by train, was met at the station by the man whose place I was to take. He had a motorcycle which had been allotted to him and which he immediately handed over to me. He seemed so excited and pleased to see me as it meant he could get away from that place, which, he said, I would find very unpleasant. He did, however, at least wish me good luck before moving off as fast as he could go.

That place was indeed a very strange spot to be in and was where the Royal Electrical and Mechanical Engineers (REME) had a large workshop some way out of town. It was set among a lot of trees, next to a paddy field and I felt it was like being in the jungle. I was shown to my accommodation, which was called a 'basher' though I never found out why. It was a bamboo hut with a stone floor and hardly like home at all. It was roomy enough for my purposes but, if I thought I was on my own, then I was mistaken. The lights in the basher were generated by a dynamo which was always switched off at 11 p.m. By then one had always to be safely tucked in bed, surrounded by a mosquito net, and stay there until it was daylight at least. The reason for this was that the region was swarming with snakes, including the notorious krait, or bootlace snake, whose bite could kill instantly. It was absolutely necessary to empty out your boots each morning in case a krait was hidden inside. There were larger snakes around, too, such as pythons and cobras, which did not make me feel too happy. But there was no choice in the matter: here I was and here I would have to stay until recalled to headquarters.

Every night, once in bed and before the lights went out, I always spotted a variety of weird creatures on top of my mosquito net, a praying mantis, perhaps, or an armour-plated beetle. Neither were dangerous but they were just not nice to look at when one is going to sleep. That is, if you were lucky enough to get some sleep, for the howls of hyenas and jackals that prowled the borders of the camp looking for food also kept me awake. Tigers and black panthers were not far away, either; as a matter of fact the local rajah often went out hunting them during the day. The idea of being eaten in one's bed by a wild cat is never conducive to sleep. No wonder I slept with two loaded pistols and a torch under my pillow.

Earlier in the evening, when I would sit at my table doing paperwork or writing home, there would usually be a semicircle of large ugly toads sitting watching me. I once screwed up a paper ball and threw it at them but they did not go away; in fact one caught it in its mouth and swallowed it. It was disturbing to learn that where one finds these creatures it was a sign there were snakes around as they eat the toads. It was bad, too, that day and night one would hear a strange squeaking sound whose origin I was unable to determine until, much later, I discovered it was termites eating away at the bamboo poles of the hut. This was disconcerting – wouldn't the hut eventually collapse? – though apparently this had never happened.

My last worrying thing I did not learn until later when I had acquired a 'bearer', or male servant, to do my chores. Baba was an absolute gentleman and I felt so sad that he had come down to this but he needed the money to survive and I treated him as a friend and helped him financially as much as I could. One morning I found a packet of biscuits which I had left on the table had been taken down to the floor at the other end of the basher and well and truly chewed. I waited for Baba to arrive and asked him if he knew what this was about. His reply was that it was rats and they lived up in the roof of the basher and only came down at nights. Apparently they were as big as English cats but were not dangerous, which I found hard to believe. I felt no easier when one day Baba came into the basher looking as white as an Indian man could. He told me that on his way to me he had stopped at the paddy field to watch all the people working. Suddenly a huge python reared up and bit one of the men, who instantly dropped down dead. He also told me later that one of the Indian soldiers in the camp had decided to get out of his bed after lights out for some reason and as he put out his arm a snake struck and he, too, died at once. After this I asked Baba not to tell me any more things as I was not a coward but we did not have these problems in England. Meanwhile, I would pray I would get out of this place alive.

The very worst experience happened one night when I was awoken by a clicking sound on the stone floor and something like padded feet moving around. I was immediately fearful and called out, but there was no reply. I thought it might be 'loosewallahs', who are men that come into the hut while one is asleep. They have the knack of touching a certain part of the neck so that one turns over so the robber can get his hand under the pillow where most people would keep valuables and money especially. I realised it was not anything like this as the clicking and padded feet sound continued with the addition of heavy breathing. By then I was bathed in sweat and even more fearful. I decided not to shine a torch, although I didn't know why, and realised my pistols were of no value if I couldn't see. I must have passed out. When I came to it was daylight and there were no signs of anything having been disturbed. So I got ready and went for my breakfast and in the middle of it one of the men came in and asked me if I had seen anything of the tiger in the night. He occupied the next basher to me but was on searchlight duty, which all the men had to do in turn in order to check security. On the roof of the main building was this very powerful searchlight and he said it picked out a big tiger right in front of my basher and it suddenly disappeared so he thought it might have visited me. I did not find his joking attitude funny as I told him what had happened and then knew it was the tiger. He said it was lucky I did not shine a torch as it might have attacked me. He also said if I had used my pistols it would not have stopped the tiger. I decided to put on a brave face and laugh it off, though inwardly I wondered how much longer I could stand all of this.

The heat was terrific and reached 130 degrees every day, which meant I had to get up very early in order to do my work and be back before the midday sun. After lunch, or tiffin as it was called, it was necessary to take a siesta until around 4 p.m. when it would be cooling down and one could take a shower. But it never really seemed cool to me, especially as even back in England I had been wont to complain of any heat, though how I wished to be back home now! There was no chance of that for some time, even if I were to survive this period, so there was nothing to do but see it out as best I could. I took my meals with the REME men, who at first viewed me with great suspicion as they thought I had been sent there to spy on them. Apparently the man before me had let them think this, so I assured them it was not so with me. Gradually they came to accept me, though I rarely joined them in the mess as I was usually too tired for drinking and playing around. They were a good bunch of men but had been out there for a long time and some had become quite 'puggled' which is a condition caused through being in the heat for a long time. It seemed to make them fearless, as was demonstrated one day when one of them saw a snake wriggling towards his basher and simply fetched a hatchet and chopped its head off. When I asked him how he could do that with such a dangerous thing, he merely said one shouldn't be afraid. He told me how the major in charge of them had a set of snake guns and loved to shoot snakes, so if I ever saw any crawling through the walls of my basher then I should let him know and he would shoot them. I replied by saying I would run a mile if I saw one and I would not wait for the major.

I had to visit various camps around the area and check their security, which was not very exciting but which at least tested my ability to do that which I was trained for. It often required tact and careful handling because I had to deal with superior officers who resented a sergeant telling them what to do. Even though my rank in Intelligence was supposed to equal that of a lieutenant, although not in pay, it took a lot of courage to face a ruddy-faced brigadier and give him a polite telling off. One example of this was when I checked a certain camp, supposedly known for its efficiency and security, and I found a hole in the fencing which was big enough for a man to get through. I was not even challenged by the guards as I went in. When I was allowed to see the officer in charge I gave him the customary salute whereupon he looked at me and said, 'What are you snooping around for? Haven't you people got something better to do?' He was very fierce-looking but I decided not to be put down so I replied, 'I am only doing my duty, Sir, as I am sure we all are, and I have to report certain things to you which I feel you must know and deal with.' I expressed myself as politely as I could and watched his expression change to as soft as one might expect a brigadier to be. In fact, he invited me to sit down for a man-to-man talk and when I told him what I had found he became quite furious, not with me but to think there was slackness in his camp. He assured me it would all be seen to immediately and then added, 'I suppose you are going to report this?' I told him it was my duty to do so, as I'm sure he would agree, but I would say that his cooperation was excellent and this was a one-off slip. He was so relieved I was not going to make a big fuss, that he beamed and told me I was a good man, different from the rest of my lot, and I would be welcome to drop in for a chat any time I was in that area. I went on my way, feeling very proud of myself for having proved I could rise to the occasion no matter what the circumstances.

This gives a general idea of all my work there, which on the whole is not worth writing about, other than what I have already said. There was very little recreation but I did for a while make friends with a man named Ross who was running the army mobile cinema. He was in the same camp, from where he travelled to different places to show films to the troops. It was mostly for the Indian soldiers but he asked me to go with him and have the experience of seeing how it all worked. I remember only that the film was in Urdu, which I could not understand, but I was amused at the excitement these films caused. It was a pleasant diversion for me and good to be with Ross as we seemed to share a lot of the same interests. It was all too short a friendship as I was soon recalled to headquarters and, though I was sorry to leave him, it was a huge relief to leave behind all the snakes and tigers and so on, not to mention the intense heat and boring routine. I will never forget Ross as, although perhaps neither of us would have understood why we got on so well for that short time, there was an unusual bond between us which we both accepted could not fully materialise. Not having his home address once I got home again, there was nothing I could do to get back in contact with him, but the memory lingers on.

Ross kindly drove me to my train in the early hours one morning and I immediately dropped off to sleep and awakened as we pulled into Ranchi station. I was met by Barry who drove me back to the bungalow where I met all of the gang including Jerry who greeted me with 'Oh it's you again! I suppose you feel cocky now you have been out on detachment, but it is nothing really.' I could not resist replying, 'If you think so much of it, then why haven't you been out there?' One of the other men observed how much weight I had lost, adding, 'You look as if you have seen a ghost, too!' As an explanation of my sorry state, I gave them all an account of what it was like and of the prowling tiger and all the other things. Even Jerry admitted that it must have been horrible. He said they had received a very good account of my work there and so I should be pleased. In truth, he was merely trying to cover up his own fears of having to do such things, while all the others were wondering who would have to take my place there. Little did they know that the replacement had arrived the day before I left, and came from a different detachment, who, I rather suspected, had wanted to get rid of him. He was a most obnoxious man and did nothing but try to put me down by saying I was like a little boy to be so afraid of snakes and tigers.

Once back and settled in I had to take my share of duty visits to various units and deal with their problems – not just checking security. One problem happened in a Sikh camp where the soldiers were threatening rebellion if they did not get the cloth they needed for the special underpants they had to wear. Here I must go back a little to explain an incident in Karachi which helped me to understand what was now happening. I had been invited to dinner with some Indian officers and afterwards was approached by one of them, a young and very handsome man, who asked me if I would like to sleep with him and make love. I was rather taken aback and explained that I was not interested as I was not of that persuasion and was surprised that, being of a different race and religion, he would ask me anyway. He apologised profusely and told me that the Sikhs believed that the second Messiah would be born of a man and it would not matter which race, colour or creed. He said he would have been honoured if I had accepted his offer but asked if we could still be friends, which we were for a short time before I left for Ranchi.

Well, back to the Sikh camp. The very kind officer in charge, after I had checked security in the camp, explained that the soldiers used special cloth to make the underwear they needed as part of their religion. Apparently between the two legs of the garment there had to be a special bag which, according to their belief, would catch the new Messiah when he was born to man. It seemed very odd to me, but then there are so many different religions and beliefs all over the world, and my duty was to try to understand and help. It seemed that they had repeatedly asked for more material but had been refused or told to wait. When I reported back to Jerry he laughed his head off and said I had better deal with it as *he* wouldn't. So I rang headquarters and spoke to a senior officer who told me not to be so stupid. I don't think he believed me but I was not prepared to be put off and told him the Sikh soldiers were on the brink of rebellion and it must be dealt with. He then accused me of being insubordinate. I responded by telling him I would make an official report saying what had happened including his own part in the affair. Suddenly he calmed down and told me he was sorry and that I was an excellent negotiator; the matter would be treated with the utmost urgency. Which it was, the very same day, thus saving a critical situation and the face of one staff officer. He made me sound like a hero and even Jerry had to admit I knew how to do my job.

For me it was a lesson in tact and diplomacy – qualities I was developing and which would see me through many an awkward situation. One day I was driving out to a place which could be approached only by a long road full of potholes. John came along as a pillion rider but kept on begging me to let him drive. As we were on an open road and far away from camp, I foolishly agreed. After a few hairy moments I decided John was a danger and transferred him to pillion again. He kept shouting things like, 'Mind that pothole!' or 'Slow down!' In other words he became a back-seat driver and if there is one thing that makes me nervous and annoyed it is that. And so the inevitable happened when he screamed for me to avoid a hole which I would have missed had he not grabbed hold of me in fright. I went straight over the handlebars whilst he fell off sideways.

Luckily we were wearing crash helmets and no damage was done, at least not to us, but the bike was a mess and all the gears were broken. It could not be ridden and there seemed nothing to do but walk in the hopes of finding some help. From the distance there appeared a huge lorry. It stopped and several Sikh soldiers got out and asked us where we were going and, as there was nowhere to go but back to base, they said they would take us. After they loaded the machine and us onto the lorry we were safely delivered to base where Jerry went quite mad and told me I would be in dead trouble and I would have to report to the commanding officer. At least that is how he made it sound, all the time rubbing his hands in glee. John, by contrast, was told how lucky he was not to have been hurt by this madman. I did not say anything as I realised I would have to take responsibility; I would not tell what really happened.

The commanding officer appeared to be a pleasant man, bearing out the fact that some officers are human. Jerry had assured me he would tear me apart and it would be the end of my career, but knowing Jerry as I did, this dire warning had no effect on me. The officer simply asked me what had happened, so I invented a version of the truth and told him about the dangers of Indian roads and how I had had to swerve and consequently went into the pothole. Jerry had said I would have to pay for all the damage and probably be put in the guardhouse; instead the officer sympathised with me and said it was damn bad luck and I had acted in the right way. In fact, he said he would give me an excellent report. If you could have seen Jerry's face when I told him: it was pure delight to see him put in his place! He could not say any more as a little later the officer phoned and told Jerry the results and how I was an excellent soldier and good at my job, and that it was just an unlucky thing that happened and a new motorcycle would be issued. Jerry said I must have told lies or crawled round the officer, to which I said I had simply told him the truth, all the while crossing my fingers knowing I had bent it just a little.

5

An Austrian Idyll

My stay in Ranchi came to an end soon after the motorbike accident when, along with some of the other men, I was sent back to Karachi. We were to be prepared to leave India, which was now about to gain independence. There was some time to be spent there more or less just enjoying leisure pursuits but still having to attend lectures and be drilled occasionally. As we were not yet going to be demobbed, it was announced that our work would still be continued elsewhere – perhaps the Middle East or Austria. In the army there is very little choice and one has to go where and do what one is told. As luck would have it I was posted to Austria with a group of men that I very much liked and got along with. I am not usually lucky but this time I felt it was meant to be.

As we sailed away from Bombay en route to Port Said, I could not feel anything but joy in getting away from India as it was at that time in history. I did feel sorry that, in my dislike of being there, I had not taken any advantage of the wonderful sights to be seen, but being still nineteen I only wanted to get back to England and home, and away from the army and war. It was only much later that I thought maybe one day I should go there as a visitor and it would all be different, but it has not come to pass and so all I can do is to see it as a valuable experience which no doubt helped me to find myself.

Port Said did not seem especially inviting to me and, although the Egyptians were interesting people, and despite the pyramids and other wonders, I only wanted to get away from there as soon as possible. From Port Said we sailed up the Suez Canal only to be deposited in a transit camp made of tents and with very crude conditions. It was hot and smelly and sleep came fitfully, especially when we discovered a fearsome white spider crawling up the tent walls. It was fuzzy and had evil red eyes and always managed to escape our attempts to kill it. There was sand everywhere and it got into everything, but, despite all this, we were given lectures and things to do to keep us on our toes. As time went by it felt as if we would never get away from there. Suddenly one day we discovered that the Intelligence branch was in fact trying to keep us there despite the fact we had our official orders for Austria. Our man in charge fought long and hard to get us back on our original route and finally succeeded one month later, when we found ourselves on another boat to Venice, our next stop before Austria. It was a tremendous relief and as the boat sailed out into the Mediterranean on 1 June it was happily a gloriously sunny day.

It was not a troopship but quite small, more like a pleasure craft except that the cabins did not have bunks but hammocks. There was great fun to be had as we all tried to get the hang of getting into them and, more to the point, staying in. I found it very difficult but once achieved it was surprisingly comfortable although the swinging about took some getting used to. There were only thirty of us men, which had its advantages as the food was good and I figured we were getting special treatment as the crew said it was better food than usual. We were only to be on board for three days with no duties to perform and so our man in charge told us we could treat it as a pleasure cruise. As though we could! For on that first day we had not gone very far out when all of a sudden the sea became very rough, although the sun was still shining. The boat was tossed about and rolled from side to side. Someone said it was lunchtime and so we trooped into the mess where everything on the tables was rolling from end to end. Even if one wanted to eat it would have been a case of catch it if you can. Some tried but for me just one look at food made me rush to be sick. I was soon followed by all of the men except one who must have come from a seafaring family as he was able to sit and have as much as he wanted. The rest of us found positions on deck where we could lay down, though not for long as there was a continual toing and froing as we were sick again. In the end it became a contest to see who would be sick the most number of times. Needless to say I won with a score of thirty! After that first day things settled down and it was possible to enjoy the trip to some extent but I longed to get off the boat and realised I would never make a sailor.

It was a beautiful sight to behold as we sailed into Venice but once docked and landed we were taken to yet another transit camp at Treviso, not too far away. We were able to have a day trip to Venice but it was wet and cool, not very good for sightseeing. Nevertheless we saw most of the important sights and had a chance to barter with the Italians for things on sale, but it seemed as if the people did not trust us and the aftermath of war seemed still to hang heavy over everything. At that time, I suppose, I had a prejudice against the Italians and mistrusted and disliked them. I was very young, after all, and only over time did I develop a feeling of comradeship with and love all my fellow men. Perhaps at the time I was just like all the other men, prone to fall for the temptations that lay in my way and liable to follow common opinion. Being young, one rarely understands or thinks about the rights and wrongs in life.

After two days in Treviso we boarded a train and headed northwards into the Alps and into the region of Carinthia and the city of Villach. It was a pleasing journey through the most beautiful scenery with snowcapped mountains and shimmering lakes, Tyrolean chalets and meadows of wild flowers. I wondered how any of my companions could have failed to be thrilled by all this but surprisingly quite a lot grumbled and wished they were en route to England. At the same time, however, many were determined to get the most out of this next posting, especially as they had heard that real Intelligence work took place in Austria; so far there had been nothing they could get their teeth into. The thought of having to do spy work and such like seemed to me to be only a remote possibility and slightly absurd. Despite the fact that I had done what I had to do so far with excellent references, I did not feel cut out to be an Intelligence man.

In Villach we were given some talks on how life would be and what was expected of us before being transported to a village called Steindorf on the edge of the Ossiachersee, a lake five miles long, amidst the most beautiful scenery one could wish for. Almost immediately things took on more of a holiday atmosphere, especially when we were billeted in a hotel which had been converted for the troops. It was right at the edge of the lake and all one had to do was to walk out of the back door and jump into the lake for a swim; there was even a boat for our use whenever we wanted it. Also in the camp was a very beautiful chalet with lovely grounds which actually belonged to an Austrian princess and was being used as the sergeants' and officers' mess, plus another building which was used as an office and interrogation room amongst other things. One could not have wished for anything more comfortable or pleasant, especially with a canteen very close by where one could go in the evenings. It was the equivalent of a NAAFI but far superior. Once a week, dances were held there when trucks were sent out to collect all the girls from local villages.

There was a cinema not far away, too, though unless one knew much German it was not very enjoyable unless you had a girlfriend to take your mind off the film. I experienced this joy just once but apparently there was a warning that a lot of the local girls had been infected by venereal disease during the war, as many had had to sell themselves in order to survive. So passion needed to be cooled. I had a list of all the girls known to be questionable which was very useful and it became one of my duties to make the men aware of who and what. So it was back to being a sort of nursemaid for that and a lot of other things. I had been there only a short time when it was decided I would be in the office for the rest of my stay as I was undoubtedly more experienced than most there. At first this did not please me but in due course I was delighted as it gave me many more opportunities to make my stay more worthwhile.

In the camp were thirty men plus a sergeant major, a lieutenant and the major in charge. Despite the holiday atmosphere, there was still a routine to be followed, though not a very difficult one and it seemed as though most of the time there was little to do. Some of us more senior ones were let into the secrets of what was going on but the important stuff seemed to be taking place at nearby Klagenfurt where they dealt with Nazi war criminals. Everything was so hush-hush that I often wondered if *anyone* knew what they were really doing. There was still a sombre atmosphere around as many of the Austrians had collaborated with the Germans and were still under suspicion. They had to be checked out and watched, which was something I did not enjoy doing but it was in the line of duty like so many other things. I learned a lot about shadowing people, interrogation and surveillance.

Life there was not without humour and many amusing things happened that helped us keep some sort of perspective. Most days those of us in the office would watch out of the window at people passing by. The locals were allowed to go through the camp on their way to work or use it as a shortcut but they did not present any kind of danger as everywhere was well protected. It was simply amazing to see the number of men who looked exactly like Hitler with the same moustache, which made us think that he was not dead at all but living, hidden amongst a lot of look-alikes. We never did find out why this was so but perhaps they had been sympathisers and still wanted to be like their hero. On the whole the local people were quite friendly, especially once they found they could trade things for soap and cigarettes and other items they had been deprived of during the war. Luckily army rations were generous and so it was a good thing to be able to help them out and profit in some way at the same time. I had a very smart suit made up by the local tailor in exchange for soap, chocolate and cigarettes. The situation of the populace was the unhappy part of my stay in Steindorf, the only consolation being that the war was over and things were now getting back to normal.

Gradually most of the men were sent out on detachment, leaving just myself, another sergeant, the sergeant major and the major to run the depot. The latter did not seem to be bothered much and so we had free rein to do what we liked. Before the other men departed we did hold some wild parties, with all kinds of drink including rare old brandies and whiskies; in fact all sorts of things one would never have tried otherwise. It is best not to go into *too* many details. On the other hand, I think we were quite well behaved, comparatively speaking. After the men had gone, we had a group of new recruits come to the camp before being sent out on detachment. I think *their* behaviour was quite disgraceful for as soon as they arrived they started chasing the local girls, getting drunk and completely disobeying orders. Some of us old stagers had to rescue them from all sorts of situations to prevent them getting caught by the Major, which would have meant real trouble. By then I most certainly had enough experience of getting drunk and getting up to all sorts of tricks, but after a time it becomes very boring and one longs for better things. With all the scenery and particularly the lake, there was so much to enjoy and I was a good swimmer as well as walker. Being out in the countryside was so uplifting and like getting away from it all. Thus when the camp was empty except for us two sergeants, things became much better and more rewarding.

Life was not without romance, too, as I had already been introduced to a very nice Austrian girl who lived in a small village not too far away. The other sergeant, Al, and I had become good friends, and as he was transport sergeant he could wangle lifts for her and anyone else we wanted. As a matter of fact we shared all the job titles between us so there was nothing we couldn't arrange for our own purposes. Not strictly above board, I suppose, but no one seemed to care. Nothing was ever checked or even recorded which gave us the opportunity to live it up. We only ever saw the major on rare occasions and he seemed satisfied to leave us to our own devices, and this also applied, too, to Jock the sergeant major. He certainly knew what we were up to but, as he, his wife and daughter were included in the dinner parties that we arranged, he was happy to turn a blind eye. He always did his nightly 'security' rounds but if he realised our girlfriends were hidden under the blankets he just gave us a knowing wink and suggested we get them out before there could be any complications.

The situation became even better when the major was replaced by a new one. He wanted to be one of the lads and insisted on knowing what we were up to, not in order to stop us but so that he could take part. When we found an emergency food store which had been hidden away and presumably forgotten, he wanted to know all about it and if there was any record of it. When we discovered there was not, he suggested we divide up the spoils and send home parcels of tea and other things that were still on ration. The new major was so impressed with us that he asked us if we would like to sign on for six months longer and go with him to Vienna where things would be a lot different and the outfit would be full of 'top brass', but where he could use a couple of sharp and clever minds like ours in order to survive. Had it been possible to remain where we were, then both Al and I would have jumped at the chance to stay in this idyllic spot, but we both felt that really it was high time to go home. I didn't want to leave the girl I had fallen in love with but Vienna would have been too far away and there would be very little chance of seeing her anyway, so reluctantly I decided to return home – though with a lot of beautiful memories.

The most outstanding of these was when my girlfriend and I climbed into the branches of a magnificent magnolia tree and shared some kisses. We could not be seen amongst the masses of deep-pink blooms and to this day I never fail to remember this moment every time I see a magnolia in bloom. I felt sure I wanted to marry this girl but it wasn't that easy and finally, after realising I had no money and my job paid only enough for one to live on, and there was nowhere we could live, I had to write and tell her. It broke my heart and in a way I felt mean as I had been in love with the girl at school.

6

Demob Happy

And so we were finally demobbed. We were brought home to England and given 'demob suits', but allowed to keep our uniforms and given three months' paid leave before our discharge became final. It was so good to see the family again and catch up on everything. It is called getting back to normal but I soon realised things would never be as they had been before. I had spent two years and nine months under army discipline, undergoing intense training and enjoying camaraderie which had transformed the boy into a man. In some ways it had made me someone I did not want to be but nothing would ever change that, so it was something I would have to deal with and learn to accept. I decided to enjoy the whole leave before looking for work, and in any case I did not know what I wanted to do anyway. I felt the army had taken a lot out of my life, or at least my mother thought so, and so in some way I felt I was going to get my own back. A lot of men felt like this: it was a disruption that left one feeling up in the air and knowing that one would eventually have to come down.

While doing my service, I had always allotted some of admittedly meagre pay to be sent each week to my mother to help with the family income. Unbeknown to me she had put it all aside for me when I got home, and insisted I take it as I would need something to be going on with. It was so nice of her but I realised it would come in useful for something I had always wanted to do, which was to take her to Devon for a holiday. Mother was born in Stockport in Lancashire but, as I have stated, her parents were both Devonshire and Mother and her twin sister often spent their holidays with their grandfather who was a gentleman farmer. Mother talked so much of Devon and I realised she longed to go there again, but there had been no chance for thirty years owing to lack of money and the pressures of raising a family. At first she was reluctant to let me spend the money but I soon persuaded her as I was keen to go myself, too. I had no idea of what it would be like as, although I had been to Cornwall, I had only seen bits of Devon through the train window. What I saw looked good but what I found later was really wonderful and at once I knew I was truly a part of Devon and it was part of me.

We set off for a week's stay in Barnstaple, which was the nearest place to the villages we wanted to see. Mother had a cousin also named Winnie who before the war had also lived in London but had later been evacuated to Devon. After the war ended she had decided to stay on and now she was to be our guide as we tried to reconnect to our family roots. Once in Barnstable, we settled into a hotel and enjoyed a good night's rest. The next day we were to take a bus to the village of Landkey where her cousin was to meet us. She had told us to get off at the top of the hill where she would be waiting so that we could take the walk into the village and see what Mother would remember. As we walked down I could see an elderly gentleman in the distance coming up the hill. Her cousin told Mother not to say anything as this was old Mr Hammett whom she would remember; we would see if he recognised her. Mother was astounded that he was still alive but as we all drew level we found he most certainly was. He took one look at Mother and said, 'Why bless my soul, 'tis Winnie Yeo!' and looking at me he added, '... And this is your son. I can see he belongs in the family!' To say I was moved is an understatement and when he started remembering all the things relating to the past, none was more amazing than when he said to Mother: 'I remember the last time you and your twin sister Mabel came down for your holidays and I met you with the pony and trap. You were wearing white dresses with black velvet buttons all the way down the front, a black velvet sash and big picture hats!' Turning to me he said, 'Your mother and her sister were beautiful young ladies and we have never forgotten them, although sadly we have lost Mabel.' He went on to speak of their grandfather, whom, he said, was a greatly respected man, and on hearing all Mr Hammett had to say I wished I could have known him as well as the others who had gone before.

The old boy chatted on for some time before telling us he had to be about his business. We continued our walk, which was full of more surprises as everywhere we went Mother was immediately recognised, which seemed incredible to me as I had not heard much about the Landkey people at home. She looked up a very old friend who asked her why she had never written. Mother could only say she had had a busy time bringing up a family and that things were difficult but here she was now and she would keep in contact in future. We finally wended our way to the graveyard attached to a small but pleasant-looking church. As we approached we passed the vicarage where we saw a man leaning on the front gate. He called out from a distance, 'Well, Winnie Yeo, what has kept you so long in coming back?' I was just dumbfounded to see and hear for myself how Mother had never been forgotten and I was delighted for her, but at the same time rather sorry that she had not been able to stay in Devon all those years ago.

When we got to the graveyard Winnie wanted to show us where Mother's mother was buried. It was a very simple grave and even then quite old, but the strange thing was that the inscription said it was Mary Buckingham, her maiden name, instead of Mary Yeo buried there and no mention of her husband called Henry Yeo. The cousin supposed that old Granny Buckingham had not liked Henry and didn't want his name on the stone, but the question remained why Henry had not been responsible for his wife's burial. It was a mystery and would remain so for a long time.

The week soon passed, although we were able to visit some of the many beauty spots and also the village of Swimbridge where my great-grandfather was buried, though it was impossible to locate the grave as parts of the graveyard were overgrown with yew trees. It seemed that almost every grave one could see belonged to a Yeo, which was a very common name thereabouts. Finally we made our way back to London and came down to earth as one might say. I had already decided, though, that I would get back to Devon as soon as I could to find out more about my family, but before that I would have to get my life sorted out, which was not going to be an easy task.

The first thing I had to do was to apply for jobs, the only ones I could consider being clerical as I had no idea what else I could try. At that time it was impossible to find anything as jobs were scarce and one needed qualifications, which I did not have. After trying and trying, I began to feel absolutely miserable as it would mean going back to my old job. There was a law at the time which said any man returning from service in the armed forces must be given his original job back within a six-month period. So there was no choice to but to present myself at the town hall and face up to something I did not really want to. I needed to earn money and catch up on what I had missed at home, which on the wage I was offered would take quite some time to do. I was welcomed back and was surprised at how many of my former colleagues were happy to see me. I knew I could no longer be considered as a junior and so found myself in the audit section again as a more senior member.

I had come out of the army with that 'the world owes me a living' feeling common to the demobbed soldier and consequently was inclined to be somewhat rebellious and bombastic. Not that it wasn't such a bad thing at the town hall as in local government one had to hold one's own and be determined not to be beaten. I hated the jealousy and backbiting that went on but it would never change so it was best to cope with it in one's own way. I have always been determined not to let anyone put me down and later I was called 'the master of the smart answer' by my friends. Fortunately I was good at my work and as I gradually lost my earlier feelings I was accepted and respected, but I would always uphold and stand by what I felt to be right.

My work took me out of the office a great deal, for which I was thankful as to get away from that atmosphere made things more bearable. I had to visit schools, swimming baths, crematoria, cemeteries and catering establishments alike in order to audit their books. Wherever money was transacted in the borough it had to be checked or audited. It was not a very pleasant job as I was often initially received with suspicion and even some hostility. However, I was soon able to put minds at rest by explaining it was a job I had to do and, unless anyone was cheating, there was nothing to fear. I gradually got to know those concerned and was received with open arms as they came to trust me and knew I would always help them rather than get them into trouble. I also had to check on school kitchens and was always pleased to be asked to have lunch with the staff, especially as we did not have the same meals as schoolchildren did (thank heavens!). All in all I learned to deal with people and understand them as they would also understand me. I gained a reputation of being outspoken but honest and caring, which made me feel good, although back in the office was a very different matter. I could not understand that even the head of office as well as most of the others were jealous and annoyed, but after a time I realised they all operated their own secret schemes and were afraid my methods would show them up. I had frequent altercations with the head man but I always stuck to my point and eventually we became good friends as he knew I could run the office standing on my head, which would give both of us a chance to do what we wanted. I must admit that I did take advantage of that but never without doing my work correctly and honestly. Because I was quick and capable there were some of the lazy ones in the office who thought I should help them out. As I did what I was paid to do to the best of my ability, I told them they should do the same, but, having a weak spot, I did sometimes help one or two.

I had not been back from the army but a few months when I received my papers to report for the army's Z Reserve. This was something introduced then but abandoned later because it turned out to be rather pointless. The idea was that men who had served should have a refresher course and know where they would have to report to if there was another outbreak of war. It was only for two weeks but I for one could not see any real point in it so soon after being demobbed, and rightly or wrongly I approached it with an uncooperative attitude. I had to report to Penally in Wales, very close to the famous beauty spot of Tenby and on a wild, scenic coastline which stretched into Pembroke. For a holiday it would have been superb but for playing soldiers it did not appeal to me. When I arrived at the depot everything seemed to be chaotic and very few knew what they were doing. We had to remain in our civilian clothes until two days later we were given some sort of uniform but no weapons. We had to pretend we had them and it began to feel like a lot of little boys playing cowboys and Indians. The accommodation was adequate and the food fair, but as there was a lot of freedom many of us would dine out in Tenby or elsewhere. It seemed we could do more or less as we pleased, so if at any time we wanted to leave the camp, no one would ever notice. There were quite a few officers around but they could not care less if the lower ranks saluted them or not, and few bothered to talk to the men and as a matter of fact they turned out to be the biggest kids of all.

On my first evening there I was told to report to a certain sergeant who appeared to be thrilled at being where we were and it was obvious he was going to take it all very seriously. There were several other men there who like me were not keen on the idea, which only infuriated the sergeant. I thought he was going to cry because we were spoiling his game, but when he said someone was going to be put on guard duty everyone murmured their disapproval. It was then I knew that he would choose me because I could see that look in his eye on first meeting. When I said it was stupid because there was nothing to guard and what would it look like without a rifle, he retorted that I would just have to go through the actions and pretend. This got me angry whereupon he said that, if there *were* another war, I would have to report to him and then God help me as he would remember me and make my life miserable! I told him this was childish and suggested he give some thought to the matter as I was sure that every man would do his duty if there was a need to. I also said that I presumed we would have real weapons and if I had a bayonet he would need to watch his step. I never have liked playing games and hate wasting time. It served no purpose at all and the government soon realised this and dropped the whole project, though unfortunately. not before I finished my two weeks in Penally.

The days were filled with endless stupid exercises, some of which we were forced to attend, but most of which we were able to dodge. I had made a good friend and so he and I often went for walks along the coast and had lunch out. Luckily the weather was good so it felt great to leave all the nonsense behind for a while. One day we thought we would see what was going on in the camp and wandered into a large marquee where a group of officers resplendent in full uniform and medals were standing around a large table. On top was a map and various other things which suggested they were plotting something. As we approached the table some of them turned and shouted to us to get out as we were not allowed to see or know what was going on. Another lot playing silly boys, we thought.

The so-called highlight of our stay was an exercise that we had no choice but to go out on. The first entailed our being taken to a certain area and split into two groups called the 'attackers' and the 'defenders'. I was in the first group and could not believe it when we were told we had to creep up the road from behind bushes and take control of a telephone box which was being defended by the first group. We all walked up the road in full view, only to come across an officer laying stretched out in the middle of the road. I walked up to him and said, 'Excuse me, Sir, are you all right?' 'Get away, get away!' he shouted back. 'Can't you see I'm dead! I've been killed by the defenders!' Unfazed I just walked up to the box, which was encircled by men, and said, 'Excuse me, chaps, I want to make a telephone call.' The 'defenders' just stepped aside and I used the field telephone to ring the remainder of my group who were hidden behind bushes, and that was that. Another fiasco! We did however receive a stern lecture from the officer in charge who told us what naughty boys we were and that we should learn to 'play the game'.

The biggest laugh came near the end of our stay when we were told it would be a night exercise. We were taken out to a remote spot where we had to sleep under the stars wrapped only in groundsheets. At four in the morning we were awoken and again split into two groups. The defenders were taken off somewhere but we were not allowed to know any details. The attackers, who were once more my lot, were taken to where there was an old mill and told that we would have to creep under cover and take the mill. Seeing that the ground was somewhat muddy and rough, this seemed to be a step too far in this whole stupid charade, so I and some of the others decided to just walk up to the mill. On the way we encountered a lot of men, including officers who were down on one knee and pointing their hands as though firing a gun, and shouting, 'Bang, bang, you're dead!' One particular officer even said to me, 'Lay down, man, I've just killed you!' and when I refused he got very upset and said, 'If this was real you would be dead by now.' To this I scornfully replied, 'If this was real you wouldn't be playing silly boys!' Somehow this whole thing did not seem real and, if I hadn't known better, I would have said I was dreaming.

The last straw came on the day we were leaving when in the morning we were taken to a field where three or four officers were seated on the ground for the purpose of an interrogation exercise. I was directed to a very fat officer who looked smug and who undoubtedly thought he was going to enjoy himself. He made me sit down and said, 'Now I am a suspect and you must interrogate me.' By then my patience was exhausted and I refused to play, expecting he might be angry and attempt some form of punishment. Instead of which he just laughed and said, 'You will be sorry, my lad. You need to remember what you have learned, but you will suffer for your actions, I promise.' My only reply was: 'No more than you will for yours. If this whole two weeks has been of any use then perhaps we have both learned something, which is not to play at things that are not really funny. We must all stick to our principles.' I then hurried away to get ready for the train journey back home.

All of the men were glad to go but there was one final irritation – while we were away on the exercise some of the men were burgled and a lot of personal things stolen. I lost a few items not really worth worrying about but others had a lot taken and, although they were assured of compensation, it was not a happy ending. It underlined my feelings about the whole thing: it is senseless playing silly boys unless you do it properly. Once on the train I could only reflect on yet another waste of my time but another lesson learned. Inwardly I offered up a prayer that there would never be another war but, if there was, then I would be serious and do my duty. Meanwhile I could use the experience for what it was worth, which was not much...but, still, every little helps.

So it was home once again and back to the town hall. This was not exactly what I wanted and after a while I made up my mind to leave and find another job. I had made a friend in one of the other offices who, when I told him of my plan, said I should stay and apply for a higher-grade position as I was a good worker and well respected. He said it didn't matter if I didn't like the work but that I would have to study, which did not please me as I had no desire to study something in which I had no interest. Then one day a higher-grade post came up in my own office and my friend literally forced me to apply. I was sure I would not get it only to be surprised to find myself on the shortlist. After facing an interview in the council chamber with a tough committee, I managed to convince them I was the man for the job and more or less promised to study and become qualified. When I discovered my salary would be doubled I was delighted as it meant I could do so much more than I expected and could therefore put up with the job whatever it entailed. Studying would be the problem but not one to be resolved immediately.

One thing I was able to do with the extra money in my pocket was to go to the theatre more often and have a good seat. This gave rise to two more wonderful experiences that would always remain in my mind as being beautiful and significant turning points in my life. The first was when I decided to treat my parents and sister to a trip to the theatre in London's West End, which we could not have afforded before. I chose a musical, *Annie Get Your Gun*, which I hoped would please everyone. It was at the Coliseum, where we had front-row seats in the upper circle. The thing I will always remember is when the curtain went up and a young lady dressed in buckskin strode out onto the stage with a rifle slung across her shoulder and began singing out the song called 'You Can't Get a Man with a Gun'. Her voice was so powerful it filled the whole theatre even without the use of a microphone. Her name was Dolores Gray, who became one of my favourite singers.

The second experience was when I decided some time later to go to see *King's Rhapsody*, which was one of Ivor Novello's shows. It was beautiful to look at and lovely to hear, but the one thing I can never forget is when the star of the show, Vanessa Lee, stood alone on the large stage of the London Hippodrome without a microphone and sang 'Some Day My Heart Will Awake'. Once again the singer's voice was glorious and, I dare to say, one of the finest voices of the age. If ever I feel in the need of hearing something to make me feel good, this is one of my three all-time choices, and although there are now so many other memories I can recall, nothing has quite the resonance these things do.

As I was now of a higher grade and presumably more responsible, I was given an assistant, which pleased me as it could be lonely travelling around on my own. Also I had acquired a motor scooter, which made it even more pleasing especially as I could claim a petrol allowance. My first assistant was a young lad called Jim Carpenter who also seemed to enjoy the idea of getting away from the town hall for a while. After a time we became good friends, and still are, and we shared many experiences. It was fortunate that we could go to his home for lunch and, once I had met his parents, I became a regular visitor there. Jim and I shared a lot of the same interests, which led to many unusual situations and interesting results, of which I will tell more later. One thing we did was to share some holidays, one of which took us to Devon where I had the chance to visit some of the places I had been with Mother. I did not have much luck tracing my family tree as there did not seem to be any church records available, nor anything else that could give me more information about Mother's relatives.

Later I had a new assistant named David Prior with whom I also became friendly. We didn't only have fun doing our work. At that time we both had pedal cycles and during our leisure time we would often cycle for as much as 150 miles in one day exploring old English villages. We also swam, rowed, went dancing and even learned to handle a canoe. David had a great sense of humour and we shared many hair-raising experiences.

Once we spent two weeks riding down to Devon with a large trailer attached to one of the cycles, which held camping equipment and food. We took turns in pulling the trailer but it seemed in vain as the weather was so bad that we got to camp only once and even then the tent got flooded out. I was taking my turn with the trailer one day and it had been raining heavily. The road was very wet and as I took a bend I suddenly saw a notice about a one-in-four gradient ahead. By then I had gathered speed and the trailer was toppling all over the place. I jammed on my brakes but they would not work having become too wet, so instead I desperately tried to use my foot realising there was a crossroad at the bottom of the hill and there would be traffic on it. I thought David would be far behind me and he was going to find me dead. Someone must have been watching over me as I went over the crossroad safely and, as the road then evened out, I was able to stop right outside a pub. When David came racing up he exclaimed, 'Oh my God, you aren't dead!' to which I replied, 'I'm not sure *what* I am but I need a stiff drink.' When we had one in that pub I was able to compose myself and gradually we turned it into a funny story. Some may think this peculiar but I have always tried to see a funny side to things as it creates a balance. By the time we reached Barnstaple, the trailer collapsed and we had to find someone to repair it. Luckily we found a place that did it quickly and so we were able to go on to Landkey where we stayed for two nights with one of Mother's old friends. It was so good to be there but I did not find out much else about my family and by the time I got home again I more or less decided to give up trying.

There were other things to do in my life, which was beginning to open out in a more promising way. I still kept contact with my old school friend Les and we would often meet for a drink in one of the local pubs. Sometimes we would visit a dance hall in the hopes of finding girlfriends but, to be honest, at that time I was more interested in dancing and could do it quite well. Geminis, it is said, are interested in many different things, are good communicators and creative, but tend to go on to other subjects before finishing the first. At the time that did apply to me, though perhaps now not so much because one reaches the realisation that if you are going to succeed in anything you have to stick with it. During my life I have wanted to be an actor, a pianist, a designer, a singer and many other things. My meetings with Les turned out to be sessions of crying into our beer and feeling sorry for ourselves, although we could still find a few things to laugh about.

One of these meetings with Les turned out to be a very important turning point in my life. I had often told him that I would die when I was twenty-five as I had a very strong feeling that something was going to happen, and it was not an easy thing to laugh off. At that point I was just coming up to that age. Sometimes we went to a pub called the College Park Hotel where on a Saturday night they would have someone to play the piano for a sing-along. It was fascinating to see so many different characters there as by this time I tended to study people and decide what sort of person they were. Even Les joined in with me and we had fun at what I thought was guessing who was who and what they did. On one occasion a lady came into the bar, leading a blind man whom she placed by the piano. She went to fetch him a drink and then sat down to accompany the singing which the man joined in. He appeared to be thoroughly enjoying himself. It made me say to Les, 'Look at that man. He's blind and reliant on others but he doesn't feel sorry for himself, while we have our sight and are able to do so much more but are very sorry for ourselves.' 'What, old Alf?' Les replied, 'He's quite a character. Would you believe that he has been told he will see again?' I was surprised and asked how Les knew this, whereupon he went a little red and thought he had better tell me that he and his mother went with the lady next door, who was a medium, to a little Spiritualist church. It seemed that Alf and his lady friend went there too and that Alf received healing from somebody who had told him his sight would be restored. Strangely enough, although it was quite a long time later, Alf *did* get his sight back.

Asked why he hadn't told me about this before, Les said he didn't think I would be interested. I demanded to hear more about it and ended up feeling I would like to go to this place and see for myself. I did have some experience of playing with the glass and alphabet, but nothing else. I sometimes used to think that my stillborn brother, who would have been a year younger than me, was watching me, but to be honest I never thought anything about another world or the continuation of life. After the frightening time at church with my godfather I preferred not to think of anything like that because I was young and life was surely made to be enjoyed. Anyway, Les invited me along, but for one reason or another it was several months before I actually went.

7

The Haven

The Haven, as this little Spiritualist church was called was just one room in a large house in Harlesden, quite local to both Les and me. It only held thirty-five people and, as I entered it with Les, his mother and neighbour for the first time, I was more than surprised to find it completely different to how I had imagined. To be honest, I hadn't really imagined anything other than something curious and way out. I certainly expected to have a good laugh, but immediately felt disappointed as it was really quite ordinary. Here there was a small altar with a silver cross and two vases of flowers on a raised platform in front of the French windows which had been covered by deep-blue velvet curtains. In one corner of the room was an organ and four rows of chairs had been set out in front of the altar plus a bench at the back of the room. Not the height of comfort but there was nonetheless a wonderful sense of peace and welcome.

We sat down on the chairs and waited for the 'service' to begin. After a while a lady came to the organ and began to play various hymns. I was immediately attracted by this lady, who turned out to be Nora Blackwood, one of the finest mediums of our time. Actually she had not been discovered at that time but it happened not long after I began to attend this church. She also had a fine singing voice and it appeared everyone there loved her. Eventually two ladies came onto the platform, one of whom was the chairperson for the evening, and the other the medium who would take the service. I was also attracted to the medium as she was a very beautiful lady and spoke with an equally beautiful voice. After the introductions, we launched into a hymn followed by prayers and a reading of some kind and then another hymn before the medium addressed us.

So far, this was better than my earlier experience in my godfather's church, as it was less rigid and had a much happier feel about it. It became better still when the medium gave her address, although I cannot remember now exactly what she said, only that it was very interesting to listen to. I was somewhat distracted all the time by hearing a voice calling my name from the ceiling at one corner of the room. It seemed only I could hear it as everybody else was listening to the speaker. I should have been frightened but somehow it seemed to be quite soothing until it eventually stopped. By then the address had finished and another hymn was announced, after which we were told this lady would give a demonstration of clairvoyance, which meant she would be trying to contact those who had passed to another world and pass on messages from them. She addressed several people all of whom seemed to be happy with what they were told; I, however, did not receive anything. So the service closed with more hymns and prayers and, although I had decided I did not want any more religion at least for some time, I felt that that did not matter as this was somewhat different and a very interesting experience.

When we got outside the little church Les asked me what I thought of it. I could only say I found it interesting but was worried by what had happened to me. When I told him of the voice calling me, he burst into laughter and said, 'Oh boy, they have got you well lined up...You're obviously psychic.' I told him not to be so daft as I had no intention of getting involved with anything like that, but was quite happy to go back there again to give it another try. After all, I had not received any messages and felt I had to hear something before I could pass judgement upon it. Les quite eagerly agreed to accompany me to the next meeting. This was to be a week later but to me it seemed a long time as something inside of me was telling me I had to follow this through.

During our next visit to The Haven we heard Mr and Mrs Blenkiron, a husband-and-wife team. Mr Blenkiron no doubt gave an interesting address but to be honest I did not hear a word of it as I was waiting for the messages to begin. Mrs Blenkiron was a little lady who smiled beautifully and as she stood up we were told she would give the messages in a trance. Suddenly she spoke just as a Chinese person might speak, though it was hard for me to believe she was in a trance. It did not really matter at that time because I was more interested in what she might say and more importantly that it made sense. Her first message seemed to go down well and then came my big moment as she pointed at me and said, 'Young man, you are very psychic!' I was stunned. 'No, I'm not,' I managed to stammer. She insisted. 'You are and what is more you will become one of the best-known mediums in this world.' I nearly fell off my chair laughing but quickly apologised by telling her I did not mean to be rude but if she was sitting where I was she would understand. Not to be put off she assured me she was right and then said she saw a gentleman standing behind me. He was wearing a schoolmaster's cap and gown, his name was Harry and he was my grandfather. I had to admit that, although I never knew him, Mother's father had been a teacher. The medium then mentioned several names, none of which I recognised, but she told me that I lived at home with my mother and that I should go and ask her.

After the service, I could not wait to get home to interrogate Mother. Les, who was absolutely gloating, came with me. Mother was surprised to see me home so early and asked why. I said I knew her father had been a teacher whose name was Harry, but was there an Uncle Willie who was a train driver in the family? I went on to mention the other names, too. She said it was all correct but was puzzled where I had got all this information from. When I told her I had been to a Spiritualist church her immediate reply was: 'Don't get mixed up in that.' I said I was an intelligent man and I had been to this place which I did not know existed before, seen a lady I never knew existed and who to my knowledge had never seen me before, and who had told me all these things I did not know and which were true. So I was certainly going there again to see what more I might discover. To which Mother just said, 'Please be careful!' If she and I had known how important this was to be in my life then she would have been happy and proud, although in retrospect I ought really to have given it very serious thought. I had a lot to learn and many experiences to go through, and I often heard Les saying, 'I told you so, I knew they would get you!'

I did go again and again, and every time I did, no matter who the medium was, I received what I called 'a star-studded message'. All the messages contained evidence of survival but always the accent was on the fact that I was very psychic and would become very well known and some even used the word 'famous'. I went twice a week to the meetings as they were called, on a Thursday and a Sunday, and as time went on I began to believe it could all be true. It became a joke with the other people attending, as they would always say as I entered the room, 'Here he comes and we know he will get a message tonight for sure.' They were always friendly people who began to look up to me as someone special, which at that time I did not want to be special, or at least I did not think so. When Les often reminded me that I was destined for something special, I always said I did not want to be, and that, although the subject was very interesting, I would only make it a little hobby. Little did I then know that if it was my destiny, so to speak, that in the end I would have no choice. I was also told I had a healing power which made me feel a little different about it all, as I have always cared very much about helping people. Gradually I became more involved with the running of the church and helped out in any way I could, including arranging the flowers – something I loved to do as an outlet of my creative and artistic side. Eventually I would became medium's secretary and then resident medium.

At the town hall I had to be so careful not to tell anyone what I was doing outside of office times. Most of the people I worked with there seemed rather biased, and there always seemed to be the same atmosphere of jealousy and backbiting. I longed to get away but as fate would have it I had to stay in that job for a few years more. However, I learned to treat it all as something that had to be done, and, as it paid good money, I was able to enjoy holidays abroad and other things that helped to broaden my experience. A part of my work was to visit all local things connected with the council. The place I enjoyed going to most was the catering department which was in a very large building in one of the local parks and which also organised wedding receptions and the like. It was there incidentally that I learned a lot about wine and food, as I was quite friendly with the manageress and her assistant and they would always keep some tasters after a reception for me to try. I had to check all the stock and often had to work with the storeman, a man named Eric Slater, and, strangely, it was he who was to be instrumental in my future as a medium.

I had not seen Eric for some time and thought he must have left the job, as he always said he was not happy with it. One day as I returned to my office in the town hall after a lunch break, I was surprised to find the only person in there was Eric. Apparently, as he told me later, he had been transferred to the audit section and was glad of the change. Before that, however, the first thing he said to me as I walked into the room was 'Hello, what have you been up to then?' I asked him to explain what he meant and he simply asked me, 'Are you a Spiritualist?' At first, I was reluctant to answer but then found myself pouring out my story, insisting it had to remain just between us. He agreed and told me that he, too, was very interested in the psychic and had known the moment I walked into the room that I had found something in my life that could not be changed. He had known since he first met me that I was a medium and would become famous, though he hadn't said anything then as I probably would have called him silly. When I told him about all the 'star-studded messages' and that I still found it hard to believe, he said he had a friend in Shepherd's Bush who was an excellent medium and that I should go to see her. I hesitated, but before I could say more he had picked up the phone and made an appointment for me the following evening.

As I approached the address he had given me I felt a certain trepidation and almost turned back. I am not a rude person and reminded myself it would be wrong to let the lady down, so I found myself ringing her doorbell, hoping that I would not let *myself* down. The door was opened by a little lady who was very pleasant-looking and spoke with a Welsh accent. I knew her only as Mrs Rosser but she made me welcome and got right down to business. First she asked me to let her hold the ring I was wearing and proceeded to tell me all sorts of things about departed relatives which by then I knew to be true. She was doing what is called psychometry, which means holding an article and feeling the vibrations from it. I wondered if it was necessary but could judge it only by what she was telling me and that was good. She then handed back my ring and just spoke to me normally and gave a lot more interesting and correct information.

By then my mind was swimming but at the same time I realised she had not said a word about my being psychic or becoming famous, and so I felt I was right in thinking it wasn't really true. As I was putting on my coat to leave she suddenly said, 'Well, young man, what are you going to do about it?' I looked at her puzzled and she then added, 'You must know that you are very psychic and must develop it. I have a development class here every week but it is too full and in any case you would have to travel a long distance each time. Do you by any chance attend a Spiritualist church anywhere? They might have a class there which you could join.' I told her about The Haven and promised I would enquire the next time I went.

As I left through the front door I met a man coming up the steps, 'Hello, young man, has the wife been telling you great things? Don't go yet, come and sit in the porch with me as I want to tell you more.' It seemed he was also a medium and was just returning from a trip so could not have known I had been seeing his wife, who had already given me ninety minutes of good evidence. He proceeded to give me another thirty minutes of the same and there was no charge; his wife had charged me little enough, so that made me feel they were honest sorts of people. By the time I caught my bus home my mind was absolutely swimming and somehow it all seemed unbelievable. I needed time before I could make a decision to join a class, as I was already aware there was one at The Haven, but I really did not want to get involved. When I next saw Les I told him about my experience and yet again he said that I didn't have a choice but to do it. I told him I did have a choice: 'I'm going to prove it by joining this class if I can and then we'll see who's psychic. I have to know one way or the other, but whatever happens I'm not going to get involved!'

The next time I went to The Haven, after the service I approached Nora Blackwood and asked her if they had a development class there. She questioned my reason for asking and I told her my story so far. 'I would like to put it to the test and find out one way or the other,' I told her finally. She looked at me and said, 'If anyone's psychic then you most certainly are, and I will be starting a class here in two weeks' time and there will certainly be a place for you. She said she would write to me with details and so I went away wondering if I had really done the right thing. Inwardly, however, I felt excited at the prospect of it perhaps being true that I was psychic. I eventually received her letter to attend one Tuesday evening at a certain time but there were no other details and I was left wondering as to what I could expect.

On the day stated I arrived in good time and found that all the chairs had been arranged in a circle with one set slightly apart from the rest. I was told to sit in one of the hard-backed wooden chairs and eventually another nineteen people arrived and all took their places. I realised they were all experienced pupils but they seemed friendly and immediately a pleasant atmosphere was created. The room was lit only by light from a table lamp, which was later covered by a red cloth, which darkened the room considerably but at the same time was more relaxing. Nora then took her place in the special chair and explained that we would play some music to help us relax, especially her as she would go into a trance and be controlled by a French nun called Sister Thérèse. After a time a voice boomed out. It was the nun speaking. At first I was somewhat sceptical but gradually became very impressed by what she had to say, which was more like a spiritual pep talk and right up my street, so to speak. After that was finished we were told to relax and let whatever would happen take place. My first thought was how could one possibly relax on these chairs, but I put my hands down on my knees, as instructed, closed my eyes and waited. I remembered no more until I suddenly opened my eyes again. I thought I must have fallen asleep and would have to apologise. It was then I noticed the room was very full of people. There had been twenty to begin with but now it appeared there was somebody standing behind each chair. There were one or two North American Indians, a nun, a Chinese man and several English people (or at least I presumed them to be such). I took mental note of everyone and everything, after which all these people seemed to melt away through the floor. I suppose I should have been more than surprised but it all felt quite natural to me.

Eventually Nora called an end to whatever had taken place and announced we would now have a run around so each of us could tell what we had experienced, so she could explain and help us to understand. When it got to me Nora asked if I had ever sat in a class before, to which I replied I had not, but she asked me if I was sure. At this I felt affronted as I told her I had no idea what I had come to that night and still did not understand. She told me how amazing it was then that on my first time I had been controlled by a North American Indian speaking in his own language. She then asked if I had any other experience to report so I said that after falling asleep, as I supposed, I had at length opened my eyes and seen all these people. I pointed to each one present in turn and explained whom I had seen behind their chair, giving very clear descriptions of them all. Everyone and everything was recognised and accepted, which absolutely staggered me. Nora repeated that it was rare for anyone to be in class for the first time and experience all this. For me it was like a switch had suddenly been pulled and set everything in motion. Needless to say, I decided to continue with the class: what else would I discover, I wondered. At the same time I still felt it would just be an interesting sideline but, as Les had said, I half feared they had got me. I would just have to wait and see. As I went home that night my mind was swimming once again with so many things. I felt I had discovered something I did not know about and supposed it must be for a purpose or some other good reason. Only time would tell and so I continued to visit The Haven and enjoyed the fact I was doing something worthwhile.

One day as I was talking to Eric in my office, we were overheard by my junior assistant, Jim Carpenter, who immediately wanted to know more about the subject and asked if he could come to The Haven with me. We had formed a good friendship away from the office and so I finally agreed. By then, I was running a development class myself and Jim begged to join. I was somewhat cautious as I had been catapulted into this position for which I did not really feel qualified. There had come a time when Nora told the class that she would have to close it down as she was leaving to go on to other things. She was much sought after and in fact became one of the best mediums and in my mind the most brilliant one of us all. The class were so unhappy and begged her not to close it, as they so much wanted to continue. As I was the most advanced pupil they asked if I could take over. Nora said she had no doubt I could do it but pointed out that it was not fair to put such responsibility on me at this stage. After much pleading with me from the whole class I agreed and so I found myself, a relative novice, a teacher. It was a daunting task as once the new class began some people decided they did not want to take orders from someone younger and jealousy figured quite strongly. This is where I had to assert my authority and to ask all dissenters to leave. Gradually the class dwindled down to ten or twelve people but it seemed all right as everyone was happy and cooperative and I was able to help all of them in some way. I ran that class for ten years before I too took off to give my time to other things. It was time well spent for the experience I gained and for Jim my assistant too. He developed the ability to heal and also to give clairvoyance but as he later married and had a family he could not pursue his gifts as he might have liked to do.

8

Taking Wing

After Nora left The Haven she still kept an interest in what was going on. She felt strongly it was time for me to serve churches and show what I could do. She called one day to say she had asked another famous medium, Eileen Blaschke, if she would give me a chance of demonstrating at her 'fledglings' meeting to be held in Caxton Hall. It would be a good experience for me but Nora said she thought it was perhaps not right to ask as it was really only for Eileen's pupils. It was a great surprise when Eileen said she would be delighted to have me, and when I met her I realised she was a lovely lady in every way. There were to be two demonstrations, afternoon and evening, and she made me the star turn in both, saying it was not only because of Nora's recommendation but in being psychic herself she just knew I had a very fine gift. When it all went so well in the afternoon session I felt it was a turning point of some kind.

While having a tea break later I was passing a recess in the hall when a stout, jolly-looking man sitting there called out to me and asked me to sit down as he wanted to say a few things. He introduced himself as Ben Herrington. I remembered reading about him as he was quite a noted figure in the psychic community. First he congratulated me on my performance and said he knew I would go a long way and would get even better with more experience. There were one or two things I did that he didn't think were right, like my saying please and thank you to the recipients of my messages. He suggested that, as those on the receiving end were getting something good then it was they who should say please and thank you. Of course he was right but in answer to his question of why I did it, I could only reply it was how I was taught and how all mediums I had seen did it. It was then he said I was an individual and should do what I *felt* drawn to do, as, although the basic gift was the same, it was mine to handle as I knew to be right. For that to happen it would soon be time for me to stand out and not be afraid to be different. He also advised me not to become like some mediums who think they know it all and are the only ones who are chosen. 'They think they are powerful but remember, young man, a little power can be a dangerous thing!' He kept me talking quite a long time but it was a very helpful and encouraging meeting someone who knew what he was talking about. I was grateful for his advice and I have never forgotten him and how he helped set me on the right road.

When it was time for the evening session I was told that the editor of what was then a newspaper called the *Two Worlds* was sitting in the front row. This was Maurice Barbanell who as well as being a fine journalist was very knowledgeable about Spiritualism. At first I was nervous, knowing that there were such illustrious members in the audience, but I soon overcame that and was able to give an even better demonstration than in the afternoon. Barbanell did not speak to me afterwards but a few days later I received a phone call asking me to go to his office for an interview. He was running an article to promote young mediums and along with three others I occupied some of the front page of the paper the following week. Barbanell was a strange man in some ways but completely honest. It did not matter whether he liked you or not; if you had a gift worth writing about then it would be done. Later he would always give me wonderful coverage and was an admirer of the work I was doing, which in later years became so much more adventurous and experimental. So my public debut was indeed a turning point and one which taught me a lot, perhaps even *all* I needed to know about working with people.

When not attending The Haven, Jim and I often travelled around most of the Spiritualist churches in London to hear and see other mediums and how they performed. The churches themselves were often dirty, makeshift places, though others were clean and welcoming. By the time we had finished both of us decided that, if we were to work for the psychic, then we would like to evaluate the subject and decide what we would and would not do. I have always been the sort of person who never takes anything for granted and wants to put it to the test. We spent many evenings in a room in Jim's home where we tested and tried every aspect of the subject often with amazing results. Unfortunately we did not have a tape recorder then, nor did we make notes, but nonetheless it was a great experience for us both, but especially me as by then I was deeply involved with the subject and needed to reassure myself I was doing the right thing. Jim shared in some of the experiences which I will relate in due course and where they tie in with my realisation that, whatever happens, it would seem our lives are already planned out in advance and that perhaps we have little free will, if any. All things are debatable and we can only truly judge by what happens to us, as first-hand experience is the only convincing thing.

During the course of my work I met Peter Ingold, someone who was to be my very best friend and with whom I would share many experiences. He was and still is my tower of strength and encouragement. He is another one who has good psychic and healing abilities but tends to shun the limelight. He also became a friend of Jim's and we were often called the Three Musketeers. At one time we ran a small theatrical company called Desperance Productions. This name was taken from a famous materialisation medium, Madame Desperance, whose beautiful oil painting hangs in the College of Psychic Studies, and was in the room in which I worked there for a period in the early days of my career. Madame Desperance means 'Mrs Hope' in English and, as we were then trying to get materialisations in the room at Jim's home, we felt it was an apt name. We did not really get much out of that. Although we tried with the help of other friends, it was not meant to be, although we did get some good advice and help from the other side. There was always a time for messages, which further encouraged us to try other things such as ghost hunting for instance. I feel I personally had so many experiences that there was very little left to try.

Many people seem to think we can demand evidence of survival through the services of a medium, but from my experience we can only hope that contact may be possible and, if so, we have to accept what comes through and consider its merits. Communication with the spirit world can happen at any time and in any way and any circumstance. This is proved by the following instances, which show the spirits know more about what is going on than we do.

I first met Peter when I gave him a sitting. One of the things I remember was when I made contact with his father, who had passed at an early age and whom he had not really known, he was able to accept what came through because of what his mother and family had told him. The most outstanding thing for him was when his

Aunt Jean communicated and did it by not giving her description so much as the manner of her passing. I had the feeling of something in my mouth that was choking me and at the same time I could smell gas very strongly. She took her life by putting a gas poker in her mouth and turning on the gas. He was thrilled to hear from her and even more so when in later years she would make herself known in various ways.

On one particular occasion when I happened to be talking to Peter on the telephone about things in general she popped in. Although I knew him well, I did not know much about his family but suddenly became aware of his much-loved aunt presenting herself in a grass hula skirt with a garland of flowers around her neck. His comment when I told him was that, although he had been close to his aunt, who could be very lively and amusing, he had no knowledge of her ever wearing such an outfit. She told me to tell him she would prove it to him. Six months later while visiting his grandmother, who had a large collection of family photographs, she decided to show him some. They loved talking about the family and happy memories, so imagine his surprise when one of the photos was of his aunt and her husband on a seaside holiday putting their heads through a cardboard cut-out which produced a picture of his aunt wearing a hula skirt and a garland of flowers. At the time of the phone call he knew nothing of this photo, but her statement was proved true.

At the end of this same telephone conversation the aunt appeared to be wearing a nurse's uniform and carrying a black bag. She said to tell Peter that she had her nurse's uniform on and she had to go as she had an appointment at midday with a friend of his who was staying in Jersey with her husband, who was performing there in cabaret. She said she was going to give the lady healing for some back trouble as she was in great pain. Peter was surprised as I knew nothing about this lady or her whereabouts. He was also puzzled as to why his aunt was wearing a nurse's uniform. As it neared midday he got me off the telephone and a while later put in a call to Jersey to ask how his friend was, not knowing there was anything wrong with her except what his aunt had suggested. Her reply was 'Wonderful, I haven't felt so well in months.' He thought the message must have been wrong until she added, 'I have been in agony with my back for some time, but especially today, when I have been crying with pain. I was laying in a strange position hoping to get relief when, quite miraculously at midday (I noticed the clock was striking), it was as though somebody put their two thumbs at the base of my spine and suddenly all the pain seemed to drain away.' So the aunt was good to her word and since Peter was not aware of this lady's problems, it was a great help and evidence at the same time. The lady herself was not aware of the psychic or anything to do with healing, which was all the more impressive. Some twenty years later Peter was talking to the aunt's daughter about psychic things. He told her I was possibly the most accurate psychic he knew but there was one thing about her mother's message that did not make sense and explained about her insisting she was wearing her nurse's uniform as though she had been one. His cousin explained her mother had been a nurse and that was how she had met her husband. This story tends to suggest that healing can come direct from the other world, though, however it happened, it was truly remarkable. The hula skirt and uniform were not in Peter's mind at the time but were verified at a much later date.

There is no set pattern as to how soon a person can communicate after passing to this other world. Some return almost immediately, others take a long time and some do not communicate at all. One assumes that much depends on the individual and there is no reason why anyone should be forced into something they have no desire to do. Much depends on the people in this earthly world because, unless anyone wishes for evidence of survival by consulting a medium, then there would be great difficulty perhaps in finding other ways for the departed to make contact. We cannot be sure of anything concerning life after death, as there are, and presumably always will be, many unanswered questions and doubts caused by what we call lack of complete proof. In my experience there are many wonderful examples of what could constitute evidence but the sceptics and scientists will always find reasons for doubting it. The human mind can play a very big part in trying to control what we would *like* to hear rather than what we *do* hear. It is difficult to set one's own mind aside, but to a very great extent it is possible to do so after a time of discipline and practice. It is something that as a medium I have learned to do but even now I cannot guarantee to empty the mind completely and not colour the communication in any way.

Having passed on and maybe finding life very different in this other world, no doubt there are those who find it hard to leave material things behind, and those who realise their mistakes and want to put things right and possibly do good to those they have left behind. It is totally wrong to suggest they can work miracles but easier to believe that to some extent they can influence our lives for the better. Perhaps it is only by thought, but thoughts can be very powerful things. There are many strange happenings that probably the majority of people experience at some time or other in their earthly lives, some of which can be dismissed as auto-suggestion or wishful thinking, but many of which are hard to explain. This story of the two aunts is one of them and offers a lot of food for thought.

At one time I was giving healing to a young boy with whose mother and family I became friendly. The mother often discussed family matters with me and would ask for advice. One day she came to me in a disturbed state as one of her aunts was in hospital and not expected to live. Apparently this lady was rather outspoken and difficult and not popular with the family, as she would have nothing to do with them. The only people she would accept were my friend and her mother, who did all they could to help her despite the fact she was cantankerous. As time went by, the aunt realised she was due to pass on and suddenly insisted she wished to leave everything she had to my friend and her mother. Unfortunately it was too late as she passed on before she could make a legal will, and her verbal instructions which she gave in the presence of two nurses were not legally binding.

As often happens in families, all the other relatives descended and demanded their share of the estate. When my friend told me all this, she also explained that her aunt had repeatedly apologised on those last days in hospital as she realised they had looked after her home and all her affairs and she wanted them to have everything. It now seemed all they would get was a small share of the estate. It was then I suddenly sensed the presence of the aunt, whom I had never met, but of whom I was able to give my friend a perfect description. She seemed agitated and insisted my friend and her mother should have what was in the little brown bedside cabinet in her home. They smiled and said they had already looked there and it was full of worthless rubbish. They had looked through all the drawers and compartments but found nothing of value. The aunt still insisted there was something inside the cabinet, so I suggested they look again. This they did the very next day and found all the aunt's things had been packed up ready to be taken away but the little brown cabinet was still there and set to one side as though nobody wanted it. Luckily no one else was around so they could take another look again. Nothing. In sheer frustration they shook the chest and it rattled, proving to have a false bottom which when removed revealed a compartment containing two hundred and fifty pounds – at that time a small fortune. So the aunt's wishes had been fulfilled in a strange way and I felt after that she was at peace.

Not long afterwards, a sister of this aunt passed on. Unlike the first one she was popular with the family and together with her husband had a good relationship with everybody. After her husband passed, she became more of a recluse, developing diabetes and having to have a leg amputated. She became strange and uncommunicative until she, too, suddenly passed on. My friend and her mother had done all they could for this aunt but she too did not leave a will. In fact, when the relatives went through the house, there appeared to be nothing of value at all, only a lot of old bits and pieces and children's books. Absolutely no money at all and, since she had taken all her money out of the bank and building society, it was assumed she had spent it.

Once again on being told this by my friend, I did not actually sense the aunt's presence but nonetheless felt very agitated. It seemed to me she was telling them not to throw out all the rubbish but to go through it with a fine toothcomb. Apparently the family had already done this, or thought they had, and so everything was packed ready for the dustmen and dealers to clear the following day. I could only beg my friend not to let this happen until they looked again. She went to the house very early the next morning, as did the rest of the family, but they flatly refused to look again. She told them about me and what I had felt but to no avail. She became angry and went to one of the boxes containing the children's books, took one out and, as she did so, a pound note fell out from between the pages. As she shook it again more pound notes and ten-shilling notes fell out. This of course got the family more interested and they went to work, going through everything and taking it apart. The search revealed hidden hoards: there were notes concealed in the backs of hairbrushes, in the lining of hats, or under the hatband, between shelves and in just about every place anything *could* be concealed without being noticed. The aunt, it seemed, had become afraid of banks and then of burglars perhaps. There were notes under carpets and under the linoleum, these having being left down for the dealers to clear. What a find they would have had! The search revealed seven hundred pounds, which in those days was quite a fortune. The interesting thing about both these stories is that I had no knowledge of the two aunts and the information received was not through an *organised* consultation but a spontaneous reaction to two urgent situations.

There came a time when, despite the fact I tried to keep my involvement in the psychic away from my work colleagues, I came to realise I would have to help two of the girls in the office who desperately needed advice. The first was Dawn who worked in the outer office and doubled as the tea lady. One day I went to the outer office for a second cup. Dawn was only seventeen, an attractive young lady and quite a flirt, both with the boys and the older men as well. I had heard through the grapevine she had given birth to twins when she was still at school and was proud of it and did not mind anyone knowing. They were being cared for by her mother and it seemed Dawn was hoping to get one of the lads involved so she could get married. I could see that deep down inside she was a nice girl and with the right help and direction could be turned into a worthwhile person and mother while making someone very happy. It was not by design but by accident (or was it meant to be?) that, as I approached her for my tea, I saw her putting her own empty cup on the tray and could not help but look at the pattern of the tea leaves left behind. I cannot really read cups by the pattern of the leaves but being psychic helps me let the person think I can, and then to pass on any relevant impressions I receive. Dawn saw I was looking in her cup and asked me if I read tea leaves. I replied no, but she was too canny to be fobbed off by this and immediately pushed me behind some filing cabinets where nobody else could see us, and demanded I read her cup because she knew I could. This I did while she listened very attentively and when I had finished said it was a lot of rubbish. I told her that she had asked me to do it and it was her prerogative if she didn't believe it, but not to ask me to do it again.

A week later when I was passing through her office she suddenly grabbed me and pushed me behind the filing cabinets again. She said she wanted to apologise as all I told her had happened and was perfectly true. She thrust that day's cup into my hand and begged me for another reading. This was when I realised that this young lady needed my help and it would be a way of getting through to her and giving her the advice and direction she needed. So hiding behind the filing cabinet became a regular feature and I could see her gradually changing and having greater respect for herself. However, one day she asked me if there was anything she could do for me as she thought I was lonely and unhappy and needed a relationship. I knew what she was suggesting and told her I was perfectly happy and that she needed to sort her own life out. Soon after, she announced she was leaving for another job and told me she was so grateful for all I had done but realised now she would never get married because no one would want her and the twins; they would think she was a trollope. I then told her to stop thinking that and I predicted that she would soon meet a very good-looking young man who would worship the ground she walked on and who would marry her and take the twins on as well. They would be so happy all together she would think it would be too good to be true. It sounded like a fairy story even to me but that was exactly what I had to say. She went off happily and I continued with my routine.

Not long after when I had given up my job in order to be a full-time medium, I was going through a bad patch as I was not finding enough work to pay the bills. Feeling very low one day I decided to go for a walk and as I left the house and started to walk along the street, I could see a figure waving at me from the distance. As it got nearer I could see it was Dawn who was running as fast as she could to get to me. As she did she flung her arms around me and hugged and kissed me and said, 'I'm so glad to have found you as I've been looking for you everywhere and had no idea where you lived. I want to tell you how wonderful you are and so right. I can't believe it is true but it is. I met and married a good-looking young man who worships the ground I walk on and he loves the twins. We have our own place together and are so happy you wouldn't believe it!' The only reply I could give was: 'Well, it shows and I did tell you so! If it is of any help for you to know, you have just cheered me up and returned a favour.'

The second young lady was Stella, who also worked in the outer office where Dawn had been but she was not the tea lady. She was a typist and often had to do some work for me, but being of a nervous disposition she often made mistakes and would get into an unhappy state and did not think enough of herself. I covered for her and tried to encourage her to do and think better. We would often have a little chat and she would tell me her troubles. Stella was a pleasant-looking girl who wore glasses but had a deep inferiority complex. She felt everyone was better than her and they ignored her. One day as we were talking she suddenly said I was very kind and asked me if I was a Spiritualist. She said her mother believed in 'all that' and that I reminded her of her mother and the things she did and said. I had no choice but to tell Stella the truth and asked her not to tell the others as it was not the place for such things. I talked a lot with her and she confided her secrets and fears: mostly at that time they were about the fact that all boys never looked at her – who would want her anyway? I did my best to put her mind at rest and finally made her a prediction similar to Dawn's that one day she would meet the most unbelievably handsome young man who would choose her from a lot of other girls and would worship and cherish her. They would have two children but only two as after that no more would be possible. It would make no difference as they would be so happy and have a long time together. Stella did not believe this but thanked me for trying to cheer her up. Soon after I left my job and did not expect to see any more of Stella.

Some time later I was reading my local paper when what should I see but a wedding photograph of Stella and her very handsome husband. She looked radiantly happy and it made me feel good. Quite a long time after that I was again walking down a street when who should I see but Stella pushing a pram with one child in it and another sitting on it. When she saw me she burst into tears and smiled saying how marvellous to meet me as she did not know how to contact me but felt I should know how right my prediction had been. I told her I had seen her wedding picture and that she had a handsome husband. She told me how one day, when she had been working at a show with several other typists, this man looked into the tent where they were, and seeing Stella asked if she would go out with him. All the other ladies were jealous and couldn't understand why he had chosen her, and for that matter neither did Stella! They got along famously and he proposed, saying she was the only one for him and always would be. She said, as I could see, she had two children and had been told she could not have any more owing to a problem which would not affect her in any other way. She said she was so happy she could not believe it at times but she trusted in all I had told her and went on her way beaming, having kissed and hugged me.

If anyone should wonder why I tell these stories it is because it illustrates what my work is all about. Mediumship does not only concern evidence of survival; it is about using one's gifts to guide and steer others through this earthly life, which at times can be extremely difficult and challenging.

During my training I was advised to do certain things in order to keep my mind clear for what I had to do. I later did a lot of experiments to see how the mind would function under various conditions, and found by and large that as long as one paid attention then the psychic flow would happen whatever the conditions. There was one thing which I overlooked, however – avoiding alcoholic intake before undertaking psychic work. Then one day I found myself having to work with a dreadful hangover.

The night before I had been to a party given by a famous medium, Stanley Poulton, with whom I was friendly and who had also given me a lot of useful advice, though alas not concerning the question of inebriation. It was a hot August evening and I was glad to get out into the garden where a young man wanted to talk to me, asking a lot of questions and pretty much monopolising me. All this time I was having my glass refilled frequently with what I had been told was a pure-fruit punch, just the thing for a hot evening. A young lady I knew came over and asked me if I knew how many glasses of punch I had drunk. I asked her who was counting and she said *she* was and I'd had ten! Unperturbed, I pointed out that it was very hot and it was only a fruit punch after all. She laughed and told me she had helped to make it and of course it had fruit in it but also lots of different spirits as well. I stopped drinking immediately but by then the damage was done!

Shortly after that, the young man insisted on driving me home as it was very late and I would not get transport very easily. We got into his sports car and by the time I realised he had also had too much to drink he had driven off at great speed and I could not get out. Luckily the roads were quite empty as he zigzagged all over the place and sometimes even mounted the pavement. Finally the nightmare drive ended and I was home, much the worse for wear in more ways than one. It was a relief to get to bed except I could not really sleep and at six in the morning I was sitting on a bench in the garden with a colossal hangover. I needed fresh air and eventually cups of coffee to try to clear my head, but it did not shift easily and I began to worry as I had to take a service that evening at Richmond Church.

Later that morning I phoned Jim and told him what had happened and that I couldn't keep the engagement. He reminded me that they would be so disappointed if I didn't, and anyway we had agreed to meet two friends in Richmond to have tea before the service. He was sure I would be all right and so I took further hangover measures and later met up as arranged. We had our tea in the little café we had chosen but the beautiful cream cakes made me heave, though the tea was welcome as I still had a thirst. Our friends laughed when they heard my story and said I looked pretty awful, which did not help matters. Jim took a photo of me looking like death on Richmond Bridge, as it was a day to remember. By the time I got to the church I felt dizzy and tired and not in the mood for anything, but, as they say, the show had to go on.

Strangely when I got there I must have looked more like my usual self as everyone was delighted to see me and made no comment on my appearance. This was a church I enjoyed working in and always had a full house with people often standing at the back. Some of my friends from the party came to see me and give their support, knowing how I would be feeling. Stanley, the party giver, said to me: 'You don't look too good, Ron, so rather you than me. I hope you can make it but you have our support.' I was truly worried and, if the church officials had known what had happened and how I was feeling, they would have been horrified as I was always thought of as a spiritual, abstemious kind of a person. When the time came I climbed onto the triangular podium and clung on to the lectern whenever I had to stand up to join in with the hymns and usual routine. I had no memory of what I said in the address and when it came to the demonstration it seemed everyone was laughing at me and the messages I gave. I began to wonder if my trousers had fallen down or something but when I surreptitiously felt around all was in place. At the conclusion I was thanked for a very evidential and uplifting service and the chairman said it was one of those evenings they would always remember. Afterwards Jim told me it had been wonderful and the messages were accurate and funny and it really was a good show because nobody would have realised I had a hangover. I felt guilty in a way but from that day to this not many people have known what happened and my reputation was better than ever.

My mind was certainly affected by the drinking – indeed, if anything it was enhanced by it. Perhaps the alcohol relaxed my inhibitions and allowed the psychic to flow without my own mental input colouring it. I believe one can work through anything if one sets one's mind to it and often certain situations make it better because one has to try harder. I have been through periods of illness where most mediums would not work, but I do not like to let people down and believe in keeping the mind occupied if possible. Under such situations the results were often better and certainly not worse; someone even told me I should always be ill if the results were going to be that good. Despite the results, I have never allowed this to happen again, not because it is wrong, but because I am someone who prefers to be responsible for what I do and say and have a clear head.

I have often been asked if animals survive. As every living creature, in common with humans, must have some kind of living force within them I think it highly possible. During the course of my work I have tried to get some kind of contact with people's pets and have produced some interesting evidence that strongly suggests they do. Of course, I cannot guarantee it, as it could, in some way, be connected with the mind of the owner. My stronger belief, based on the evidence, is that every living thing must migrate at death to the next world. The evidential messages, particularly from cats and dogs, often come through as though the animal itself was speaking directly to me. One of the most unusual instances came when a well-known man from the theatre came to see me for a sitting. He was seeking evidence from a very dear friend who had died under tragic circumstances. He passed on a lot of detailed evidence but what most impressed my sitter was when his friend told him he could see he was wearing his blue underpants. Apparently he had only decided to wear his dead friend's underwear just before leaving home and was uncomfortable as they were not the type he would normally wear. He was so pleased with his sitting he came to see me a second time and the young man communicating told him he was worried about the dog. Apparently the sitter still had his friend's dog, even though he did not really want it but had kept it only because he has promised to do so.

It was quite a time before he returned for a third sitting, but on this occasion he asked me not to try and contact his friend but a certain lady instead. Having no other details I suddenly felt whoever it was must be around, although she gave me an 'unusual' feeling. I gave all the descriptions and characteristics of this lady, who also talked about things in the home, which my sitter acknowledged as accurate. I began to feel extremely odd and, when the sitter asked what was the matter, I said to be honest the communicator felt more like a dog than a woman. He laughed and was delighted to tell me that she was the friend's dog who had passed since his last visit. He had come to love it and said she was 'absolutely human' in many ways. By passing on exactly what I felt, it convinced him it was the dog actually communicating with me and he told me it would make an amazing story and he intended writing a book about it. I don't know whether he did or not. As for me, I put it down to experience, but I was puzzled as to how a dog could take over my mind and make me think it was a person communicating.

9

The Mavis Tapes

At this time so many things were happening. I was still working in the town hall and was becoming increasingly tired not just of having to do my psychic work at weekends and often weeknights, too, but of the awful atmosphere that still existed in the office. After I returned from the army it was bad and I could not get on with my boss, the Chief Auditor, who was always picking on me for some reason. I always stood up to him, which meant endless rows. As time went on he mellowed and began to realise what a good worker I was and that I was someone he could trust. In fact, we even became good friends. When he retired he left references for the new chief telling him that I was capable of running the office standing on my head, amongst other things. The new man, however, was weird and lazy, not to mention quite vicious, and from the word go he did not like me and made it clear he wanted me out. At first I fought him and for some time remained at my post but eventually felt I could take no more. In any case, by now I was confident enough to launch myself into the psychic world full time, though I realised it would be tough. One day I heard my departed mother's voice telling me to give in my notice, so I took a deep breath, knowing I was forfeiting the right to a good pension, and did as she said. It was a tremendous relief but a new challenge was beckoning. I felt that I would rather be able to look back later and say I did something interesting and worthwhile than to have a good pension and be bored out of my mind.

I have never regretted this move, although for the first two years it was very hard going and I began to have doubts. Despite the kindness of Peter and Jim, who often paid for drinks and various cinema and theatre seats, I was too independent to take advantage of them. I had some money of my own but it was dwindling fast and something had to be done. It was then a very sad but strange event occurred, which marked the turning of the tide for me, so to speak, and which added to my theory that everything is planned.

First, though, I must tell you about what led up to this event. I was still at The Haven when I met a lady called Coral Polge who was a psychic artist and became famous for her superb work, although then she was still in the early stages of her development. She occasionally came there to conduct a circle as it was called where she would draw a picture of a loved one who had passed on, or perhaps a spirit guide for each person in the circle. She did some excellent work, though my own first experience of it was disappointing in one way and exciting in another. She drew for me a picture of a North American Indian. This was intriguing as some time before Nora Blackwood had told me I had a spirit guide called Running Water but at the same time I had hoped to receive a drawing of a relative. However, I felt satisfied as I believed Running Water would work with me in the time ahead. It seemed everyone else who was there at the time felt happy I had this drawing of someone they had heard speak through me in a trance state and whom they greatly respected. It was after the circle that Coral spoke to me and asked if Jim and I would like to visit her and her husband socially. So began a long-lasting friendship which would take me on a path I felt was very special and to the work which I could perhaps do best.

Our social evenings were very enjoyable but inevitably mostly concerned psychic things and about Coral's and my future careers, as at that time we were steadily improving our gifts. Coral used to give public demonstrations where she would draw pictures of relatives and guides for various members of the audience who could often recognise them. She was able to give broad outlines of the person concerned but at first it was harder for her as she did not normally get strong impressions, although after she joined my class her ability to do so improved until she was in full control. She often liked to work with an experienced medium who would let Coral draw the picture and then pick out whoever it was for in the audience. This usually worked well but I dare to say at no time better than when *I* worked with her as the results would be quite amazing. I think it was in knowing her so well by then that I could tune into her mind and help to guide things along.

Coral had an aunt living on the Isle of Wight whom she and her husband often visited and they asked Jim and I if we would like to go with them one weekend. I had been to the Island before but only on a brief visit and so it was a welcome opportunity to see more of it. The aunt, whose name was Doris Crouchman, lived with her two daughters, Mavis and Marian, in a house in Elmfield on the outskirts of Ryde. Apparently her husband had passed on some time before and she had the task of bringing up her daughters under very difficult circumstances and with very little money. Doris was a practical person and a firm believer in most things psychic, although her daughters, then only schoolgirls, were more sceptical. Our first meeting was indeed a pleasant one. We all got along very well and had a most enjoyable time. Doris invited us again and suggested to Jim and me that we need not always wait for Coral and her husband, Arthur, to visit as we would be welcome at any time. (Later Coral and Arthur divorced and Coral became so immersed in her work that she visited only rarely, so Doris's open invitation to us was a happy one.) Jim and I were able to spend a week or two there at times and we became increasingly close to Doris and the girls. We got to know the Island so well it became like a second home to us. We saw the girls grow up and Marian married a doctor and then herself became a well-known heart specialist. Mavis was more interested in helping people in another way, as she became an almoner in a hospital. She was a lovely young lady – just like a Dresden china doll with her long fair hair and beautiful face. I often used to call her 'Little Nell' as when she wore black stockings and a certain outfit she always reminded me of this Dickens character. Everyone loved Mavis as she made one feel like cuddling and fussing over her.

On one of our social evenings with Coral we were talking about various forms of fortune-telling and she asked me if I could read the cards, to which I replied that I could to some extent but did not really see the point because with my psychic gift it only acted, like teacup reading and such like, as a sort of focal point on which to concentrate. She persuaded me to try and when I spread the cards I strongly felt there was going to be a passing in the family of a fair-haired person which would be a shock. I must confess that in my mind's eye I had seen Mavis but just could not believe it would be her. Neither could Coral and she decided it must be her Auntie Kit, who was the only other one who had fair hair and who had health problems. It seemed that Mavis and Kit absolutely adored each other, which made it feel even worse in a way, so I suggested to Coral that perhaps I had been wrong as I was not a card reader and so we should forget all about it.

Some time after that Jim came to my home one morning and said he had some tragic news to tell me: Mavis had died as the result of blood poisoning. Apparently she had collapsed in the street and was rushed to hospital but they could not save her. She was only twenty-five and immediately it felt as if a light had gone out of this world and our lives. I felt so awful – perhaps if we had stayed with that card-reading affair this might have been prevented. But my common sense told me it could not have been avoided and there was nothing to be done but to accept it. The only consolation was that this world's loss would be another world's gain, but in such sad times it is hard to think of anything but one's personal loss. Doris came up to Coral's home in Harrow from where they made arrangements for the funeral which Doris wanted to be a cremation at Ilford, the same place where her husband had been taken. It was a long journey to undertake but it was settled, the only problem being as to who would conduct the funeral service. Coral rang me at work and asked if I would do this. I had taken other services before but I felt too upset and said no, but she said I was the only one they wanted as I was like part of the family and Mavis would want it. So I agreed and knew I would carry it off, as I saw it not only as a challenge but as a labour of love.

On the day of the funeral I went with Jim to Coral's home and as we entered the house we could hear a lot of chattering and laughing; it felt more like a wedding than a funeral. Once inside we realised that this was what Mavis would have liked as she was being remembered in a happy sort of way. Doris was a little concerned but soon appreciated it was better to laugh than to cry because nothing could change what had happened and in any case she had gone on to a better place. So at the appointed time the funeral procession moved off on its long journey to Ilford, which would no doubt seem interminable but at least it was carrying out the wishes of Doris who felt Mavis would be happy to be with her father. I rode in the first carriage with Doris, Coral, Marian and her Chinese husband, who had rushed from his work as a hospital doctor and who promptly fell asleep for the whole journey as he was so tired. As the cortège moved off at its customary slow pace until it was well past the house, suddenly a shower of white petals came down from the flowers on top of the hearse. There was no wind that day and the slow movement would not have caused this to happen. It was as though someone was throwing confetti at a wedding, which caused me to ask Coral if she was getting married again. Her reply was that she was not but told me that she had had to postpone an invitation to dinner with a friend who was also inviting a man whom she thought would be good for Coral. I thought it must be Mavis throwing the confetti. Later Coral did meet the man and they were married. As a matter of fact, I conducted their wedding ceremony.

As the cars gained speed I suddenly saw Mavis sitting on the end of her coffin, swinging her legs as she often did, looking very happy and wearing a deep-lilac dress. Doris asked me what I was staring at and, when I told her, she asked if I could describe the dress. I did the best I could after which Doris unbuttoned her coat and asked if it was the same one as she was wearing. It was identical. I had not seen what Doris had on as when I arrived her coat was buttoned right up. It was wonderful evidence as Doris explained that she had made a dress for Mavis and herself out of this same material. Mavis had never worn hers and Doris only for the first time that day. It certainly made us all feel better to know that Mavis was in this other world and was aware and happy about everything. We all felt she would be happier there as we discovered later she had been very unhappy in this world but never told anyone.

There was a crowd at the crematorium, not only family but many friends, and they more than filled the church. Any feelings of nerves with me soon disappeared and I was able to give a happy and loving service. Afterwards when we all gathered outside to see the wonderful display of floral tributes, an elderly man who had to walk with sticks drew me aside and with tears in his eyes said, 'I am one of Mavis's uncles. I loved her so dearly and I want to thank you, young man, for the wonderful service you gave. I have been to many funerals in my lifetime and every one has been depressing and not at all comforting. You made us smile and laugh with memories of Mavis and convinced us that we will all meet again one day. I wish all funerals could be like this one, especially mine, but I don't suppose it will. I won't worry because now I know that death is but a transition to a happier and better place.' I believe that everyone there felt much the same and I personally felt so glad I had done this because it helped to give me the confidence not to be afraid to move forwards.

Doris came to me and said the chief undertaker had asked what we wanted to do about the flowers, which were mostly in sprays or baskets with just one or two traditional wreaths. Everyone knew how much Mavis loved flowers so Doris felt it would be nice to send some to the hospital where Mavis worked and chose some for the undertaker to deliver. There still remained a mass of tributes and Doris said she wished we could take them all home because Mavis would hate to see them left there to die, and wondered if I would ask if this could be done. When I put this to the chief undertaker he looked at me and said quite imperiously, 'Oh no, Sir, that just isn't done.' I told him that they were not his flowers nor did they belong to the crematorium, so would he kindly take all but the wreaths back to the house. He had no choice but to obey and by the time we got back all the flowers were laid out on the front lawn, making a wonderful show and hopefully making Mavis happy. This was not apparent until later when the inevitable tea party was taking place and the noise of chatter was quite deafening. I was talking to Coral at one point when suddenly I felt a dig in the ribs and heard Mavis say, 'Oi! What about my flowers out there on the lawn?' Coral saw me jump and when I told her why she said we had all forgotten about the flowers and must do something right away. So she and others found every available empty container and the flowers were brought in and arranged in a wonderful display, with the perfume filling the whole house. When it was time to leave several asked if they could take some home, and even after that there was still a mass of blooms which seemed to fill the whole house with light and the feeling of love. Mavis was indeed happy.

Before I said goodbye to Doris, who was returning to the Island the next day, she asked me to tell her if I should get any messages from Mavis. I assured her I would let her know immediately, not realising what would happen would launch me on a new and interesting way of working. After some time had elapsed I felt I must try to contact Mavis. I realised, however, that, if I had to write down everything I got, it would take a long time. The idea occurred to me that I could maybe put some messages on a tape but then realised that perhaps Doris did not have a tape recorder, which, when I wrote to her to ask, proved correct. She wrote back to me to ask why I had asked. On the same day she received another letter from me explaining my idea a man from her local church dropped in to see her and asked if she would like to buy a tape recorder as he was going abroad and had to dispose of one. The asking price was the exact amount of money she had found tucked away in something belonging to Mavis (she had assumed to be her little nest egg), so she felt she must have the recorder and wrote to say she felt it must be a meant thing.

One morning, when I was working at Jim's home where he had a tape recorder, I put on a tape and said 'hello' to Doris and explained what I hoped to do. I expected to maybe get something from Mavis, then pause until something else came through, but to my amazement, once I started speaking, it all flowed for almost an hour non-stop. Mavis was on good form as she told her mother several things that proved true and were things I could not know about. The most outstanding thing was when Mavis asked her mother what cousin John was doing in the garden as there were lumps and bumps everywhere. Mavis then appeared to be holding a spray of orange blossom over my head and saying to tell mother about this. I noticed the time was 11 a.m. when I started the tape but did not think any more about it. Once I had finished, I packed and sent the tape off to Doris.

Her reply was one of excitement and pleasure as she did not expect anything like this. Everything was correct but especially the gardening part. She said that her cousin John, who was staying with her at the time, suddenly decided to plant a mock-orange tree which Doris had got in memory of Mavis. It was a cold and damp November morning and so when John had finished there were lumps and bumps all over the lawn, mostly of mud, but she was grateful to have the tree planted. She herself planted some blue forget-me-nots all around the base of the tree. The next morning Doris went out to look at the tree at exactly 11 a.m. and suddenly felt that Mavis would like me to have the first spray of blossom and then thought it would not be possible as that tree did not normally blossom until the second year. In actual fact, it did produce just one spray in the first year which Doris cut off and sent to me. It arrived on my birthday, the date of which Doris had never known, and so was fine evidence that Mavis was around. With this first tape's success Doris obviously hoped for more and so began a series of extremely evidential messages. Once encouraged, I felt I should be able to do more and so I decided to send tape-recorded messages as often as Mavis let me know she was around. At least that was what I intended but later felt it would be as much a question of *when* I would like to try.

So followed a series of communications which were extraordinary to say the least, all containing a wealth of evidence, detail and precognition which made Doris feel as if Mavis was there all the time. The timing of these messages was remarkable and I always felt that Mavis was happy and determined to let everyone know there *was* another world. It would take too long to tell how aware Mavis seemed to be of all that was going on in her mother's home but there are two extremely fine examples which when Doris first heard them sent a shudder down her spine. She always put the tapes on to listen to as soon as they came through the letterbox and on one occasion the first words that Mavis said were: 'I see you are making a dress for Suyin with that material with the fuchsia pattern you found amongst my things. It will be lovely for her!' At that very moment there on a table was the material which Doris had cut out ready to be sewn together and it was for a dress for her granddaughter, Suyin.

The second example was when Doris put the tape on and the first words were: 'Mother, what are you doing with all that blue stuff. There is blue everywhere and are you turning everything blue?' At that point Doris had difficulty in handling the tape as her hands were stained with blue as she had been dyeing something with that colour and had thought that while she was at it she might as well do several things. She admitted it was a mess but was so surprised that Mavis knew in advance exactly what she would be doing and also that she had maybe somehow influenced the arrival of the tape at the appropriate time. Over the course of time these tapes became invaluable to her, making it more bearable to carry on with her life. Always the communications were absolutely correct and it seemed as if Mavis had some extraordinary ability as a communicator. I wondered then if it was because I had known and loved Mavis that it made it easier for her to get through. Later I realised it must help but often it was better when I did not know anything about the recipient of messages or whom they would hope to hear from.

By that time my friendship with Peter Ingold had become much stronger and he had actually met Doris, as he often came to stay with her when Jim and I were visiting. We had some wonderful times on the Island, especially when we were doing all sorts of experiments with Doris and various aspects of the psychic. We tried things like flower sensience, blot reading, psychometry, palm reading and even sand reading. We all had psychic abilities and it helped us all in different ways, though we often felt Mavis was looking on with slight disapproval as when she was in this world she had accepted our interest in the subject but sometimes considered we were playing around with it. I feel sure once she passed on she must have seen there was nothing wrong with what we were doing but now she had shown us how it could be done in a straightforward way.

Here I should add that I had actually introduced Peter to Doris. We were staying in Portsmouth and, being at a loose end one evening, I asked him if he would like to come across on the ferry to the Island and meet her. He was happy to do so and when I actually introduced them Peter said, 'You don't have to introduce us. We know each other!' to which Doris said, 'I'm certain we have never met before.' Peter remained convinced they had, though he could not remember any details. The subject of reincarnation is questionable but there was certainly a particularly strong feeling between them that was hard to explain. There was no romantic connection but by that time I think we had all come to the conclusion that we had all been drawn together for some purpose, though, even if it was not so, then it was still good to be friends.

One day Peter came to me when I was doing my work at Jim's home. By this time he had heard a great deal about the Mavis tapes. He had just returned from the Island where he had been staying with some friends in Ventnor. He said he knew I only did the tapes for Doris but wondered if I might be able to try it out with one for his friends as they were having an extremely difficult time and really needed some help. I told him I would think about it and see what I could do. All he had told me was that his friends were called Jess and Ken. The next day I decided to give it a try as I could see no reason why I might not be able to help them. If Mavis could help her mother, then there was no reason why someone would not be able to help Peter's friends. I always think that anything is worth a try, so I put a tape on the recorder and began by saying, 'Hello, Jess and Ken', then gave my name and the date and an explanation of what I hoped to be able to do. As with the first tape for Doris the information just flowed for almost an hour but I had no idea if it would make sense. By then I had realised the way in which I work would not require any previous mediation, or thinking about it, as all I had to do was to open my mouth and just say whatever came through. This may be hard for some to believe but it is the truth. When I had finished the tape I packed it up to send, though until the following day I had no address or surname with which to send it. When Peter arrived I asked him for the necessary details and he was amazed when I produced the package with the tape. He could not understand how I could have done this without knowing any details and I must admit I wondered too. It was posted right away and I anxiously waited to hear from his friends. When I did they said the tape was wonderful and very helpful, as well as extremely evidential, adding that it was 95 per cent accurate. In fact, a little later they traced some of the information and found it to be true, so it was a 100-per-cent success. Needless to say, I found this very encouraging: it would be something to give me confidence if I decided to take things further. In the end I did not have much choice as when Peter found out about it, he said I should tell the *Psychic News* about the tapes as it was a truly amazing story. I have never been one to push myself and when I told him this he begged me to let *him* write the story and I agreed.

It took a while to put together as Peter went through all her tapes with Doris and selected the things he felt made the best story. He had worked for *The Times* newspaper in the communications department and I had always felt he should have been a writer himself. Finally the story, along with photographs of Mavis and me, was sent off to the paper and I was later told that, although the front page had already been prepared for that week, the editor Maurice Barbanell had told his staff to clear the front page and to print my story instead. When his assistant produced the new layout she had included a large picture of Mavis and a smaller one of me. Barbanell told her to swap them round, with a larger one of me, as he considered me to be the 'story', while Mavis was the subject of the story. He was a master journalist and knew what he was doing and thereafter showed the greatest respect for my work, always giving me good coverage, mostly front page.

I had in fact pioneered what would become known as tape-recorded proxy sittings or readings, which would become my main work from that time on. To be honest, I did not really want to go in that direction, but it is said, 'By your work will you be known,' and it was only natural that many people would hear about the tapes and ask for my help, so I could not refuse. In many places people did not have access to mediums and psychic matters and so here was a 'remote' service which I could provide, so I accepted whatever came my way. Besides which it was going to help me make a living as, having given up my job, I really needed to earn enough to keep myself going.

10

In America

It did not take long before I was inundated with requests for my taped readings and eventually I found myself with a nine-month waiting list which gave me little or no chance of a holiday or doing what I wanted. I did eventually manage to re-organise things but what with demonstrations and private consultations it created a heavy workload which put me under great pressure. Being young and reasonably fit, I was able to cope with all the demands, but it helped when I received opportunities to travel – not that this meant less work but it was a chance to expand my experience and to see how others worked in the psychic field.

I had been doing tapes for a lady called Mary Sharp who lived in Michigan. She belonged to the Spiritual Frontiers Fellowship and had been a secretary and help to the famous medium Arthur Ford. She was most impressed by my work and felt it was time America should see and know about it. She told me that in her opinion I was a better medium than Arthur Ford but I could not believe that as I had read about him and felt he was truly excellent. In any case I do not care to make any claims to greatness as I feel that I will be acknowledged according to what I can do. I have found that mediums all work in different ways and have different ideas, and I believe this provides for a variety of needs. All through my psychic career I have done whatever I believe to be right and have accepted the responsibility that has been placed on my shoulders. I have always told the truth as far as I have known it to be, and if I have been wrong in anything whatsoever I have always accepted it and changed to another track. One learns by experience and mine has been greatly helped by Mary Sharp, who became a dear friend and with whom I later conducted many psychic tests. I believe we had much in common and both shared the same ideal – to try to advance the cause of psychic research so that it could be universally accepted and used for the good of mankind.

My first trip to America was when Mary asked me to attend a seminar at Gettysburg College where I would be a speaker and teacher for a whole week, after which I could travel on to Harrisburg in Pennsylvania and do some private work. It was a very exciting prospect and I gladly agreed. On the day I arrived Mary took me to lunch before going to the college to settle in. Part way through our meal, a lady rushed in, quite breathless, and asked Mary if I was Ronald Hearn. She said that a huge crowd of people were demanding to know 'if that man from England is here'; no one, she said, would book in to the seminar until it was certain I was here. She rushed back to give them the good news and in the end well over eight hundred had enrolled for the whole seminar, with day attendance taking it to well over a thousand. It was a pleasant shock for me as well as filling me with trepidation that I would have to live up to my reputation.

Once settled in and given quite a pleasantly comfortable room, I was introduced to the officials and told that I had been booked for a class on psychic development every afternoon. I was allowed to have only forty pupils, about which I was quite happy, but then on the second day, the first class having been very successful, I found the classroom full of young people sitting and standing everywhere, at least twice the number I had expected. I asked to know what was happening and a chorus of voices begged me to let them stay as they had heard what a good teacher I was. Apparently they had been put in other classes which they did not like and their teachers had agreed they could come to me, if I agreed. With such a compliment I could not refuse, as long as they behaved and some of them did not mind standing. They *were* well behaved and each day at the end of the lesson I received applause. On the last day there was thunderous applause and it seemed everyone was happy, especially me who had found my ability to teach had progressed somewhat.

During the seminar I had also agreed to give a lecture in the college chapel, which was attended by over a thousand people, including religious ministers, doctors and scientists. This was the first time I had lectured to such a huge crowd and to say I was nervous is an understatement, but once underway my confidence grew and it proved to be a tremendous success. I cannot remember what I said but was gratified when I received three bursts of applause during the lecture and at the end a standing ovation; there was even some cheering. It went on for quite a time and I did not know what to do, whether to bow or wave or what, so I stood and smiled until it all died down and people began to leave. Or so I thought. It was then that Mary got hold of me and said, 'Ronald, put on a good face, smile and be prepared to talk with the people who are so appreciative of your being here and what you are doing.' It was then that I realised a huge queue of people had formed, down the long aisle of the chapel. I whispered to Mary that we would be there all night and she replied by saying, 'No one will leave so you have to talk to them!' I certainly did and it was a very heart-warming experience as everyone shook my hand and told me how much they had enjoyed the lecture. It was around midnight before I could get to bed!

After the seminar I went on to stay for a few days in Camp Hill near Harrisburg in order to do some private readings. When I arrived I was told I would have a very busy schedule, which proved an understatement as I found myself often starting at 8 a.m. or a little later and working through the day. It was hectic in a way but my kindly host and his wife, Harry and Blanche, made me very comfortable and managed everything so I would have no problems. Blanche acted as a sort of a secretary and often was very troubled because so many people wanted to see me. If they couldn't have readings they wanted to take me out to dinner, but there was only so much time and so many meals I could eat! I was treated like a superstar and news travelled round that I loved lobster and Planter's Punch, so I was hardly ever offered a menu as it had all been arranged for me. Only on one or two occasions did my hosts seem to think I would give them readings but always understood when they realised how hard I had been working. I must admit that on most of those occasions the Planter's Punch was very helpful as it enabled me to sleep well! I was not sorry to return home as I felt in need of a break as my trip was very demanding. It was, however, a wonderful experience and certainly one which helped me to realise just how much potential I had, and something which would yet again be more character forming. I felt as if I was beginning to find my real self at last, having wondered for a long time what my life was really all about.

In a strange way my friendship with Mary helped me to experience things of great depth which I doubt I would have been able to otherwise. There was a time when Peter and I went to stay with Mary and her husband, Al, in their home in Macatawa on Lake Michigan. It was a most beautiful spot and very peaceful. Al asked us one day if we would like to go out on the lake in his speedboat and we were happy to. Mary came along and explained a lot of things of interest. I noticed the sun was beginning to set and, when it seemed it was dropping below the horizon, Al turned off the engine so the boat stopped and Mary asked us not to speak but to witness something truly out of this world. Suddenly everything stopped still and there was a terrific sensation like being between heaven and earth and near to creation and perhaps nearer to God. It lasted for a short time but I can never forget that experience. Much the same thing happened once when I was on holiday on the Greek island of Rhodes. I used to go swimming most days and often, just before sunset, I would have a similar experience. Everything stood still and there was no current or waves in the sea; it was though time was standing still and maybe taking a deep breath. Here again it felt as though I was between heaven and earth when perhaps the Creator had paused to take breath. I was the only one swimming at the time and most of the other guests were in the bar drinking. They used to laugh at me when I told them what they were missing but no one ever joined me.

There was another experience just as wonderful as the others but different. When I was in New Zealand on a tour with friends, we visited the Franz Joseph Glacier and I was lucky to be able to take a flight in a little six-seater plane to the top of it. It was one of those occasions which seemed as if it was meant to be, as when my friends booked the flight for me it was uncertain if the weather would be good enough. When checking in the morning they were told the early flight should be all right but the weather would get worse later. So I found myself in this little plane flying over the glacier and landing on virgin snow. When jumping out of the plane the snow came up to my waist but a track was soon made so all the passengers could walk along. The other five passengers were somewhat noisy and not very interested, so I got well away from them so that I could commune with nature. It is terribly hard to put into words what I felt. As I looked at the beautiful blue sky and drank in the peace it was indeed like being nearer to God and creation. At that time I was not sure if God was a man on a throne of judgement or the power of life. Now I am sure it is the latter. When the plane landed my friends met me and told me I had been lucky because the weather was now changing and there would be no more trips that day. It felt as though I was meant to have that trip, one which was quite unforgettable. Although I could never be a mountaineer, it made me realise why men climb mountains – it is like getting away from everything and everyone in order to feel and know there is something greater than us all.

Mary and I worked together trying to prove the continuation of life for quite some time. She was a great believer and refused to be beaten. She was one after my own heart but sadly she departed this life before we could accomplish anything of significance. She had told me I was expected to be the replacement for Arthur Ford after he passed on and, although many people begged me to do so, I had to decline. I was offered no less than five places in which to live which would all be paid for, including a penthouse suite in New York. First I knew that Arthur Ford had been bothered day and night by clients who, because they were paying his living expenses, felt they were entitled to use him. He tried all sorts of things to stop this like charging very high fees, so not many could afford them, but nothing seemed to work. That could never happen to me and in any case my home was in England, which was where I have always wanted to be.

I liked America and the whole affair did not stop me from going again. In many ways American people were far more appreciative than the English and they were happy to hear as much as I could give them. I found then that in England people are not overly keen on addresses or lectures and will leave before the end to catch their buses or trains, even though they lasted thirty minutes at the most. In America one was expected to speak for at least an hour or more. At first I found this hard to believe but it was proved to me not only at Gettysburg but later during one visit to Allentown. An impromptu lecture was arranged at the home of a German lady who hastily contacted seventy people whom she managed to seat in this fairly large house. I spoke for two hours non-stop and nobody seemed restless or attempted to go; in fact they created a very interested and enthusiastic atmosphere. After finishing, I asked if anyone would like to ask questions and there seemed to be a long silence so I asked again. It was then a lady stood up and said, 'Mr Hearn, I think I speak on behalf of everyone here when

I say that you have already answered every question anyone could have and we thank you for a wonderfully enlightening talk.' There was a burst of applause and an invitation to come again whenever possible. They say practice makes perfect and I went away feeling pleased that all this hard work was bearing fruit and I was making progress.

I have never been afraid of hard work, and this was put to the test on another visit to the United States when I was invited to do a whistle-stop tour of some of the states. This was arranged by the Spiritual Frontiers Fellowship and in particular by a lady named Edith Roman who lived in Chestnut Hill near Philadelphia, and with whom I was based. The idea was that I would do one day in one place and maybe two or three days in others while giving lectures and demonstrations plus private consultations. I would travel by train to most places and a system of delivery and pick-up was arranged so a tight schedule could be kept. At first I was not too pleased with the whole idea. However, Edith Roman had a sweetener. She had a friend who at one time had been a professional photographer and he would accompany me on the tour, taking photos of me at work, as well as unofficially watching over me. George Burns was quite a character but fun to be with and, of course, he knew his way around. He took remarkable pictures many of which were subsequently published with articles about me in *Psychic News* and other publications.

Edith was quite a smart lady and had good ideas about what was to be done, although at times I felt angry at being pushed too hard. In the end I had to recognise that she was right; she just wanted me to get the best out of the tour and told me she had great respect for me and my abilities. In fact, she arranged some extra events other than those the Frontiers had organised. Again, this did not please me at first but they turned out to be very rewarding and worthwhile.

On my first day there a man from a local TV station, who was also an extremely good artist, was invited to Edith's home to do a charcoal drawing of me. I was suffering quite badly from jet lag and not disposed to sit still, especially when I would rather be asleep. Edith told me in no uncertain terms that it was all arranged and I should not be so ungrateful. She was a regular sergeant major but, although it took a bit of getting used to, I realised she had worked hard to help me and eventually we understood each other

120

and had a lot of fun. The portrait when finished was well executed but I thought it looked rather somber, not to say miserable. I felt sure I didn't really look like that and I asked the artist if he could make me look a little more humorous. He managed to alter a few lines which made a difference but I never really liked it. But, then, we never see ourselves as others do. Edith thought I would like to hang it in my home for everyone to see but I said I could not do such a thing and I would hide it away. She managed to get the last laugh on me as the next day I was scheduled to appear on the *Connie Roussin Show* in Philadelphia.

When I arrived at the TV studio it seemed that Connie Roussin had not arrived and had phoned in to say she was running late. I was asked to sit in a room to wait for her and finally she came rushing in, quite breathless, and began to take off her coat and tidy herself up. When she noticed me she said, 'I suppose you are the person I am going to interview but I know nothing about you so we will have to make it up as we go along!' I took one look at this quite beautiful, well-dressed lady and said, 'I refuse to go on until you sit down and make a few notes about me. The viewers will be expecting to hear something interesting about me, so let's give them something good.' She apologised and quickly made some notes and then said she first had to interview two baseball players and I would be called in for the second half of the programme. When I walked on set I almost burst out laughing: there on a wall was the charcoal drawing of me. Edith was clearly determined it would be seen by what was a very large viewing audience on a very popular show. The show was repeated three times by public demand after Connie, a consummate professional, had excelled herself in the questions she posed and I, fortunately, in the answers I gave. When I went on set I was surprised to see the two baseball players still there as they were supposed to vacate their seats but had begged to stay and listen to me. Not only did they like me but raved about the drawing, so I had to admit Edith was clever. She certainly would and did handle everything very well and, despite my saying I could not handle such a tight schedule, she said, 'Oh yes you can! You are the star of the show and you will do it.' I have a lot to thank her for.

My tour included places such as Harrisburg, Wilmington in Delaware, some towns in New Jersey, New York and Baltimore, to mention but a few. It was one continual round of getting up early to catch trains and as soon as I arrived at a place I would have to immediately give readings or lectures, sometimes a demonstration or be taken to meet people who just wanted to meet me. Ladies gave potluck parties for me, which meant that all the ladies would bring along their speciality which they had cooked with enough for everyone. It seemed nice at first but when I found I was expected to sample everyone's efforts, I decided such parties were not for me because, although the food was wonderful, there is a limit to how much one can eat at one go! I much preferred when I was taken out to dinner as, although it was squeezed in between engagements, it meant I could choose what I wanted and how much. I cannot deny that Americans are wonderfully friendly and hospitable people.

It was when I was getting near to the end of the tour that Edith announced that she had arranged an appearance on *The Saturday Night Show* in Toronto and they would like me to do a chair test, which meant that I had a plan of the seating arrangement for guests on the show and had to select two seats and write out some messages for whoever would be sitting in them. This I did and they were sent off to the TV company. It was then that I realised I was supposed to be in Baltimore on the day of the show. I told Edith it was not fair to have to cancel that day because people would be disappointed at not being able to see me, to which she said she had been on to Baltimore and they understood and agreed that, as I would be there for a further two days, what I would have done on the first day could be fitted into the others, so no one would lose out. I was angry and asked Edith if she thought I was some sort of machine, but again she told me I could do it and asked me how I could contemplate missing a break like Toronto. I had no choice but to concede gracefully. The day before the TV show I was working in Harrisburg and giving a lecture in the evening. It was arranged that a car would collect me immediately the lecture was over and take me to Edith's home in Philadelphia. I arrived at midnight and went straight to bed but not for long as I was awoken at 5 a.m. and taken direct to the airport where I caught a plane to Toronto.

It was a long journey, which gave me a chance to relax, and I arrived in Toronto around midday. I had been instructed to take a cab to the studios at a certain time, which gave me a chance to see a little of the town and have a light lunch. I arrived as directed to find a very busy scene. Technicians and all sorts of people were getting the set ready for the evening show, which had to be filmed in the afternoon. I gathered the male workers were upset as they would be missing the big football match, so at first I felt rather ignored and not very popular. I was soon put at ease by one of the interviewers on the show, who explained the procedure and what I would have to do. Apparently the subject of the show was about death and the continuation of life. Five guests had been invited comprising an undertaker, a mortician, a coroner, an author who had written about the subject, and a religious minister. They would all be interviewed in turn after I had been interviewed and the results of the chair tests had been announced. I always felt nervous about doing these tests but after the first one, which was for one of the interviewers, I had no need to be as it contained a lot of accurate information which could not be refuted.

By far the best of the chair tests was the second one which was for the author, and here one must remember that I knew nothing about anyone on that show or what it would be about. The messages he received were that he was a well-known author who had just had a best-seller published. He had arrived late and thought he would not get to the studio on time. He was having some trouble with his hair and there was some alteration connected with his plane ticket and time of departure, amongst other things, which all proved to be right. He *had* just written a best-seller, and he *had* only just got to the studio in time and had had to go hastily to the cloakroom to try to do something with his hair. He had washed it the night before but on the day it would not settle down. He did not, however, understand about the time change and his plane ticket...

After the show had finished I received quite thunderous applause from the technicians who then wanted to ask me lots of questions and shake my hand. I had to be hurried away from this in order to get the plane back to Philadelphia. As the author was going to the same airport, the company arranged for a car to take us and paid for us to have a meal together before we departed. This was not to be as when we reached the airport the author said he would like to check the time of his departure and make sure his ticket was in order. He came back to me looking very flushed and hurriedly said he could not have dinner with me as his departure time had been altered and the plane was leaving almost right away. Also there was something to do with his ticket, which, however, was easily settled, so all of his messages turned out to be correct except that one had yet to happen after he left the studio. Not many would know about this but to me it was interesting and encouraging, more so when I heard that the show was a great success and attracted a large viewing audience.

I enjoyed a good meal on my own and then flew back to Edith's home, where I did not get much sleep and was up and on the train to Baltimore the next day. It was a jam-packed schedule in those two days but luckily everyone was highly satisfied with my work, although by then I felt ready to drop. There were so many nights on this tour when before going to sleep I mentally asked someone to help me to get through it all and that, if I did, I would never allow such a thing to happen again. Surprisingly, Edith told me after Toronto that she and George were taking me to Montreal for three days where I could take it easy as all I had to do was a recorded radio interview. I must admit it was good to see this place and we had quite a lot of fun. The radio broadcast went quite well, although I did not know until after I got home that a disc was made of it and they sent me a copy. I believe it was played over the radio quite often and several of my clients, especially in America, told me they heard it on their car radio. The tour was a huge success and, despite the fact that when Edith and George accompanied me to the plane home I was almost asleep, I went with the feeling of having achieved something worthwhile and that I was now truly established in my profession. Nonetheless I needed a long refreshing sleep before I could fully evaluate it and face whatever else was to come.

Some time before this, I had been asked to appear on the *Betty Hughes Show* in Philadelphia; it was when I was staying in Allentown with some friends whom I had made through the tapes I had been sending them. They had lost a son and I was able to give them convincing evidence of his survival. Actually it was the first TV appearance I had ever made and it was at what to me was the unearthly time of 9 a.m. A few weeks before when at home I had been asked to do a taped reading for Betty Hughes but I was not to know the results until that morning. I arrived at the studio a few minutes early and saw people running around doing all sorts of things. No one noticed me and I stood wondering what I was going to do. Suddenly a young man came up to me and asked if

I was Ronald Hearn. When I assured him I was, he took me to one side and said, I am not supposed to tell you this but I heard the tape you sent to Betty and it was fantastic and you were right about everything. She is saying it was not and she is going to say so on the show. I don't think this is fair and so I want you to know but please don't tell anyone or I will be in trouble.' I was very touched by this young man's gesture as he genuinely seemed to care and was obviously upset by the situation. I told him not to worry as I could deal with it, but what he had told me would be helpful and he had my grateful thanks.

Soon after that the producer called me and explained what would take place, and then some technicians asked me to sit in a certain position on the sofa. They played around with the lighting and then asked me if, when talking to Betty, I could look towards a certain spotlight though it did not matter too much if I couldn't. I assured them I would do it and then the set was cleared and a blast of music heralded the opening of the show. I must admit that, while I had felt nervous before, the moment we were on the air something inside me seemed to switch on and I felt wonderful, as though I had been doing it all of my life. It must have been the frustrated actor and showman in me but I felt completely confident and hoped I might be able to do more of this in the future.

The programme was divided into three parts and in the first Betty had to interview me and supposedly talk about her tape. With every reply I gave she appeared to become somewhat confused, especially with regard to the tape. She could not in any way show me up and had to admit that the tape was interesting and, to a point, accurate, but her comments were quite begrudging. In America it was then the custom for the interviewer to do the adverts in the interval and apparently Betty made a mess of them as she seemed flustered and confused. The second part was yet another interview which might have been a little better than the first had not Betty continued to try to put me down. Once again she fluffed the adverts before we got to the third and last part, which was to be a chair test. Prior to my coming I had been sent a plan of the audience seating and asked to send two separate messages in writing for any two seats I chose. This I had done and they were duly produced and given to the two people occupying those seats. They were asked to open them and study the contents. The first one went to a lady who broke into a huge smile and said everything I had written was right on the nail. The second one went also to a lady who said nothing applied to her. Immediately I could sense Betty feeling triumphant that I had been proved wrong at last.

Any feeling she had was soon shattered when a lady standing at the side of the packed hall raised her hand and told Betty that she could understand and accept everything the second lady couldn't. She was an usher who had sat in that seat until she realised there was no more room and so gave up her seat to the second lady. It must have been very upsetting for Betty to hear but this was a fine example of someone knowing beforehand who would be sitting in that seat and who *should* have had that reading. As I was about to leave the studio I was told that the telephone lines had been inundated with calls complaining about the way Betty had tried to put me down because they all thought they had witnessed an amazing and very interesting person who should have been allowed to talk about his gifts without such rude behaviour from her. Although that was fair comment, I felt somewhat sorry for Betty as she had brought on something for herself that she would regret and there was no apparent reason why she did it. Even more sad was the fact that this lady was always top of the ratings but the next morning it appeared she had fallen to the bottom. I never knew if she climbed up again but rather hoped that she did and had learned a lesson. I felt that through this experience I had gained a great deal of confidence in my beliefs and that I could stand by what I believed and act accordingly.

During one of my stays with my friends in Allentown, in order to try to help me they had told a radio station I was in town and they invited me to do a fifteen-minute talk. It was only a small station and I agreed, knowing it would be my first time on radio and something that would add to my experience. It was late night and I found myself wearing headphones in a very cramped little studio and feeling very hot. The announcer told listeners who I was and asked me some questions about my work which seemed to go down well. As there were a lot of people phoning in to ask questions, I agreed to answer them and they extended the programme for as long as I would care to be there. It seems I made a lot of people happy with answers the like of which they had never heard before and the lines were busy, with quite a waiting list. After ninety minutes I had to stop, being tired from previous work and because it was so late; I felt I could not do justice to my readings any more. They would have gone on all night asking questions but I needed my sleep. This was another milestone in my career and something to be proud of.

The station gave me an open invitation to broadcast whenever I was in town which gave me a great feeling of satisfaction. My friends also had a sudden idea about my possibly doing a TV show called *Into the Valley* while I was there and called the station to ask if they would be interested. Such was their enthusiasm they said they would set up a special episode the next morning which would be recorded for broadcast one evening. It was a twenty-minute programme where someone of note who was in town at the time would speak about what they were doing, and mostly it would have some sort of religious connection or something to do with life and death. The next morning one of my friends drove me to the studio, which was quite small but a hive of activity as the technicians were hurriedly setting up. I was greeted cheerfully and asked to wait until my interviewer got there, which wasn't until the very last minute as he arrived all hot and bothered. He explained that he had been asked to do this at the very last minute and even then he did not know exactly what he had to do. I told him who I was and what I did and then it was time to go onto a platform in front of the cameras. The interviewer was still uncertain but I said, 'Just introduce me and I will do the rest.' And so the cameras rolled and twenty minutes later it was in the can as they say and I was receiving a warm round of applause from all the staff there. The interviewer was amazed and said how impressed he was and how controlled I had been. He had thought I would never do it and asked me if I would like to see a playback of the filming.

Both my friend and I were amazed and delighted at how excellent the programme was. It was good to see myself in action as it gave me further encouragement to carry on with the good work. I had to leave for England and home before it was shown, but I heard later it was put in the usual slot the next week and proved so popular they had to repeat the programme no less than three times! They had also asked me to do a whole series of programmes should I ever be in Allentown again. Unfortunately this is something I have not been able to do but that one time is something I will always remember.

Perhaps, after all, it is in the United States that my work has always most been most appreciated and respected. A somewhat unusual honour was afforded to me there when I was made a Kentucky Colonel for my work in the psychic field, and, as far as I know, the first medium to be given that honour. The Kentucky Colonels is a charitable organisation which does a lot of good work and affords to each nominee the freedom of the state of Kentucky. Among the many illustrious holders of the title Kentucky Colonel are General Eisenhower, Winston Churchill and Princess Margaret along with many other celebrities, and I have always felt that, if *they* were happy to receive it, then why shouldn't I?

11

Challenges and Experiments

I have always felt that, in the field of Spiritualism and the psychic, things do not seem to be advancing much, if at all. It always seems to me that mediums are too content with what they have achieved without realising it could be better, and that many are too eager to use their gifts for big monetary rewards. I have never charged extortionate fees, as this would mean a lot of poorer people would not be able to get help and I have tended to think of myself as the poor man's medium. Not that I did not help celebrities, with some of whom I became quite friendly, but I have never been a name-dropper, as I see and treat everyone on the same level. It does not matter about one's position in life because we all have problems and difficulties, whether we like it or not, so everyone is entitled to help in whatever form it may be. When I give consultations I do not really look at the outer person but the inner one where it is possible to find the real individual. I tend to call it contacting the soul and invariably people feel I understand them as, like them, I have suffered too. In order to understand what makes people tick I have done things I would not normally do but which have made it possible for me to meet them on their level. I care very much about people and like to quote an old Paul Robeson song: 'If I can help somebody as I pass along, Then my living will not be in vain.'

Lecturing and teaching became two things which I could do extremely well and I've always thought that perhaps I inherited these gifts from my mother's father, Henry Yeo. I did want to be a schoolteacher at one time but that proved impossible, so I decided I must already be on the right pathway for me. I was often asked to give lectures at the Spiritualist Association where I worked for a time after I gave up my job with the town hall. I also gave demonstrations and readings and at one point I was considered to be a future top medium who would be giving demonstrations at the Albert Hall – the highlight of the psychic year. It would have meant having to stay at the Association on a more or less permanent basis but I could not do that as I did not enjoy being there with a tight daily schedule which made me feel hemmed in. I used to laughingly call it the sausage factory because it was like churning out one thing after another. While I was there I learned a lot about other mediums, although I was often put in my place as being a young whippersnapper, but, despite the jealousy which often surrounded me, I was able to prove I was as good as anyone and began to make a name for myself. Before I left the Association the President, Tom Johanson, husband of Coral Polge and a good friend of mine, asked me if I could think of anything different which could be done to improve the way things were done. He felt people were tired of the same old methods and he knew I was all for trying some new ideas like my tape-recorded sittings. I suddenly had the idea of tape-recording a meeting in advance. Eight weeks before, I would sit in my home with a plan of the Association hall and give messages for whoever would be sitting in certain seats which I would choose. It was rather like a chair test only on a bigger scale and more in keeping with a Spiritualist meeting. Tom was all for the idea which he thought was wonderful and agreed to send me the plan and cooperate with me in whatever way I needed. I had a sudden feeling that it might not work, but I adhered to the principal of one never knows what one can do until or unless one puts it to the test by trying.

The first time I did this it all went well at first. I sat with the plan of the hall and the numbered seats and the messages flowed whenever I chose any particular seat. After I had finished I asked my friend Peter to witness my putting the tape into an addressed envelope so that it was in effect signed and sealed, and it was posted to the Association where it was locked in their safe until the evening of the meeting. On the day of the meeting I began to feel nervous and questioned what I was doing. I did not like the idea that I would have to sit in front of the audience and listen to my own voice as the tape played, but I had no alternative. When I arrived and went to the reception desk, the man who was to be chairman of the meeting took me aside and said he had some bad news: the upstairs hall for which I had recorded the demonstration had been booked for something else, so I would have to take the lower hall. I was quite angry as the layout would be different of course and I said I would cancel the meeting. He looked at me and said he was very surprised, as I was someone he knew who would always accept a challenge, and didn't I think that the greater plan would know about this in advance; it would work whatever the circumstances. He cheerfully said I must go on and do it, which of course I did. I have always refused to be beaten so there was really no choice.

At the start of the meeting the chairman, who was rather aptly named Leonard Jolly (he was always relentlessly optimistic), explained what was to take place and then told the audience that tonight they were to witness something unusual: Ronald Hearn, he said, was the only medium he knew who was prepared to stand or fall by what he had done. A nice compliment which made me cross my fingers tighter than usual, although I am not really superstitious and firmly believe in precognition and predestination. So the tape recorder was switched on and my voice boomed out, first making an opening announcement and then calling out the number of a seat and asking whoever was in that seat to listen carefully while the message was relayed. At the end the recorder was stopped and the occupant of the seat asked if they understood what had been said. It was a tremendous relief to hear them say it was absolutely correct about details of people who had passed on and messages of comfort and guidance. Then followed several more seat numbers and every occupant was able to accept what was said. All these seats had been numbered as near to how they would have been in the upper hall and it was amazing to find they fitted with what I had previously recorded. Also no other person in the hall but those sitting in the chosen seats could accept the messages, so every one had been a direct hit.

In this lower hall there was a long bench at the back which could be used to take more people if necessary and on that night it was fully occupied. I remember that when I originally did the recording at home, for the very last message I could not choose a number, so it was not really surprising that my voice could be heard on the tape saying that there was only one foreign visitor in the hall that night and it was an American lady. The messages contained communication with some relatives who said she had only arrived in London the evening before and had experienced some trouble with her hotel; the bellboy had tried to get fresh with her and that her camera had jammed, amongst other things. She was astounded as everything was true and needless to say she was sitting on the bench at the back and was the only foreigner in the hall. It was also interesting to learn that she had no intention of coming to the meeting and she had only called into the Association that day in order to find out what was going on there. While she was having tea in the café she sat opposite an elderly gentleman who happened to know me very well. They got talking and he said he supposed she had come for the Ronald Hearn meeting. She asked him who I was and what I did as she had no idea and didn't even know about the meeting. When he had explained and said he felt she should witness this, she hastened to the reception desk and managed to get the very last ticket. So, it seemed, she was meant to be there. To think these things were known eight weeks in advance and before she even knew she was coming to London was quite something and to me it meant that, even if it did not prove life after death, it did at least prove there must be some greater force at work.

I did several of these meetings all of which were great successes and at one point I could not cope with the demand as there were other challenges I wanted to take on. One especially stays in my memory, which was when I was asked to do one of these tapes for the Portsmouth Temple of Spiritualism. This was to be over a longer distance in effect but by then I had learned that time and distance are not a problem where this other world is concerned and if one approaches it in the right way something will always come through. On the due date I travelled down to Portsmouth where I often stayed with the then President, Len Slark, and his wife, Raie, who lived right next door to the Temple. That evening the church was packed full except for one seat which remained empty. I felt acutely aware of it and hoped it would not be one I had chosen. However, its number *was* called out and I think a lot of people thought things had gone wrong, myself included. I asked those who were sitting around that seat to all listen to the messages and tell me if anyone could understand. At the end of the recording a lady who was sitting directly behind that seat said she could understand everything and it was uncannily accurate. She went on to explain that the empty seat was the one she always occupied when she came to the church, but as it was a special evening her friends who were sitting in the row behind had saved her a seat with them and insisted she move to sit with them. So the message found its way to the right person and it suggests that the greater force finds its way to whomever is meant to receive it, even if they have changed their seat. The tape, which lasted eighty minutes, had been recorded and witnessed thirty-six days in advance and every message fitted to the person occupying the chosen seat number and no one else in the hall. Each message averaged fifty different statements which were given without me pausing for breath.

The very first message was given to a gentleman who was told about two people I thought were his parents but turned out to be grandparents who had acted as father and mother to him. He was very surprised to hear that an accident in which he had burned his arm in steam from some boiling water had been seen by the communicator. A lady, who described her message as 90 per cent accurate, heard from her dead father whom she resembled very strongly and recognised when I told her he was rubbing his hands because there was something wrong with them; she said he was partially paralysed. A stillborn brother who sent his love was accepted as well, as was a woman who had lung trouble and who kept talking about her cats. She was recognised as a mother-in-law who had kept seven cats. One lady was told she had something wrong with the left side of her face and her wedding ring finger, to which she agreed. She had crushed the finger in a church door when she was a child. She recognised her father who said she was bothered about aeroplanes. She refused to fly. He spoke of his earthly leg trouble and a penchant for highly polished shoes, both of which were correct. Another lady's deceased husband was described as good-looking, dignified, fairly tall with well-defined eyebrows, prominent nose, broad mouth and dark, slightly wavy hair brushed back. He was a proud man who did not like wasting time. He also mentioned his internal trouble, which had caused his passing, and showed a detailed awareness for her current problems. The lady who should have been in the empty seat had a man described to her as a dead brother linked with the RAF who had a prominent nose and large expressive eyes. He was shot down over Germany and said he did navigating, though I, as the medium, thought it was not on that flight. The lady said it was not *her* brother but her mother's, but he was more like a brother than an uncle to her. He was shot down on the way to Germany and later passed on. He was a navigator but had acted as bomb aimer on that particular mission. Another lady's father used to sing music-hall songs on stage and mentioned 'Let's all go down the Strand', 'My old man said follow the van' and 'It's a great big shame'. She said these were all his favourites and when he said he had a big Adam's apple she said there was no one with a more prominent one. Yet another father said something funny about a Black Maria, which, apparently, was his party piece. He mentioned his daughter's back trouble and a purse with lots of old papers and a receipt which should be thrown away. I felt there was an interview at 11 a.m. on a Tuesday which she should know about. After the meeting this lady opened her bag and took out a card with details of an appointment with a specialist to see about her back trouble at 11 a.m. on a Tuesday. She also opened her purse which was crammed with papers and a receipt for a bicycle which she had bought for her granddaughter. She also received a message from a grandmother on the tape which made her close her eyes and feel just as if it *was* her grandmother speaking. She was reassured her back trouble was not permanent as she had already spent five weeks in hospital with it.

There were many other evidential and reassuring messages which contributed to a highly successful demonstration, showing how much was apparently known in advance by people in this other dimension. There is no way this experiment could have been 'fixed', as when I made the tape it was witnessed, signed and sealed and sent immediately to the church where its receipt was witnessed before it was locked away until the day of the meeting. Also it was shown to the audience as not having been opened until that very moment. I must admit to heaving a huge sigh of relief after it was proved to me that once again a challenge accepted had been a worthwhile effort.

During the course of my work there have been many aspects which I did not particularly believe in but had to find out about them nonetheless. One of these was predestination. I had been giving a demonstration in the Richmond Spiritualist church on one occasion when, after it was over, a lady approached me and asked if I believed in predestination. I said I did not to which she replied, 'Well, listen to what I will tell you and I think you will change your mind. A few weeks ago when you were last here you gave me a message from my father who had passed on. You saw a lot of privet hedges with him and felt he was a gardener, which he was. You described both him and his character so well it could not have been anyone else. As you concluded the message you said that he was watching over me and would protect me, which sounded very nice and comforting, although I did not think it was anything important. You then saw a motorcycle laying on its side by some broken steps with a privet hedge overhanging them. The road was completely deserted and once again my father said he would protect me. I work in catering and am employed by a company to work in their canteen. Every day I leave at 4 p.m. and as I go through the main entrance I always say goodbye to the doorman and then turn left through the gates into the roadway where I catch my bus a few yards along. One day as I was walking to the bus stop two young motorcyclists came roaring down the road at breakneck speed. As they passed me I thought they were silly young lads who would probably kill themselves but they had gone in a flash and my mind turned to other things. The next day when it was time to leave I felt my father around and it was as if he was telling me not to leave yet. So I busied myself with a few odd jobs until it felt all right to go. When I reached the front entrance the doorman said it was unusual for me to leave this late and asked if I had heard about the silly young lad on a motorcycle who had got himself killed. There had been an accident. There were two of them but one went off the road and crashed and was instantly killed. As I walked along to the bus stop I saw the motorcycle laying on its side, the broken steps and the privet hedge in a completely deserted road. Next day I had to find out exactly when it had happened and it was at the exact time I would have been going to catch my bus, and when I would have been in front of those steps. I then realised why Father insisted in saying he would protect me. It's so strange that I should be protected and yet that poor lad was not.' I had to agree it was something to think about and could only feel there was something in the old idea that when your time was up you would have to go, but not before. However, it is very hard to accept our lives are mapped out to that extent, but for me this story caused a change of mind, enough to help me see other things more clearly in future.

Precognition, or fortune-telling, was a subject I had often read about. I had had my palm read before I had even become involved with the psychic but cannot claim I was told anything significant, just a lot of trivial things which did not really apply and could have fitted other people. I will not say I was sceptical but at that time it was more or less just for fun. After becoming a medium I was obliged to look into the subject and decided to do an experiment which, as my friend Leonard Jolly had said, I would have to stand or fall by. I had agreed to give a lecture at the Spiritualist Association on the subject of precognition but decided to try the experiment with it. Some weeks in advance I took fourteen pieces of paper and wrote on each of them fourteen statements about whoever would receive them. They were very simple: 'You are a lady wearing glasses', for example, or 'You speak French and have just returned from France' or 'You are wearing a blue dress'. I then put each one in an envelope and sent them all to the Association where they were locked in the safe until the evening of the lecture. I managed to give an interesting lecture to the audience who at that stage were not aware of what was going to follow. I explained what it was all about and then asked the chairman to hand out the envelopes, as that way there could be no collusion. I told him to hand an envelope to anyone he was drawn to and, when they were ready, each person was asked to read out in turn what was written on their paper and say if it applied to them. I was astonished when no less than twelve said everything applied to them and no one else in the hall could claim it applied also to them. That just left two which seemed to have completely missed, or so I thought. After the meeting was over, a lady came up to me and said she was very sorry and embarrassed because one of the envelopes had been given to her daughter who came with her, and the girl did not really understand what it was all about. The most outstanding statement on her paper was 'You have been doing something connected with balloons.' Mother said her daughter was training to be a ballet dancer and only that afternoon she had been doing an exercise called 'balloons'. Then the next day a Portuguese man whom I knew as a client but whom I hadn't known to be at the lecture telephoned me to apologise for not speaking up when he received a set of statements because his English was not good enough to immediately understand them. Now he had studied them they were all correct and he said very unusual things were mentioned. So in the end every statement was true and the experiment an unqualified success.

Another interesting example of my experimental period was when I was going to stay with some friends in Allentown in the States.

A journalist named Anne Kovelenko who was connected with the *Allentown Call Chronicle*, a very popular newspaper, had got to know about me and asked if I would do an absent proxy test. The idea was that I would record messages for twelve people who would be in a group and send the tape to her well before my arrival in America. This I did without any difficulty as by then I had done enough to encourage me not to doubt my ability. On the night of the group meeting which was held in someone's home, I found twelve people sitting in a circle waiting anxiously to see and hear if I had pulled it off. A problem arose as the hostess asked me how were we going to number the people so each one would know if their message was for them. I suggested she write numbers from one to twelve on a slips of papers and hand them round, but as she had just finished writing the numbers she accidentally dropped them all on the floor. As she tried to apologise I told her not to worry but to leave them there. I then asked all the group members to just pick any one of the papers they wanted to, which they did and then sat down to listen to what my recorded voice would tell them. One by one the messages fitted only the numbered recipient and all of them contained amazing evidence which showed without any doubt that everything was planned and known in advance. Experiments such as this gave me a great deal of confidence to go full steam ahead with the work I was doing, though I knew I would never be fully satisfied as there was still so much I had to learn. Just as one thinks one has all the answers then something else comes along that sets one fresh questions and challenges.

They say all work and no play makes Jack a dull boy, but luckily I have always tried to keep a balance and have time to myself. Even my leisure time, however, tended to tie in with the psychic at times and it usually threw up other new ideas that perhaps I would not have thought about otherwise. On one occasion Peter and I had arranged with our friend Jim and his wife to go to Greece on holiday, which was something I had so wanted to do for a long time. We chose a place called Loutraki on the Gulf of Corinth, about an hour's drive from Athens, and made our arrangements. At the last minute Jim's wife, Gwen, had to cancel as she was pregnant and so Peter and I went alone. When we stepped off the plane in Athens I had a powerful feeling of coming home. Peter did not feel exactly the same but he was quite thrilled.

We were both even more happy when we found ourselves in a delightful small hotel, in a room overlooking the hotel's swimming pool and with a beautiful view. Once settled in we went to the dining room for an evening meal. While we were wondering where we should sit, a man and his wife came up to us and asked if they might sit at the same table. We were happy to share a table with this charming couple and were shown to what would be our regular spot. As we began chatting, it turned out that the man was a university lecturer and his wife a child psychiatrist, very interesting people who like us wanted so much to see Greece and enjoy a break. They said they had not intended to come to Loutraki but as it was a last-minute decision this was the only place they could get and they felt they had to be there. During the course of the holiday we went around together and enjoyed their company very much. It felt as if we had known them all our lives.

At the next table were two young girls who seemed to be very happy and laughing most of the time. They kept looking at Peter and me and after the meal they spoke to us and said they wished they could have been on our table as they had seen us on the plane and thought we looked like two really nice men who had a sense of humour. After that we often saw them on the beach and they sometimes came on the same trips as us. They told us that they often came to this place but always at a different time to now. Owing to some problem at home they had to come at this particular time but were glad it happened this way as they felt we were all meant to meet. At another nearby table were a young man and his girlfriend who seemed to be glad to be there and to be able to meet us. They only decided to have a holiday at the last minute and Loutraki was the only place they could book, but as soon as they arrived they felt it was a meant thing. We thought they must have got Gwen and Jim's cancellation which made it seem that all eight of us had been meant to meet, if only for the reason we all got on so well and took a great deal of pleasure in each other's company.

Normally neither Peter nor I like to be in groups and prefer to do our own thing but this time we were rarely on our own as everybody concerned wanted to go places and do things as a sort of party. We did actually have a tour guide staying in the hotel, a beautiful young lady who felt immediately she too wanted to be with us, and we all had a great time doing all sorts of things. She said she had never had a group like us before and also felt that somehow it was meant to be. It would be hard to say why we were all drawn together and had to meet. I have no doubt the others all found something special had taken place, but Peter and I experienced some interesting things to make us think more about what we believed in. I decided we would all think back on this holiday after we got home and realise how important it had been to us in some way or the other.

One day Peter and I were sitting on the beach looking across the Bay of Corinth. Although he claimed not to believe in reincarnation, he suddenly said to me, 'If there is any truth that we have lived before then I must have been in Corinth.' I was surprised but inwardly very pleased as I was longing to go there and, although I supposed it was to see the place itself, I felt deep down inside there was a reason for it. So we found a trip was possible and the next day found us on a coach full of people and heading for Corinth. We had a tour guide who was an extremely interesting person and who knew just about everything there was to know. We followed her at first but gradually found ourselves dropping back a bit so that we could get to see some things she hadn't told us about. At one point I stopped dead in my tracks and suddenly felt very angry, so much so that Peter asked what was upsetting me. I said: 'What have they done to the road? There used to be a road here that led from the Triumphal Gate into Corinth and down to the sea.' Peter seemed puzzled, saying there were no signs of a road nor of a Triumphal Gate so perhaps it was my imagination. That only made me more indignant until quite a while later we caught up with the party just as the guide was saying, 'Ladies and gentlemen, you are now standing on what once was a road which ran from the Triumphal Gate, which also no longer exists, right down to the sea. If you could dig deep enough you would find the remains but it would be very deep down as they disappeared a very long time ago.'

After that I felt relieved, as the sensations were so strong and personal to me. It could have been a psychometric impression but the feeling of somehow belonging there left a strong sensation that I was connected in some way with this place. Even Peter was beginning to feel something stronger within him but at that point he still had reservations. We continued on, still following the guide, until we came to a sort of cliff with what seemed like a place someone might have stood. As soon as I stood there, I felt as though I was preaching to a lot of people who were standing below and it truly felt like a wonderful platform. I even felt this might be where St Paul had given his Epistle to the Corinthians and indeed it was, as we found out later. I do not mean to suggest I am a reincarnation of the Apostle, but certainly it was a fine experience which gave an extra dimension to the history lesson the guide was giving. On another trip we took a tour to the temple of Delphi which is in ruins but still retains a wonderful atmosphere. When we came across the altar where the priestess gave her predictions, we felt such a tremendous power that I think I could have gone into a trance. Peter still laughingly calls me the Oracle of Clapham, which is where I live of course. Another experience was when we visited the Acropolis and the Parthenon in Athens. We both felt absolutely at home there and when we saw the amphitheatre of Herodes Atticus I nearly passed out and had a strong urge to go down to the stage and act. These things may not have had anything to do with reincarnation but were certainly what one could call psychic phenomena. I have told only a few people of these experiences, which were no doubt needed to hold my interest and make me fully accept the psychic world.

12

Music and Laughter

Having spent almost sixty years in service to mankind, I have met many interesting people and done an enormous amount of work in trying to help them and in promoting what I believe to be the truth as far as I know it. Apart from doing readings, sending tapes, and giving lectures and demonstrations, I have had to write thousands of letters in connection with these things, and this has been very demanding, not to mention tiring. I have never had a secretary or indeed a great deal of help; it has been a case of 'do it yourself'. I have, moreover, given a lot of unpaid help to people in need.

At one time a man from Canada used to come to me for readings but never answered anything I said and just sat staring out of the window as I talked. After a time I became frustrated with this and when he next came told I him it was not good enough and I would not do any more readings for him. At this he became very upset and begged me not to stop and said the readings were absolutely wonderful and accurate and he acted as he did only because he did not want to put words into my mouth or lead me in any way. He then said that he always took the tapes back home to Canada where he played them to all the people in the village where he lived and often in places further afield. He said that many people were benefiting by this and it was teaching them things they should know. It was only then that I understood why he never wanted me to record the readings on a tape for him. I had noticed he always carried a black case which he just put down by his chair when he came in. I just assumed it was a business case but apparently it had a tiny built-in tape recorder which he switched on without my knowing. I should have realised he could not possibly have remembered all I said but I always try to go along with whatever a client wishes. In reality, I should have asked him to stop doing this, but I find it hard to say no and disappoint people, especially if they are in need of help.

The Society of Psychical Research is a body of people who investigate all aspects of the psychic and who are very difficult to impress. I have worked with them doing some tests and sometimes their members would come to me without saying who they were. I think it is true to say that I was able to impress most, if not all, of them, which is proved by the fact that Maurice Grosse, the one-time President, gave a quote for the cover of my first book in which he fully endorsed my mediumship. Another Society member was Guy Lyon Playfair, himself an accomplished author and investigator, who asked me if I would try to get messages for someone and the only clue he gave was a date of birth. Knowing how expert this man was, having written many influential books on different aspects of the subject, I felt this would be an enormous challenge but I was ready to try. The first tape I did turned out to be successful and Guy was amazed I was able to get on track, so to speak, having so very little to go on. He had asked me to do it for a neighbour and friend of his who had lost her husband. She was a well-known actress named Hana Maria Pravda, wife of an even better-known actor named George Pravda. She was, as I found out later, a very sceptical lady and not always the easiest person to deal with. So I tried another tape with even better results and thus began a whole series of communications with George, which were quite amazing as he was a marvellous communicator who seemed to know exactly what his wife had been doing and also knew what she would be doing. Hana was a most amazing character as she had undergone great hardships in the wartime and had been in Auschwitz from which she escaped, though some of her family were not so lucky. Her first husband had been tragically killed before they could be reunited. The tapes also gave her contact with family and friends, and over a long period of time she received strong evidence of survival. We also became very good friends, although always there was that professional side to both of us that would not allow our friendship to interfere with or affect our work together. It is interesting to note that, after a few tapes, Hana, who was still somewhat sceptical, asked if she could come to see me for a consultation as she felt it would produce better results. I agreed as at that point I felt she did not really understand the whole process and I could explain it better to her. When she arrived and I started to make contact for her, she just sat with eyes closed and did not answer anything but asked me to just say all I had to say. It was absolutely impossible and I had to explain that she was effectively putting up a barrier and there was nothing more I could do. All the same, she begged me to keep on with the tapes.

This experience shows how some people approach the subject. Hana was a very clever and intelligent lady who through her hardships had shown remarkable courage. I have no doubt that she believed in me and what I was doing, but she had to put everything to the test before she could completely accept anything. So we went back to tapes and she was able to fully accept there could be no other way of my knowing about her and all she was doing and going to do other than some psychical explanation. Guy Playfair lived close to her and they were good friends. He wrote a very interesting account of her tapes which he subsequently referred to as the 'Pravda Tapes' when his story was published in the *Light* magazine of the College of Psychic Studies. He also lectured on the taped communications. Hana often told me I had a wonderful speaking voice and that I would make a marvellous actor. She had hoped to stage one of the plays she had written for a pub theatre and wanted me to take part in it. I was almost persuaded but unfortunately it did not happen and I concluded that I was meant to go on doing my work in the psychic field, as perhaps that was what I was best at.

Strangely enough I was told by other people I should be an actor, which pleased me, but I never received any offers. One man who was a Broadway producer in America came to me for a reading and after it was over said, 'You are a brilliant psychic and I have enjoyed my reading, but if I had to put in order as to what you should do, then it would be an actor first and a psychic second.' He went away, saying he would remember me if any parts came up, but I never heard. Another producer, this time on TV, said much the same when I went to talk about the possibility of doing a programme concerning many aspects of the psychic. He asked me to show what I could do by giving three members of his staff, including him, some messages from the 'other side'. When I had finished he said it was not quite what he was looking for, although he was impressed by my work. He then looked at me and said, 'You should be an actor as you have the gift.' I replied, 'If you think what I came here for was to become an actor you are mistaken.' He said it was not meant to be an insult but he really could see me as an actor. When I said I was too old, he said there were plenty of older parts I could play but declined to make me an offer saying it was not in his power to do so.

I have had other people say I really should have been an actor and after a while I began to get very annoyed as I thought the suggestion was that my performance as a medium was purely an act and to me it was never that, even if it appeared to be. When communicating with the other world I am always open to connect with anyone who wants to get through regardless of their many different characteristics. Mostly the messages which come through cover a wide range of emotions, from laughter to anger, and as a medium I convey exactly what I feel. An actor plays out what has been written by someone else whereas a medium gives it straight from the horse's mouth, in a manner of speaking

I can't imagine any world without music and have often said that, if there is none in the other world, then I don't want to go there. Music plays a great part of my life, as does humour. Without these two things I would be lost. Shakespeare famously wrote, 'If music be the food of love, play on. Give me excess of it...', which to my way of thinking means you can't have too much of a good thing! From a very early age I loved music-hall songs, which although very rumbustious were easy to remember. It was the same with the songs and music from films and shows as they stayed with me. Even now around seventy years later I can remember the words and tunes of so many numbers, many of which are forgotten by so many others. For quite a time, and especially in my early teens, I did not like classical music or so I thought. At secondary school when I sat next to my friend Les we were always singing songs made famous by Peggy Lee and various other artistes. This tended to annoy the girl who sat in front of us. I had a crush on her because she was so beautiful and I hoped she would be my girlfriend, which finally happened after we left school. She was very fond of classical music and was always telling us we should listen to it and discover what we were missing. This fell on deaf ears, at least for me, as I could think only of what I already liked. So what else could there be? I was to find out in a surprising way.

In my teens I used to go to stay with a friend of Mother's who lived in Princes Risborough in Buckinghamshire. She had been in service to his family and they had all kept in touch in later years. For me it was a special treat and this man, whose name was Bert Trotman, introduced me to some of that beautiful countryside and some of the people who lived there, including Stanley Holloway the actor whom I was delighted to meet. Bert lived in a pleasant house which offered interesting walks. He was a man of great ability but never seemed to bother about doing anything with it. The one thing he loved was music and especially the organ which he could play really well. He actually had quite a large organ installed in his lounge and would sometimes play for me, which I loved. On one occasion Bert had to go out on some business which he said would take him two or three hours and so I would have to amuse myself. When I asked him how, he pointed to a pile of records beside a wind-up gramophone and told me to take my pick. I was not amused at the idea as when I sorted through the records they appeared to be all classical ones. However, in sheer frustration I put on a record of Tchaikovsky's Piano Concerto No. 1 in B flat minor and as the opening chords boomed out I had to sit up and listen. It was exciting and wonderful and suddenly it dawned upon me that I had been missing something and that my girlfriend Margaret from school had been right. I made up for lost time and listened to many more records. I could not get enough and when Bert arrived home he thought I was in a stupor as I hardly noticed him. When I finally explained my great discovery he played me some pieces on the organ that appealed to my new-found passion.

From then on my life seemed to have changed – when I listened to any kind of music, but especially classical, it seemed to reach down into my heart and soul. It began to make me realise just how sensitive I was and after I left school and went to work I found myself able to buy records for myself. What's more I could finally afford to go to the ballet and opera. At first my friends teased me and said ballet was a sissy thing, but I did not care and gradually realised that dance was the purest expression of music and that I would always have to include ballet in my life. It was much the same with opera. I have happy memories of fine performances at which I always stayed right until the end. Watching the artistes taking their bows made me realise how important it was to be recognised and to know that one has been able to communicate something of value to other people. Deep down inside I knew I envied what was taking place but was not jealous of it. I would have loved to have been a concert pianist, a great dancer or singer, and perhaps above all a great actor, but it seemed it wasn't to be, but there have been compensations. What I feel I have achieved in my life is to be able to help my fellow men, to understand anyone who comes to me for help and, on occasions, to save lives even. Through my work I have prevented people from committing suicide and sometimes from making disastrous decisions. I have guided many and set them on the right course and brought hope to many lost souls. This I say in all humility, not to boast, as it has taken hard work and dedication.

Mostly because of religious teachings many people think that any loved one who has taken their own life is in some sort of dark place. I know from my own religious upbringing that suicides can only be buried in unconsecrated ground, which always struck me as being unfair and far from what any god would want. If God is love then there should be forgiveness for all, if it be necessary. I have never been more thankful than to break away from organised religion and think for myself. I was made to think more about suicides when giving readings to people who have had communication from friends and family who had taken their own lives. I never found a suicide to be unhappy or held back in any way. Most of them said they would not recommend anyone doing what they did as once anyone passes over then they have to put their house in order and sort themselves out. Suicide can make it more difficult to do so, though not impossible. I once gave a lecture on 'What happens to the suicide' and expected only a few people to turn up. I was delighted to find the hall was full to overflowing; some even had to be turned away with the promise I would give a repeat lecture, which I did, and still the hall was packed! It seems that people found such comfort in knowing what I had proved, which was that every person that passes on is able to communicate if they so wish.

On a cheerful note I often tell a story of a personal reading I gave to my friend Betty. At one point I made contact with a young man called David who had taken his own life. He truly appeared to have been the life and soul of the party but it transpired that he had been very unhappy while going through a very personal and difficult situation, which resulted in his not being able to take any more. He gave a lot of evidence to Betty but the most happy and convincing part was when he asked her if she would like to buy a garden gnome. He was laughing and reminded Betty it was in Selfridges. That had been the last time she had seen David. She had wandered by accident into the gardening department and a young man had come up to her and said, 'Would you like to buy a garden gnome, Madam?' She suddenly realised it was David and they both burst into laughter and talked of old times. In his communication there was nothing to indicate he was still unhappy and for me it was encouraging to find something to uphold my beliefs and a story which could help others to find comfort and joy in knowing they would meet their loved ones again regardless of what they had done.

For all that, suicide can provoke uncharitable reactions. I found it very sad when I learned that Nora Blackwood, who in my opinion was one of the world's finest mediums, had taken her own life. She was suffering from mouth cancer and, having nursed her husband, who had also had cancer, she felt she could not burden her family with her problem. This I could understand and I felt she was entitled to do what she did, as we are all entitled to make our own choices and should be responsible for our own actions. However, it seemed that the Spiritualists in particular felt she had let the side down and even the psychic press implied as much. Perhaps because of the manner of her passing, she was soon forgotten and the wonderful work she had done over the years was ignored. I had one special client who knew Nora extremely well and had done a lot of work at the church this lady ran. She had fairly regular tapes from me and she told me she hoped that Nora might communicate. She did not really need to ask as almost immediately Nora came through with some very indignant messages. She was fully aware of how people were reacting to what she had done and went on to explain why and how she had taken this step. She gave a lot of wisdom and sound advice as to what it was like in the other world and why suicide is not a sin. To say her communications were instructive is probably an understatement. The lady asked me if I would agree to her taking the tapes to the Spiritualist Association where Nora had worked for so long, as well as to the psychic press, as she felt the messages should be published so that people would understand and be helped by what Nora was saying. Unfortunately they did not want to know and since then nothing about Nora has been published. It was something that amazed and saddened me, as she was instrumental in helping so many people, including me. It seems that Spiritualists, in line with orthodox religions, prefer to bend the facts to fit their theories rather than adapt their theories to fit the facts. No matter what they think, I would certainly listen to Nora anytime. This incident was pivotal in my ceasing to call myself a Spiritualist.

Through my experiments I firmly believe our lives are predestined, in which case suicide must be within some people's destiny. The sooner Spiritualism separates itself from religion the better; only then will it evolve without bias and allow the truth to shine through unimpeded. Many people are inclined to think that life after death is purely a serious thing and because of religious beliefs they find it hard to accept that there might be a humorous side to it. I believe that we all retain a sense of humour (that is, if we had one here!) and if not then one would soon develop one once we have come face to face with the truth. Many of the messages I have given certainly uphold this idea and I will quote some examples.

One particular message comes to mind that I gave to a lady called Marjorie Backway, during a demonstration I was giving at the Richmond Spiritualist church. She was with her daughter Clare. It was about Clare's grandmother's funeral. After giving what Marjorie called a perfect description of her appearance and strong personality, mentioning her large family and various other memories, 'Granny' said Marjorie was at her funeral which was in the country and 'what a performance that was!' She then described the ancient village church and how her coffin had been put on a very old bier with creaky rusted wheels and had been trundled along a narrow alley in the churchyard in order to reach the church. It wobbled all over the ground, which was very bumpy, and the coffin looked in danger of falling off. Granny appeared to be highly amused by this, even though she probably would not have been when in this life. She said there was a small retaining wall on the left with graves in the ground above it and that a cat that had been asleep on one of them was glaring down at all the commotion. She was laughing at what she had heard Marjorie say to her sister as they followed behind side by side. Granny had always disliked cats and when they ventured into her garden she always made what her family called 'the cat noise' in order to shoo them off. This noise was almost a quack like Donald Duck used to make. Marjorie had forgotten this incident but now remembered how she had said to her sister as the cat arched its back as they were passing by: 'I wonder Mummy doesn't put her head out of the coffin and make her cat noise at it.' This certainly was a good example of a very individual and unusual piece of survival evidence. It also demonstrated that Clara had witnessed her own funeral and was able to let her daughter Marjorie know that fact.

After this I became close friends with Clare and her family, as it transpired they were Devonshire people and lived near to where my mother's family came from. I think we were meant to meet as I have been able to be of some help to Clare. We have enjoyed many psychic experiences together, which have encouraged her to develop her own gifts and help other people. She has a great interest in the psychic and now Marjorie is watching over Clare just as Granny watched over Marjorie. I often feel that very little occurs without reason and most things are predestined.

One of Clare's and my shared experiences took place when we spent a holiday in Cornwall with Peter and my sister Winnie. We had rented an old farmhouse just outside Bude but as we journeyed there Clare felt unhappy and had an unpleasant feeling about the place, even though we had not yet seen it. She did not want to go there but as we had paid for the rental there was little else we could do. When we eventually located it I must admit that all of us were surprised and disappointed as it appeared to be very old and somewhat run down. However, all apart from Clare thought it was only for sleeping and we would be out and about most of the time. We saw the owner, a very strange-looking farmer's wife with a quaint old Cornish manner, who gave us all the necessary instructions. Once we were settled in, it was a case of making the most of it, though we all agreed it was certainly not de luxe. Peter and I shared a room with broken windows, which was draughty to say the least. The ladies had separate rooms at the top of a rickety staircase which had to be negotiated carefully. Our first problem came when the lights suddenly went out and, although we knew we had to put money in the meter, we spent several minutes before we located it in the strangest of places. It seemed as if there were all sorts of odd occurrences but all of us except Clare decided to laugh about it. She was convinced the place was haunted and some strange things happened that suggested she was right.

One morning as we all met for breakfast, Winnie and Clare seemed to be arguing about something which had happened during the night. Apparently Clare was accusing Winnie of opening her bedroom door during the night but Winnie denied doing so. Their rooms were directly opposite and Clare said her door was definitely opened as she could see light coming in as though from Winnie's room. There was no earthly reason for this to happen but as she had also heard footsteps it was hard to convince her otherwise. One could only assume there was a ghost. Another incident confirmed that it might well be, as before we had breakfast one morning Clare wrote a card and put it on the mantelpiece ready to post when we went out later. After breakfast we all walked into the room to find the card on the floor over the other side of the room in a far corner as if it had been carefully laid there. We all checked and realised there was no way that could have happened other than perhaps by ghostly means, as all the windows and doors were closed and no draughts could get through. Nothing could have shaken it down and across the room, and it was too carefully placed to be accidental. Nothing *very* ghostly, to be sure, but even so it was interesting, although Clare became even more eager to get out of the house.

There was another strange happening before we left Bude, but not in the house. One afternoon we thought we might all sample a typical Cornish clotted-cream tea. As Clare preferred to go for a swim, the rest of us left her to it and agreed to meet up later. We three had already spotted a nice place to go and so we found ourselves in a lovely café run by an elderly man and his son. The man told us that after his wife had died he and his son had decided to carry on as usual; he was doing the waiting and his son made all the scones and the cream. When we entered the café and sat down the owner seemed to ignore us and we had to call him over to order. He asked us where the other lady was. He had been waiting until she joined us as he had seen the four of us get out of the car. We told him there was no one else with us but he insisted he had seen the other lady arrive with us and gave a good description of Clare. It was hard to make him accept Clare was not with us but in the end he laughed it off. When we told Clare what had happened and that we were going for another visit the next day she said she would come with us. As soon as we entered the owner came up to us and said that Clare was the lady he had seen on our previous visit. A good example of thought projection as Clare did say that as she was swimming she had thought about us as she did not want to be late meeting us. We all found this incident very interesting and for Clare a happier phenomenon, though she was still relieved to get away from Bude.

Above:
Great
Grandfather
William Yeo

Left:
Grandfather
Henry Yeo

Right:
Grandmother
Mary Yeo

Below:
Mother's wedding
L: Uncle Percy
R: Father

Above:
Ronald's Mother, Winifred
(one of identical twins)

Left:
'The lady with the white hair'
– Mother

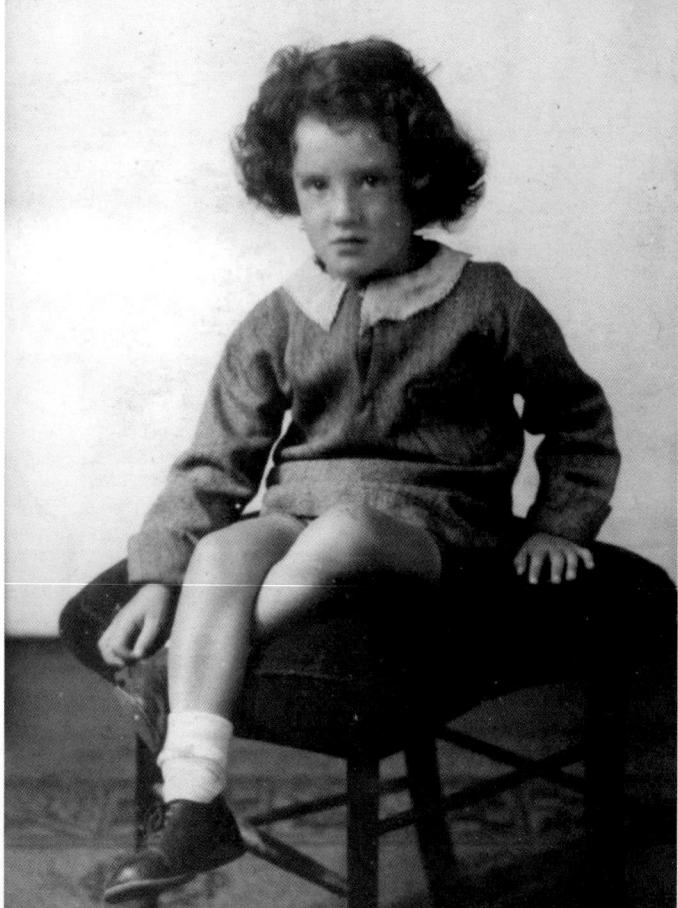

Above:
Ronald and sister Winnie

Right:
Ronald, aged 4.
The first photo ever taken

Left:
Sergeant Ronald Hearn,
Intelligence Corps

Below:
Ronald's Sister,
Marjorie Yeo

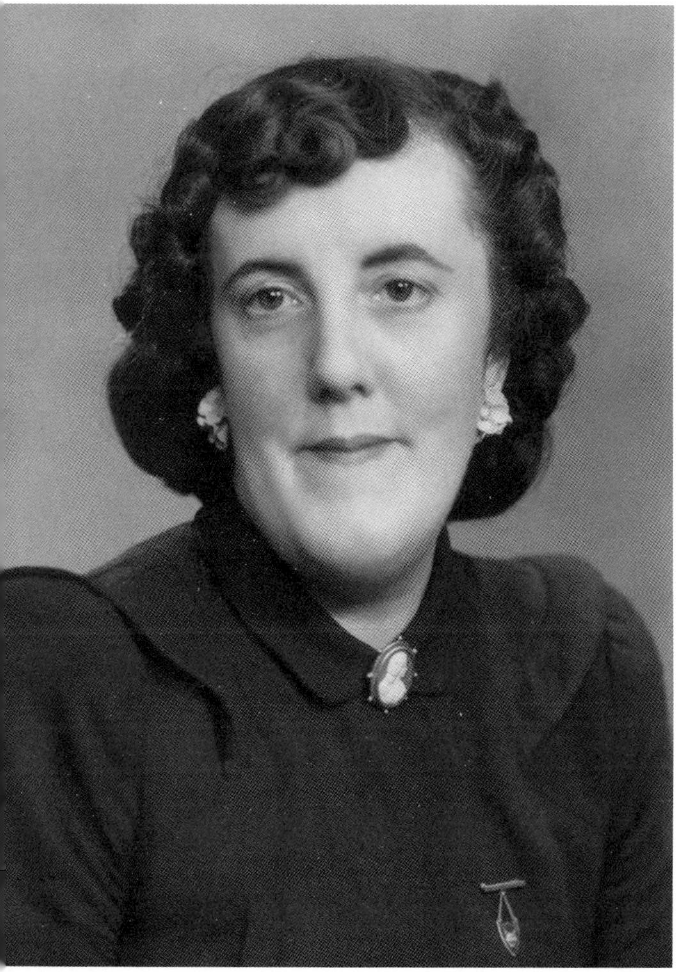

Right:
Ronald's brother Bill

Below:
Ronald's sister Winnie

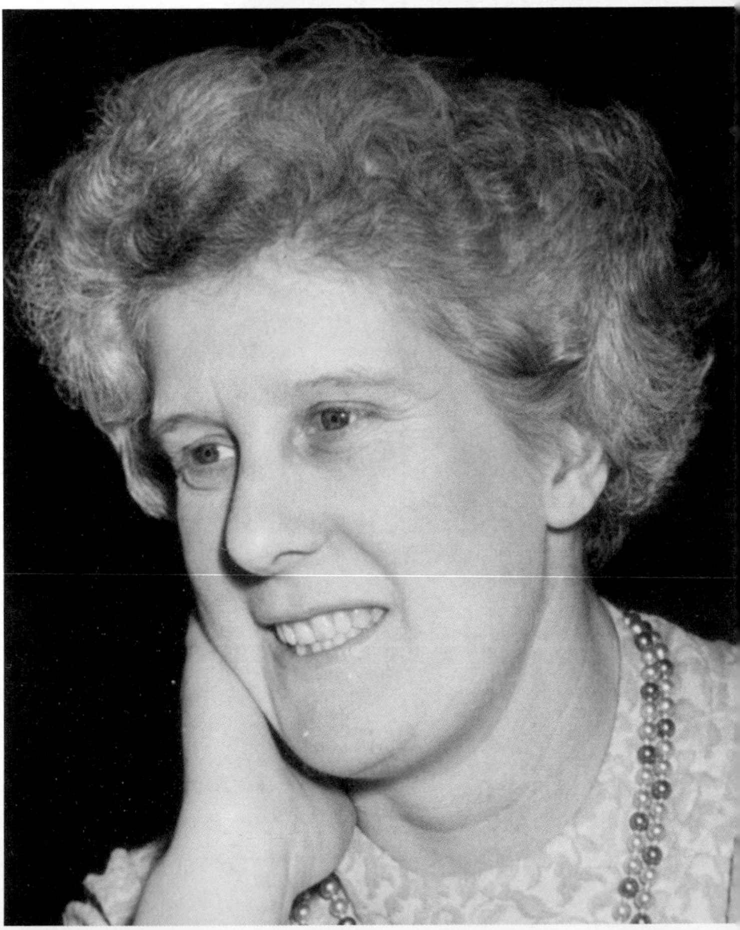

Left:
Corporal Ronald Hearn

Below:
Ronald with
L: friend Norma Williams,
R: sister Winnie

Ronald Hearn: Medium

We also stayed a few days in Paignton where we had yet another curious incident. One evening we decided to attend the local Spiritualist church where a very fine medium named Lillian Hurst was giving a demonstration of clairvoyance. I had met 'Auntie Lil' as she was affectionately called but did not at that time know her that well. As we entered the church I suggested that Winnie and Clare sit on one side while Peter and I would sit on the other. This was because Lil might recognise me but she would not know who Winnie was nor would anyone else in the church. Lil gave a really sparkling and extremely evidential demonstration during which she picked Winnie out for a message. She described our mother to a tee and then said she was holding out a yellow duster to her, adding that she was a very hard-working lady who loved dusting and polishing among other things. After a while of waving the duster to her daughter it seems that Mother directed Lil over to me. Lil said, 'I know you, Ron, but it may seem strange but this lady wants to shake the duster at you and says you should know why. Is there some connection?' This most certainly was the case because not only was I the lady's son but earlier that day all of us had been trying to tidy up the bungalow where we were staying but could not find any dusters anywhere. When we got back that night and entered the kitchen, there on a towel rail was hanging one yellow duster which had not been there before. Certainly a sign from Mother who always had to have yellow dusters near at hand. Full marks to Auntie Lil for her message!

On another occasion back home, when Winnie, Peter and I were attending another church, Father decided that this time *he* would have something to say. Margaret Pearson is a very well-known and highly respected medium whom I knew quite well, but she would have had no idea that I had a sister who was sitting on the other side of the church. First she gave me a message that was very evidential during which Father took over and then he drew the medium across to Winnie. Margaret asked why this man would also have something to say to her. When Winnie explained our relationship Margaret asked if we had been arguing about something to do with a cross on our father's grave, as he didn't seem to care what was being or not being done about it and so we should please ourselves. Father had been buried but I knew he did not want a stone erected, but Winnie felt something should be done. She had got hold of a wooden cross, which I thought inappropriate as Father was not religious. In the end, it seemed, he didn't really care less either way. The spirit world had clearly given him a new perspective on things. I could hear him laughing and saying he appreciated the thought but it really did not matter!

On another occasion Margaret Pearson was instrumental in giving another interesting and evidential message, this time from my brother Bill. She began by saying that she knew me but my brother was calling and saying his name is Wilfrid. It is Wilfrid, she insisted, spelt with an *i* not Wilfred with an *e*. He was actually christened Wilfrid but I had mistakenly had Wilfred put on his gravestone. An easy mistake, as he had always been known as Bill, and in any case I am sure he would not have minded because he was not especially fond of being called Wilfrid. Margaret went on to say that Bill had watched me that morning when I was planting something in a round bowl and was then holding out a coin to me which was an old shilling which he knew about. I had that morning been planting some flowers in a rather unusual sort of bowl and had got into a bit of a mess with it. The coin is a somewhat strange story in a way as a few days before I had been in a department store and visited the cloakroom for a tidy-up. While washing my hands I suddenly spotted a shilling coin in a somewhat unusual place. I thought someone must have left it there but could not see why anyone would or could do such a thing. After some deliberation I decided to take the coin home with me and perhaps I would get to know more about it sometime, although I did not for one moment think it might have some psychic connection. I can only conclude that Bill must have been behind it all and it was a sign that he had not forgotten me.

Another humorous communication occurred when I gave readings to a group of people that included a woman named May Gostling. She was a sweet soul with a great sense of humour and a caring nature for others in need. She was a Red Cross nurse and did what she could to help but always wished she could do more. The important thing was her sense of humour, which was shown when she received a message from her grandmother who was laughing loudly and showing me a huge chamber pot which was decorated with flowers. She eventually said to May: 'It's not what they' – meaning the rest of those present – 'all think it was used for as I used to grow flowers in it.' Not being content with that, her grandmother started to wave a huge pair of bloomers around (of the kind that ladies wore at the time) and reminded May of a time when she burned a hole in them while ironing. All this amongst other things caused everyone to laugh heartily, but May apologised to me because she thought it was rather rude and thought people in the other world would not do a thing like this. I reassured her and all the others that this was not rude but perfectly normal; it was something that happened and was as good evidence as anything else. From my angle it is a good thing to know those who have passed on do remember most things and it helps if we can laugh about them. I have been told by other mediums that the guides would not allow such things as I have quoted but I always give what I get. Such humorous communications only strengthen my belief that, if there is another world, it is as natural and everyday as this one.

13

Ivor Novello . . . and Me!

I have always enjoyed meeting people from every walk of life and especially those who have connections with the things I love. I was very privileged to meet Margaret Rutherford, whose films I have always enjoyed so very much. It was at a meeting of Spiritualists when I asked the organiser if he would introduce me to her. She was at the time talking to a group of people but as soon as the organiser went over to her she immediately excused herself from them and came over to me and my friend Jim. She said she was pleased to meet us and wanted to ask questions about us but we managed to ask her about herself and found her to be a wonderfully interesting person. I was bowled over by her peaches-and-cream complexion, which was that of a young lady. She still carried that eccentric air which one always saw in her films, but she was a highly intelligent lady and eventually steered the conversation back to Jim and me because she was very interested in the psychic and wanted to know what we were doing. She asked if we were interested in ghosts, which we most certainly were, and she told us about various ones that appeared in theatres. In fact, she claimed to have seen one herself. After half an hour she was persuaded to meet other people but we felt sure she would rather have stayed with us for longer still. I told her she was a pin-up girl for many people like me, which rather shocked her until I explained that just to look at her picture made people laugh. I personally, but also on behalf of countless others, thanked her for the endless hours of pleasure she had given us.

It was an experience I will never forget but I did see her once again when she was the guest speaker at a Spiritualist dinner and dance. As we sat waiting for her to arrive, there suddenly a huge commotion and in flew, for that is the only word one could use, the dear lady dressed in a long black cloak which billowed out behind her, exactly like the character of Madame Arcati in one of her films, She was followed by her husband, Lewis Stringer, carrying an armful of cushions and trying to keep up with her. It was a sight to behold, but it was even better to hear her speech as it was surprising just how much she knew about Spiritualism. Of the many people I have met I think she was the most memorable.

One of the most important encounters in my life was pivotal in showing me I had something else within me, other than the psychic, that would prove interesting and worthwhile but would never take me where I wanted to be, although it would afford me great satisfaction. Just to know I had it gave me infinite pleasure but it also meant I would find a wonderful friend who would help me and that together we would achieve something good. They say exchange is no robbery and indeed that proved to be true when I met Betty Lawrence, who was the catalyst which really opened up something in my life that proved to be of mutual benefit. Not in a personal romantic way but more do with the romance of music. While still working at the town hall, I was doing some checking in an outer office and was singing away to myself, as was my wont. I was surprised when a lady from the adjoining office came in and said I had a lovely voice. I did not think anyone could hear me but it did not matter anyway as she asked me if I would like to join her choir and also sing some solos at some of the concerts they staged. I was embarrassed and said I could not really sing and my voice had never been trained. She thought that this did not matter but I had to decline as I thought it was not for me. For a while I thought that perhaps I should go for training, but then I decided not to bother. Somehow, however, I could not stop thinking about the idea, though I decided to leave the matter in greater hands, so to speak, and to let something happen if and when it might. The solution came eventually in a very strange way. I say strange because in a sense everything to do with the psychic seems to have a way of happening under unusual circumstances.

One day, at a social gathering, I met a young lady named Pat Ashton who was a beautiful and vivacious actress and singer, and we were drawn together in a friendly way. I was invited to her home and became aware of the fact she was very interested in the psychic; in fact she often got strong feelings and could have become a good medium herself. One day my friend Peter asked me if I would like to go to a musical show called *The Match Girls* at

Shaftesbury Avenue's Globe (now Gielgud) Theatre in which Pat was starring. He and Betty Lawrence, whom he met at a psychic event, had become good friends and she had suggested going to the show, as she knew and often coached Pat. Peter had told Betty about me and she wanted to meet me, so the show was a chance for everyone to get together. Peter was surprised I already knew Pat. It felt from the outset it was something very much meant to be and after an enjoyable show we all went for a drink to celebrate in a pub near the theatre, where we also met some other members of the cast. Betty singled me out and said she was happy to meet me and heard I was a very good medium – perhaps I would give her a reading. Remembering that Peter had told me she was musical director at the Players Theatre in London, which specialised in Victorian music hall, I realised that here was a chance that should not be missed. I said I knew about what she did and wondered if she could give me an audition and tell me if I really had a voice worth training. She said she was not a teacher but did coach a lot of people and, as long as I understood that, she would be happy to exchange a sitting with me for a session with her.

Betty was a little lady with bubbly blonde hair and tended at first meeting to be somewhat formidable, but after her sitting (which she said she was delighted with) she told me things about herself. She was not modest and rightfully so, as not only was she a fantastic accompanist and an authority on Victorian music hall, but a composer who wrote some of the most beautiful tunes I have ever heard. She had been a child prodigy and there was very little she did not know about music. I was indeed lucky to have met up with her and our friendship lasted for many years during which we had many psychic experiences as well as cooperating on musical projects. I recalled that, some time before we met, a medium had told me I would be visiting someone in Ladbroke Grove to which I replied I most certainly would not as I hated that area. He insisted that it would be so and he saw me going there very many times. Needless to say, Betty lived in that area and I spent so much time there that eventually I began to like Ladbroke Grove. She lived in what we all laughingly called the Bassett Basement, which was the basement flat of a large house in Bassett Road. The front room was her music room and housed her grand piano, on which she produced the most beautiful music with her uniquely magical touch.

The big day came when I had to face the music and when I

would learn her opinion of my voice. She had asked me to lunch first, which was one of her famous fry-ups, she having claimed that she was no cook but could just about manage this. People like Les Dawson the comedian has tasted them and when I once met him he told me Betty was like a mum to him and was always helping people out, especially when they were on their uppers. After lunch she said we should get 'this' over with, meaning my audition – at least that is what it felt like. She led me into the music room, sat down at the piano and asked me to let her see my music. When I told her I did not have any as I couldn't read music she asked how did I suppose we were going to manage. I took a deep breath and told her she surely must know a few songs she could play without music and she said to tell her one I would like to sing. I suggested 'If I Loved You' from *Carousel* and she thought she could remember that and so we started. I was very nervous and wishing I hadn't come but by the time my first song was finished I felt completely at ease. She made no comment and asked what else I would like to sing. I went on to sing a couple more slow ballads. She then asked me to sing a hymn, something which I felt might be more in my line, and all went well, though there was still no comment. Finally she asked if I could sing anything 'in character', by which she meant music hall numbers. This I could do and when we started belting out some raucous songs I even surprised myself at what came out. It was a very different voice and with a strong cockney accent. Betty was shocked. 'Where on earth did that come from?' I explained about Father taking us to the music halls. She then said, 'Well, darling, I couldn't teach you anything about that! It was quite unexpected and astounding. As far as those ballads are concerned you have a very powerful voice but I think it needs harnessing.' I felt so relieved and immediately asked her if she would take me on as a pupil, to which she agreed if I would be her psychic advisor. In the end I think she had more sittings and help than I had lessons, but everything worked so well and led on to other extraordinary things that I really didn't mind.

As time went on, Betty and I formed a very good partnership which became more interesting and creative each and every time we met. By then Peter and Jim were frequent visitors to the Bassett Basement, with Peter often helping to record some of Betty's music and even some of my songs. We had lots of fun and adventures even to the point of us three men forming a company called Desperance Productions, as I have mentioned before. The idea was to put on a two-woman show to showcase Betty's talents, the other participant being Nancy Nevinson, a very well-known actress and close friend of Betty's. The show gave me an opportunity to test my skill as a director, something which I had always wanted to do. Nancy was a wonderful actress and along with Betty in the show called *Truths and Trifles* they made a formidable team. It was hard work directing as artistes are often temperamental but I succeeded and learned a great deal about the theatre in the process, although I have not had the opportunity to do anything similar again. It was rewarding to know the show was a success and gave the public a chance to hear this wonderful little lady. I am sure our meeting was meant to be and part of the greater plan, as, on looking back, it seems there was a certain inevitability about it all. It was a friendship that also led to another experience which would give me not only great satisfaction but also another means of expressing myself.

One evening after I had sung with Betty I gave her a trance sitting with my guide called Running Water. She had become very fond of this guide who always seemed able to give her the help and guidance she needed. On this occasion he had told her that she should write some songs for which he gave her four titles. When she discussed this with me later I felt it was a good idea and that she should do it. However, Betty explained that, although she had no problem with the music, she was not really any good at writing lyrics. The first title was 'Born Again' and I made various suggestions about what she might write. Suddenly she asked me to excuse her a moment, left the room and returned soon after carrying a large notebook and pen, which she laid on my lap: 'There you are, darling! *You* write them.' When I said I couldn't, she refused to take no for an answer and left me no alternative but to try. I was absolutely amazed to find myself writing the lyrics to this first title in exactly four minutes flat. I handed the notebook to Betty who was already sitting at the piano. She looked at it and told me not to speak. I looked at my watch as I realised something remarkable was going to happen, and exactly three and a half minutes later she had set the lyrics to the most beautiful melody. She loved the words and then told me I was definitely the lyric writer she needed and gave me the other three titles. As it was late I took them home and by the time I saw her the next day I had written three more lyrics, which she put to music almost immediately. So began a fine partnership in which we wrote many songs together. For me it brought out my gift of composition, and for Betty it gave her some inspiration around which she could wrap her wonderful music. I had always been able to write funny little poems and compose letters for people, plus verses for weddings and birthdays, but it had never occurred to me that I could become a lyricist. At this point my cup was full and about to overflow because, with my deep love of music and the many different guises in which I was now able to express it, I had found an outlet for pent-up emotions that needed to be released.

It was some time later that I talked to Betty about various musical shows and told her I thought we ought to write one together. She was surprised and yet interested when I said I would have a go at writing the story or 'the book', as it is called, about reincarnation, a subject in which she completely believed. I called it 'Born Again', which was the first song title she had been given. We had already written other songs which could be used and so we were both taken over by our terrific enthusiasm, as this could prove to be a worthwhile venture. I realised this had been planned some time before and was meant to be. It also suggested to me that 'the greater power' was behind it and so I took the bull by the horns and accepted the challenge, which I instinctively knew I would enjoy. Although I really had little or no idea to begin with as to how to write a stage script, I found myself being subtly guided and everything began to fall into place. In fact, it was quite easy and progressed far more quickly than I would have expected – it seemed as though I was somehow in tune with someone who knew what it was all about. It turned out to be Ivor Novello, who when in this world had written some of the most beautiful music and songs that have ever been put into musical shows, making him world famous. Betty adored him and his music, and I had seen him in one of his shows just before he died. I was not impressed by him personally, although the music was beautiful and was something I would never forget. I did not realise at the time that Ivor was ill and I have often mentally asked his forgiveness ever since, which presumably he granted because there was no doubt he was guiding both Betty and me. He gave evidence of this in a very unusual and striking manner.

One day I was sitting in my garden trying to write a certain lyric which would not come. After what I thought to be several futile attempts I suddenly realised I had an engagement to fulfil and was running late. I jumped up with the lyric sheet in my hand and said out loud, 'Well, Ivor, if that's the best you can do then I don't think much of it!' I then hastened to get ready and managed to arrive for my dinner engagement on time. It was with another medium called Mabel Batkin and her daughter Grace, who strangely enough was a singer and always sang Ivor's songs. As soon as I took off my coat Mabel said to me, 'I must tell you that Ivor Novello has been waiting around for you to arrive and wants me to tell you he wrote a song called 'Keep the Home Fires Burning', which he thought was rubbish but which sold a million copies. He thought you would understand this.' I most certainly did and when I got home and looked at the lyric again suddenly it seemed to be perfectly all right.

On another occasion, during a sitting, Mabel saw Ivor holding a spray of white lilac over my head and then he showed her a picture of guardsmen wearing red tunics and busbies. He told her that he felt someone needed encouragement and inspiration. At that point it did not mean anything to me but by the time I returned home I felt I had to phone Betty and tell her. She was absolutely amazed as that afternoon she had been at a society wedding in Mayfair where the floral decorations were quite wonderful and contained a lot of white lilac. Betty could not believe the lilac was real and pulled a piece down to smell it. It was not plastic but fresh and with a lovely perfume which made her think of Ivor as she always associated him with white lilac, a fact I had not known before that moment. She then went on to say that someone had given her two tickets for the evening Ice Show at Wembley and when she and her friend settled in their seats the very first thing they saw was a lot of guardsmen wearing red tunics and busbies skating out onto the ice. This gave her great encouragement as only that day she had been writing the music to one of my lyrics and felt it was not quite right. So it seemed to both of us that we were being inspired and helped by this great man.

We had many other connections with Ivor and his music, one being a client of both mine and Betty's. This was a lady called Margaret Burton who had a most glorious voice and had starred in both opera at the Coliseum and musical shows in various West

End theatres; she loved to sing the music of Ivor Novello. She often rehearsed with Betty and, being interested in the psychic, had some of my recorded readings. I knew her through another client whose son she had been very close to at one time but we finally met at Betty's home where the delightful Maggie, as we called her, came one evening for a rehearsal. We asked her if she would sing a song that we had written. Betty and I had argued over the lyrics and thought we would ask the professional's opinion. Maggie loved it and thought my lyrics were perfect. The song I mostly associate with Maggie and Betty is 'I Can Give You the Starlight', possibly the most beautiful song Ivor wrote.

This determined man made another contact when I was giving a sitting to Sally Miles, the daughter of Sir Bernard Miles, and he gave her evidence which meant so much to her because she said he was helping her with her career as an actress and singer. Apparently Sally had met Ivor at parties held at her home, as well as at other celebrities', and he often gave her advice then. She became well known for her one-woman shows and in one of them she sang a number which Betty and I had written. She never denied her belief in personal survival; indeed she had every reason to be grateful that Ivor and others were watching over her. When she was told that she and her family would shortly be going to live in the country, she emphatically denied this was possible as she and her husband were negotiating for a terraced house in London. I had told Sally in the message that I saw her in the middle of a lot of green and a long way out of the city. And, indeed, the London plans fell through and she moved to a home in the heart of Suffolk which was surrounded by acres of cornfields and meadows. On another occasion she was warned to be careful as I could see a mass of smashed milk bottles. This puzzled her. Shortly after she was due to appear in her one-woman show in Worcester, with Betty Lawrence as her accompanist. Walking along the street together one morning, Sally had good cause to remember the warning when a milk lorry suddenly stalled at some traffic lights as they went past. Dozens of crates of milk bottles crashed down to the ground raining broken glass over a large area and luckily just missing the ladies. So, although the message gave no details as to what to expect, it nonetheless showed them both, but especially Sally, that they were being watched over.

Apart from Sally and Maggie, from time to time other people

turned up who also had strong connections with Ivor, leaving no doubt in my mind that he was of great help and an inspiration to both Betty and me. Needless to say, Betty made me sing many of Ivor's songs during my lessons and I loved them. Through all this I was gaining valuable experience because it seemed as though everything I had to do would be somehow connected with the psychic and helpful to people in the other world like Ivor. To me it seemed so wonderful that people like him would still try to carry on the great work they had done when in this world.

There was one other person connected with Ivor and me and that was Isabel Morrow who has the most wonderful voice and who often sang one of Ivor's songs, 'Fly Home, Little Heart', which is another great favourite of mine. I met Isabel through Betty when I happened to call in to see her. She was in the middle of a coaching session with Isabel, who was singing that song. She and I were immediately drawn to each other. It was as though we had known each other all of our lives and we developed a sort of brother-and-sister relationship. If one can accept the possibility of reincarnation, then it could seem that Isobel and I had met in a previous life. I had given the charcoal drawing of me which was done in America to Betty because she loved it and she had put it on the wall of her music room. When Isobel walked in and saw it she was taken aback and quite overcome, and she had to sit down for a while. She could only say that it was like looking at the face of her mother, which was confirmed later by others who saw it. Isobel was convinced that we had known each other before in another life and some time later I was told by a medium that she and I were brother and sister in an incarnation as Incas. Once again this connection had been made through Ivor, even if only in a round-about way, and I often wonder just how many people in this world he does help.

14

The Art of Teaching

If sometimes I felt I would like to get away from my life as a psychic, deep down inside I realised I had no choice. There were so many people who needed the help which I could give to them, and I found it very difficult to say no, even at the cost of my own private life. At one time I found myself booked solidly with work for nine or ten months ahead with no spare time at all. While it is good to be recognised and be in demand, I realised that my health could be at risk without some breaks, so I tried to get away for holidays and to resume my theatre going. But enjoyable as it all was, I invariably found there would more often than not be a psychic connection. I accepted this as I realised it would often teach me a valuable lesson in some way.

I have had so many young people come to consult me over the years and have always managed to reach out to them and their needs, and direct them towards the best pathway for them. In order to understand them I have listened to the most awful music, been to see films which I hated but knew were a part of the modern scene, and in general have studied all aspects of life which might enable me to sympathise with or encourage them. I have applied this technique to adults as well and so many people have come back to me time and time again and said, 'You understand and know me better than I know myself.' This has given me a feeling of satisfaction and has left me with an even deeper and warmer feeling in knowing I have been successful in my endeavours. I can truly say I care about people but the danger with this is that one can care too much and take on board what should really remain the responsibilities of others. One has to be very disciplined and learn to shut down. It is one of the hardest things to do, but if one doesn't it can become very draining and one's health suffers. A lot of mediums will say that the guides and people in the spirit world will replace your spent energy, but I have discovered this to be untrue. I have found the spirit world will use us as long as we are willing, and that it is up to us to know our own limitations.

It is only on looking back I realise that I have had a very eventful life and done far more than I thought, although at the time it was happening it seemed rather mundane. It has not been easy but I have always realised there are others worse off than oneself, and as long as I am able to help myself and carry on, then I have a lot to be thankful for. Such thoughts have kept me going and, thinking back to the Second World War when I was just a boy living in London under dreadful conditions with bombs and all sorts of things being hurled at us night after night, I remember the wonderful British sense of humour and how we laughed and sang rude songs about Hitler and the enemy in defiant refusal to be beaten. I had no idea about life after death at that time and one did not think about dying but more of survival, so crying would not have helped. I often wonder whether it would have made any difference had I been aware of my psychic gift in childhood. Although many mediums have told me I am a natural psychic and was born with the gift, it seems I had to wait twenty-five years before I was made aware of it. Which rather confirms the idea that nothing will ever happen until, or unless, it is the right time for it to manifest. It happened with me after having gone through various life-changing experiences and coming to my own conclusions about orthodox religion.

Many people have asked me if we live more than one life on this earth, in other words is there such a thing as reincarnation. It may appear I have already declared a belief in this by writing a musical play about the subject, but what I have written might be accepted either as factual or as an escapist fairy tale in the best tradition of musical theatre. Despite Betty's unshakable belief in the subject, I still, even after experiences such as I had in Greece for instance, remain unconvinced as so far it seems no one has been able to come up with absolute proof. There are many explanations as to the experiences I and others have had but I never claim to know all the answers to anything, so I continue with an open mind and a readiness to listen to others in the hope of eventually uncovering the truth and adapting my beliefs to any new evidence. Betty told me she was born with the conviction we come back to this world many times, and nothing would ever change her mind. She had many earthly experiences to tell which were very interesting but could be explained in other ways. She often recognised members her family and friends as people she knew in her past lives but, although I could often see her reasons for this, it somehow did not really convince me. To be honest, I have never had any deep and certain feelings on this controversial subject. Most people have at some time or other felt that they had met someone before yet they were strangers at that time. I once had the experience of being in a cathedral with some friends and, as we walked down an aisle one way, we passed a young man and his parents going the other way. As we passed my eyes suddenly met those of the young man and I experienced a sensation which was indescribable and I knew he experienced something similar. It was like something I had never felt before or since, but as soon as we passed it disappeared. It so touched me that I wrote a poem about it and to this day it still has an effect when I read it. I cannot be sure it meant we had met before, but here I feel it is important to remember we are often drawn to people because perhaps they are on the same wavelength as we are.

Betty had a very interesting story to tell about reincarnation. Her father came from Germany and had emigrated to England before she was born. She kept in touch with a cousin there and was invited to stay with her on one occasion. Betty had been told by my guide that she had lived a previous life in Spain about four hundred years ago where she was known as Donna El Piroth. I probably would not have told Betty about this in my normal state as I would have felt I was making it up. She apparently argued with the guide that Piroth was not a Spanish name and he probably meant Perez. He would not budge on this and said it was the name he had first given. After much thought and experience, I do not now accept a trance state as being taken over by someone else but think it is more a self-induced trance which releases what I call a secondary character. Nonetheless, it is interesting that this happens, especially when it reveals things I would not agree with. It is something that has underlined my firm belief that a part of me, at least, is unbiased and therefore does not stop anyone from receiving whatever is communicated to them without my mind colouring it.

One evening when Betty was about to retire, her cousin asked if she would like to read what her deceased husband had discovered about the family history. He had traced it back quite a long way and found some interesting facts which he had written down together with the family tree. So Betty took it to read in bed and was astounded to find a member of her family had married a lady by the name of El Piroth four hundred years. By the name was the word 'Spain' in brackets denoting a Spanish lady had married into a German family. It does not necessarily mean Betty was a reincarnation of that lady as it could have been a psychometric link, or there could be other explanations. She was very cross with me because I chose to keep an open mind on it, and more cross when she at a later date went to Spain and stayed in Torremolinos, from where she tried to trace a village she had been told had connections with her past. After a great hunt for this she almost gave up until one day she was in a shop looking at some old maps of the area when she suddenly saw one with a bay of the same name as the village. No one could tell her whether there had been a village of that name but presumably there must have been because a bay would usually have a town or village of the same name. The name dated back a long way and there would have been a lot of changes, so nothing was certain, but on the other hand there must have been some connection. It still does not prove reincarnation, but then neither does it disprove it. After meeting so many people who claim to have been Cleopatra, Jesus, Nefertiti, Moses and a variety of other famous people, it tends to make one laugh at the idea. It should be obvious that one spirit cannot inherit several different bodies at the same time so when one meets say several Cleopatras in the same day, there has to be something wrong. I have been told I am a reincarnation of Jesus, the man who worked the guillotine in the French Revolution, a monk, one of the Apostles and various other things, which I choose not to remember as my contention is that it is enough to live this present life without worrying about the past. Many believe in karma, which means we are working out what we have done wrong in previous lives and addressing the balance in this one. Unfortunately it is often used as a convenient excuse for our shortcomings. Or could I perhaps have been really wicked?!

The human mind is a very powerful thing and needs to be controlled. Not an easy thing to do always but necessary if one is to find peace and happiness not only within oneself but also when dealing with other people regardless of race, colour or creed. I have an extremely vivid imagination and am also very disciplined in every way which has helped me to channel my ideas in a creative way. No doubt my army training helped with this but I have long since realised the only way to get through anything is to be determined to do it and to keep it in the right perspective. Also, if anything we hope to achieve cannot be fulfilled, it could be that it is not meant for us and we should cut our losses and find some other way in which we can express ourselves. When I left the army it was my hope to go to university and become a teacher, but I was not lucky enough to secure a place there. At the time all vacancies were allotted by ballot and my name did not come out of the hat. I was told to apply again the next year but that way I feared it could take for ever. I don't think it was meant in the greater plan, although I did end up teaching in a different way. I enjoyed giving lectures and talks within my work especially the ten years of running a weekly class at The Haven, where I helped many to develop their psychic gifts including healing. Many have been kind enough to tell me I am one of the best teachers in my field. In my opinion, a teacher's task is to teach their pupils all they know and have learned, and then encourage their pupils to assimilate it and go on and do better. There is much jealousy in the psychic field and some mediums dislike the idea of their pupils being better than themselves, which, if you think about it, really does take the 'spiritual' out of Spiritualism. By contrast, I find it encouraging to hear what I have taught has been assimilated and improved upon as I think it reflects well on my teaching and indeed my own practice. This is just natural progression.

I have done a lot of teaching in private as well as in public, which I found to be a most enjoyable experience. My first big experience was when Rudi and Inge Schneider, a couple I met in London, invited me to take a seminar in Munich where they lived. At first I thought it would be too difficult as I did not speak much German, but as Rudi and I seemed to have quite a good rapport, he said he would act as my interpreter, which proved to be successful as he instinctively knew and interpreted my words almost before I actually said things. The seminar took place over a long weekend: on the Friday evening I gave a demonstration of clairvoyance to a packed hall, and then on Saturday and Sunday I held a class for 150 people. At that time this was extremely rare, as normally classes would probably be for no more than twenty people. I had some reservations at first but, once I got into my stride and with

Rudi's invaluable help, it was a great success. By the end of it every one went away from there with something. They all had discovered more about themselves and what they could do, and some were even able to get psychic messages for other people. I was moved by the generous applause I received at the end of the seminar, which made it all worthwhile. I was delighted to be asked back again and managed to go two more times, something I will always remember for the welcome I received and for the sheer enjoyment I got out of it.

I found a great rapport with German people, but later found it was the same with many other nationalities. My reception in Sweden was quite touching, and in Australia and New Zealand I was welcomed in their own traditional ways. Of course in America it seems everyone loves an Englishman and loves to hear him speak, which was a great attraction to say the least. Everywhere I went I gave personal readings and interviews and can say without wishing to boast that everything I did was a complete success. If I mention here that out of the thousands of tape-recorded readings I have done, I have never had one failure, as most were 80 or 90 per cent right on first hearing and then eventually hit full marks as time proved predictions true. Naturally there were some lesser percentages at first but I cannot remember one that did not work out to the recipient's satisfaction in time.

During the course of my psychic career I have done a huge amount of personal interviews, or sittings, as they are generally called. In one way it is helpful to do a face-to-face reading as one can get immediate answers. There is sometimes a snag dealing with people face to face as their reactions to things can be very strange and off-putting. I can truthfully say however that I have had very few like that and even those I have had I always managed to send away happy and satisfied, even to the extent of their coming again. Mostly, private interviews are just that, private, and so it is therefore not possible for me to say much about them here. However, I would like to include one very amusing story which I will always remember with a smile. Not so much about the sitting but the way it came about.

I did most of my private work from my home in Clapham Common and was kept very busy. One evening I received a telephone call from a man who sounded extremely brusque and who more or less ordered me to give a sitting to a certain lady, for whom he worked as secretary. When I told him I was solidly booked up for some considerable time he became most angry and said it was for the sister of a South American president and I had to do it. Not being one to give in easily, I argued with him until he told me it had to be within three or four days as she was returning home but wished especially to see me. At this point I gave in and told him it would have to be on the Saturday morning which was the only time I could rearrange things to fit it in. He was so rude that when I put the phone down I felt sorry I had agreed. Came the appointed time and my front door bell rang at exactly the time agreed. When I went down to open it there was the man who said he would be coming in with her. I told him I would not allow it as he was so hostile it would not help. Whereupon he said that the lady did not speak English and he was also her interpreter, so he had to come in, but he also agreed he would not be any trouble. Having ascertained that I was ready to receive the lady, he told me to wait there and he would fetch her. I watched him go over to a huge black limousine which carried some diplomatic flag or other, and immediately two armed guards got out and opened the door for the lady, whom they saluted and then proceeded to flank her and march over to me, led by the secretary. At the door the guards marched away while the secretary introduced me to the lady, whom I sensed immediately was a very sweet and charming lady. She did not mind there was no lift but happily climbed the two flights of stairs to my flat. As she came into my lounge she immediately saw a table on which were displayed several pots of South African violet plants I had grown myself and went over to them to admire them. She was so enchanted that she told the interpreter to tell me that I must be a kind and charming man as only someone like that could have produced such beautiful plants.

To say I fell for her at that moment would be an understatement, so that giving her the benefit of my psychic ability proved a great pleasure. Afterwards she told me through her interpreter she was absolutely bowled over by the sitting. She had asked a lot of questions and kindly said that nobody had been able to answer them before and she would never forget this meeting, which filled me with pleasure. I was sad that it all had to be done through an interpreter but happy it had gone so well. Afterwards the secretary shook my hand and said that he had interpreted such things for Madam, as he called her, many times but had never heard anything as good as this before. He apologised for his earlier rudeness and explained that Madam, who had heard about me somewhere or other, had set her heart on seeing me and, knowing how important it was for her, he had overreacted somewhat. I almost wished Madam did not have to go as she was so sweet and a joy to work for, but I finally took them down to the front door where the secretary signalled to the waiting guards, who marched over to take Madam back to the car under escort, followed by the secretary. It was all quite a performance and probably something not seen in the Crescent before. I hoped that some of the neighbours might have been watching but if they were I never heard any comments. Unfortunately most of the residents of the big houses tend to look on people like me as 'one of those flat dwellers' and rarely speak to any of us, but it does not really bother me. I regard Madam's visit as something unusual but satisfying and it goes down in my memory as something I won't forget because it was a lovely experience.

Wherever I go and whatever I am doing, I always try to incorporate some philosophy into my work, but I do it in what I call a more up-to-date way. I found that the Germans in particular appreciated this. For example, when giving one particular lecture I said that one of my very favourite popular songs was 'Why Don't You Stop and Smell the Roses' sung by Cleo Laine. I then explained that the lyrics are good advice for us all. We spend a lot of time buying and planting things for our garden, and in tending them, but do we really appreciate them? We should in effect stop and smell the roses and enjoy the full beauty of what we are doing. We need to get away from life's hustle and bustle for a time and appreciate the real meaning of what we are attempting to do and how that can help us. Another thing I teach does not come from music but just good common sense. We should always stop every so often to ask ourselves a most important question especially when we have decisions to make: is what I am doing or thinking going to hurt, first, anyone else or, secondly, myself? If the answer to this is yes then we should not be doing or thinking it. I find a lot of people appreciate being advised simply to stop and think.

15

Ghost Hunting

As a child I was like most, rather inclined to be afraid of ghosts and there were lots of stories, often blood-curdling ones, that made me afraid of the dark. Where we lived at the time there were two long passages in the flat and between them was the toilet. The rooms were lit by gaslight but there was none in the passageways, so in order to go to the toilet it was necessary to carry a candle. I would not go on my own as I was too scared, so my sister always had to accompany me carrying the light and then wait nearby until I was ready and then see me down again. I remember Mother telling us children that if we were not in bed by eight o'clock then Wee Willie Winkie would be cross and come for us. Wee Willie Winkie appears in a Scottish nursery rhyme about a character who '...runs through the town, Up stairs and down stairs in his night-gown, Tapping at the window, crying at the locks, Are all the children in their bed for it's past eight o'clock.' Wee Willie wasn't a ghost, of course, but the rhyme made me still more terrified of the dark.

As I grew older I lost all those fears and ghosts became just a subject for amusement. It was the same with horror films, which made me laugh more than tremble. So by the time I was introduced to the subject of ghosts after becoming a medium, I was quite prepared to deal with anything that came my way, although I never envisaged becoming a ghost hunter. One evening I received a telephone call from the Secretary of the College of Psychic Studies asking me if I was prepared to go on a ghost hunt. When I told her I had never done anything like that before and was not really qualified, she insisted, so, as usual with me in such instances, I ended up agreeing, though, I admit, with some trepidation.

A man named Hans Holzer, who was apparently a famous ghost hunter and author, was coming over from America the following day and I was instructed to ring him at his hotel at 7 p.m. and introduce myself. He would not know who he was getting until I called. He would give me instructions as to what it was all about. This turned out not to be exactly true as, when I phoned him, all he told me was that I was to meet him at the hotel a short time later and that I would be out very late.

At the time of my phone call I was in the middle of a game of canasta with Jim and his parents. Shortly after I had put the phone down I said to them out of the blue: 'I know what this is all about tonight – it has something to do with Nell Gwynn.' I told them I could even smell oranges but that seemed so ridiculous that we all started laughing and I said it was probably just my imagination. When I arrived at the hotel I found Holzer with two other men who he explained were cameramen as they were filming something about ghosts of England for American television. He would not tell me where we were going but there was a taxi waiting outside for us and it would be explained as we went along. During the ride the cameramen kept taking photos of me with infrared light, which became somewhat annoying. It was a relief when they stopped and I was blindfolded, as I was not meant to see where we were – being a Londoner I would probably recognise where I was and know too much in advance.

Once the taxi stopped I was helped out and led into a building where the blindfold was removed. Had I been allowed to see the outside I would have known I was in the Nell Gwynn Rooms, which was at the time a striptease club. I was introduced to the owner who seemed to be a very pleasant man and who was also interested in the psychic. He took us all upstairs where he said he would like us all to come out onto the roof, which meant going up some sort of back staircase with an iron handrail. Holzer and the three men went up the stairs and out onto the roof quite easily, but as I climbed I could hardly make it as my legs were leaden and I had to pull myself up by the handrail. Once out into the air I felt fine but no one had noticed what happened to me. Holzer had a tape recorder so he recorded my experience and then taped what I told him about Nell Gwynn and the oranges. He was quite excited and asked for Jim's telephone number so he could get confirmation about what I had said.

By this time I knew where we were and I was told that we were indeed looking for the ghost of Nell Gwynn, the actress and mistress of Charles II. We were asked if we would like to have tea while we were waiting for the girls to finish their routine in the theatre, as we needed to be in there for a seance. As soon as we were settled and before I got any tea, the owner asked me if I would go and sit at a certain corner table and see if I sensed anything. The whole place was very old with raftered ceilings and an air of bygone days and once seated I could see a lady standing in front of us. The owner could not see her and asked me to describe her. She was very beautiful with red hair that fell in ringlets round her shoulders. She was wearing a high-waisted long dress which allowed her ample bosom to make an appearance and a large black picture hat. The owner said it was Nell and began to ask me to ask her questions at which point I went into a sort of trance and could hear myself saying things though not very clearly. The owner was very satisfied as he had asked her where the armoury would have been in the building and she said it was directly below where we were sitting, and then she even gave the name of the man in charge of the armoury. Also when asked where the river ran, she said it was directly beneath the house running from east to west, which was true. It was embarrassing to find all the staff watching me when I came back to myself, but equally exciting to know we must have been in contact with Nell as all her answers were correct. I could not have known anything about the house, especially as it was in former times.

I was now allowed to have my cup of tea, though soon after the music stopped and we all went into the now deserted theatre to hold the seance. Holzer asked if one of the showgirls could sit in but I said no because she had no experience and it might frighten her. He asked as apparently several of the showgirls had seen the ghost and more or less accepted her as a fixture of the place. One even had had her life saved by Nell when there was a fire. The girl was trapped at the end of a corridor and couldn't get out until she suddenly saw Nell beckoning her to follow and she led her to safety. So it seems that so-called ghosts do some useful things and in this case was not frightening anybody. Some of the diners had seen her but the owner had asked for Holzer to come along as he felt Nell's appearance might frighten them and be bad for trade (though I could not help thinking it would be an enormous attraction). For me it was going to be something to be able to boast, *if* I was successful, that I had laid the ghost of Nell Gwynn to rest.

175

The seance was not helped too much in my opinion by the two cameramen who had no interest in the subject but were obliged to sit in on it. With Holzer and the owner this made just five of us. However, as soon as we sat down around the table there was a sudden eerie sensation. I soon went into a trance and could remember nothing until afterwards when I heard one cameraman say to the other, 'If that was Nell Gwynn she was a pain in the arse!' I then learned that the owner felt sure it was Nell but no one else was certain, at least not at that point. Apparently whoever it was speaking – and we thought it could possibly have been an actress who was very jealous of Nell and who used to impersonate her – seemed to know the answers to all questions put to her. The communicator certainly knew there used to be a theatre almost next to the building we were in, which she claimed to be a gift from King Charles to her. So when the voice said it was her house and she was going to do what she liked there, it must have really been Nell.

I must recount an experience which took place before the seance began. We all heard noises coming from the back stairway to the roof and there was a sound of clanking swords and footsteps running up and down. Holzer and the others all rushed to the stairs to find out what was happening but when I tried to get out of my seat to follow, I couldn't. It was as though I was tied in securely, so I had to miss the fun. Even now I wonder if I might have seen something. There was no doubt that a sword fight was being re-enacted on those stairs and when Nell was questioned about this later she said that a Captain Molyneaux from a certain regiment had been sent to guard her when she fell out of favour with the King, but they fell in love and were planning to run away together. The King discovered this and being a jealous man sent a member of his personal bodyguard, Lieutenant Fortescue, to kill her lover and they clashed on the back stairs where a sword fight took place and her lover was killed. Nell was turned out of her home and banished to the country. History has it she died a pauper. It was a very eventful evening and I got home quite exhausted but knowing I had now become a successful ghost hunter.

Some time after this Holzer obtained access to ancient military records which were not normally available for inspection and had not been viewed for many years. He found the exact names and regiments that Nell had mentioned, which leaves no doubt that what she described happened on that fateful night was authentic.

There has always been a mystery as to what really happened to cause Nell to fall out of favour with the King and this seems a very fitting explanation. It was a great pleasure to work with the world-famous Hans Holzer who has written many books on ghosts including this story, which is told in one of his best-sellers, *Window to the Past*. For me it was one experience amongst so many which I will never forget and most certainly the best example of my ghost-hunting exploits. At one time I used to think my life was empty and I had not achieved much at all, but being one who is never really satisfied I now feel a bit closer, perhaps, than many to understanding what life may really be about. There are so many aspects of life to comprehend and ways of looking at things, and we always need to sift and search to find what we really believe is in us.

A very interesting happening took place on the Isle of Wight when Jim and I were staying with Doris and her two daughters near to Ryde (about whom I wrote at some length in an earlier chapter). Doris believed in Spiritualism but for the family as a whole the subject of ghosts was a bit of a joke, until, that is, the girls came home one evening carrying a large dusty old book and seemed to be very excited. When asked what they had been up to they confessed that for some time they had been exploring the ruins of Appley House which was quite near by. Their Mother told them they were taking chances and they should not take things which were not theirs. The girls said the book was on a pile of rubbish and nobody would go there anyway as it was almost completely ruined (though there was talk that it was to be demolished in order to make way for holiday homes). The girls had been trying to trace its history at the local library but had not found anything helpful, nor could they find any local people who could remember that far back. The girls also said there was a powerful atmosphere there and that it might be haunted. At that time for some reason I did not feel very interested and it was not until a subsequent visit that their mother and a cousin suggested I ought to go there, as a definite date had now been set for the demolition. So I agreed and the following day we organised a party of interested people and decided to split into two groups, as ten people would maybe make too much noise and I needed to be able to handle things my way. The girls and their friends might be too excitable, so I suggested that their party go round a different way.

As it would have been too difficult to explore in the dark we went during the afternoon, which fortunately was a sunny one. We soon reached Appley House, or Appley Towers as it was once known, and found the old lodge gates still in good order. We could immediately see this had once been a beautiful place, especially with its extensive grounds running down to the sea. The house itself was surrounded by trees and gave out a powerful feeling of 'come near if you will but I do not want to be disturbed'. This seemed to be a challenge to me as I wanted to know why. It was hard to imagine how the house would have looked before it had fallen into ruin, but we all felt sure it would not have been very large nor very grand though there appeared to have been quite a number of rooms. However plain it might have been we all felt it was a great pity this lovely, lonely scene had to be destroyed.

In my party I had Doris, her niece Coral Polge, soon to be known as a world-famous psychic artist, and my friend Jim. Since we were all connected with the psychic field I felt happier because whatever did or did not happen would be taken seriously, and also I would have reliable witnesses. Mavis and Marian preferred to be with their friends and, while they were not entirely convinced about ghosts, it was better they explored on their own. I take my work very seriously, as it requires a lot of concentration as well as quiet. I am not entirely certain of this but in one's mind perhaps it is possible to 'hear' echoes of the past.

So our ghost hunt began and we carefully made our way across a lot of rubble into what was left of the house, though I immediately felt like an intruder. After all, we had not been invited and were, I suppose, actually trespassing, The hostile atmosphere I experienced underlined my feeling of trespassing and there was most certainly no welcome mat. As we entered through what could once have been the front door I heard the most blood-curdling scream which seemed to come from the lower part of the house. Apparently no one else had heard it and I said nothing for fear they would laugh at me and think I was getting carried away. I knew that I was cool and collected and was acutely aware, moreover, of being watched. It felt like eyes were following me everywhere and they belonged to a tall thin lady with sharp angular features. She wore her hair piled on top of her head and appeared to have what one could only describe as a regal bearing, as well as being very domineering. I was the only one to see her but when I told the others, they confessed to also sensing a presence.

The strange thing about ghosts is that experienced psychic people like me can see them but others are not necessarily aware, so the fact they had sensed something was good because I knew I had their full attention and cooperation. I felt the lady must have been mistress of the house and would probably follow us around to keep an eye on us, as no doubt she watched everyone and everything when she was in this world. She certainly was giving us a very chilly reception as the temperature appeared to have dropped quite a few degrees. This is often a sign of psychic activity and suggested that further exploration could prove more fruitful. So onwards we went.

Next I heard a name called which sounded like Edward but which I instinctively knew was not quite that name. We noted it down and decided to find our way down some stairs from whence I had heard the scream. Picking our way over more rubble and an odd assortment of broken furniture, we found ourselves in what at one time must have been the kitchen. It was very dark and could in no way be described as a dream kitchen; it was more of a nightmare place, dank and foreboding. The atmosphere created a horrible feeling and I felt something unsavoury had happened there. Again I heard the terrible scream and realised it came from a man. I could see blood everywhere and it was difficult to breathe. We ascended the stairs from a freezing-cold atmosphere into lighter, warmer air and as we reached the top, with the sun shining through the ruined house, it suddenly felt as though my imagination had been running riot. The rest of the party felt just the same. All was peaceful and quiet.

As we had made our way up a few more stairs, I again had the sensation of being watched. Not just by the lady, but by a man as well. He was not very tall and had a weak-willed sort of face. His straggling moustache just about joined a straggling beard. He looked dirty and unkempt and seemed to emanate evil. I felt very uncomfortable with him there; it reminded me of the kitchens, and I was convinced there had either been a murder or a very violent death in that house.

We had to be careful where we walked as some of the flooring was giving way, making it hard for me to get impressions in case I missed my footing. One thing I could be certain of was that we were still being watched by penetrating eyes, yet the watchers said nothing. It was as if they were hiding guilty secrets and didn't want anyone to find out about them. Perhaps they thought that by creating an extremely unpleasant atmosphere they would get rid of us, but by then I was aware that these ghosts or shadows from the past had created this atmosphere long ago and were now stuck with it. *We* could leave the scene anytime, but could they? If they were 'haunting', why were they doing it? Of course we could not be absolutely sure there were really ghosts around. It could have been some sort of 're-enactment' as buildings and places where important or dramatic events have happened can hold some sort of vibrations which can build into a seemingly real picture. I had little doubt there were ghosts among those ruins and after subsequent experiences there was no room for further doubt.

A little later in our explorations I suddenly sensed something about a duchess and supposed it could have been the lady who had first watched us. My friends laughed and suggested it was all going a bit too far. But then later, when we turned into a corridor, we saw a bell board on the wall, still in perfect condition. Marked on the board was 'Her Grace's Bedroom'. It was no laughing matter now and so we decided to search for the bedroom itself. This proved to be quite easy and I had quite a strong feeling it would have a secret room behind it and told my companions this. When we saw a four-poster bed in one of the rooms, it was reasonable to assume it must be the Duchess's. The bedroom, however, did not appear to have a secret chamber but when challenged by my party to show them where it was, I felt compelled to go to the head of the bed where I found I was able to walk behind it into a smaller room. The walls had been designed to make it look like one room but they ran parallel to each other, thus providing a clever opening. This secret room was quite fascinating and had a fine view. It also overlooked the servants quarters, which I felt to be quite significant. I felt that the Duchess had had a secret liaison with the butler who, it seemed to me, held great sway in the household. Perhaps the two of them were able to check on the staff from the secret room as it would be easy to see the comings and goings of all the servants.

After climbing yet more steps we once again found ourselves in the fresh air and standing on the parapet of a tower from where there was a beautiful view. I could not enjoy the view, however, as I felt an overwhelming desire to throw myself over the edge. Although I normally have a fear of heights, this was different because I had the impression that, if I did do such a thing, I would not be responsible. We returned to the house and started to descend some stairs when suddenly I became paralysed from the waist down. Luckily Jim caught me in time or I would have fallen down the stairs. The others said I had turned a ghastly shade of green and I must admit I felt awful. As soon as this wore off, Jim began to experience a feeling in his left leg, which he could not move, and soon after everyone felt similar things. After it all quietened down and we felt more normal, the ladies suggested we abandon our exploration for fear of worse things happening, but I felt in having come this far we should continue. To me at least it was exciting as the house was beginning impart its secrets and tell us a story, and the others, with some persuasion, agreed. We all felt an acute curiosity and, despite the prevailing atmosphere, we just had to see it through. There was a sense of danger present not only because of the state of the house, but because one felt that whoever was watching might have hostile intentions. All in all, I believed that what we were experiencing should be put down to 're-enactment' rather than ghosts. We would have to wait and see.

As we found our way down various corridors the atmosphere lightened considerably as though we were approaching happier places in the house. We looked in several rooms but none seemed to say much or have any special pull. For some time the song 'Oh No, John!' kept running through my mind, with particular emphasis on the line 'my father was a Spanish Captain'. It was being sung by a girl with a wistful but pleasant little voice. There seemed to be a number of names being called, mostly Christian names. I was more impressed by what sounded like the Duke and Duchess of Beaufort, or it could have been Bedfort. By this time we had come down to the ground floor where everything seemed to have a much grander air. I now felt the house could have had some connection with royalty.

It was not long before we entered a room which must at one time have been very beautiful. There were even some faded full-length mirrors on the walls and one could imagine it had once been completely mirrored, like the Galerie des Glaces at Versailles (though much smaller of course), and I felt it could have been a robing room. One could sense royalty and a feeling of preparation as though people would go from this room to an adjoining one to dance. We did find a very large room close by, but if it had been the ballroom, and I believe it was, there was no invitation to the dance now. In the autumn breeze the tinted leaves on the trees outside were doing their own dance, all around, like a dance of death, as they fell from their lofty perches, perhaps to join the echoes of what once had been.

This 'ballroom' offered us perhaps a glimpse of happiness, but the rest of the house, or what was left of it, reeked of unhappiness and misery. It made me feel very disappointed as on approaching the house I had felt enchanted with its setting. It seemed so wrong to find such a heartless shell, but the heart of the house had certainly been torn out. Perhaps it was for the best that the building should be pulled down and I hoped that whoever haunted or stayed in this place would not remain to witness the changes but move on to a happier plane of existence. After the ball is over, there is no use in hanging around waiting and regretting. With these thoughts in mind there was nothing more we could do except to go home and leave Appley to its fate. We met up with the other party who had not had any experiences like ours, but their laughter suggested their exploration had kept them amused all the same.

As we walked through the lodge gates, some of us turned back to take a last look at the house, and it seemed as though from some of the windows we could see ghostly faces staring out at us. Perhaps they envied us in some way, or resented the invasion of their privacy. We will never know, yet I often think of them and hope they found some happiness and were able to hold on to their better memories.

On the way back to her home Doris said to me, 'It was all a fairy tale, wasn't it?' I was rather cross at this comment, as to me it had been a real experience and not a product of my imagination. She felt it all had been like some novelette and therefore could not possibly be true. Once out in the air, and the farther away we got, even I began to feel it could have been a flight of fancy, and in any case how could we prove anything that had happened? The subject was dropped and we spent the rest of our break doing other things.

On the Monday that we were due to leave it was raining, and there was little else we could do except to sit and talk. We were about to have a coffee break when the doorbell rang. On answering it Doris found a lady from her local church who had called to tell her their afternoon meeting was cancelled. She asked the lady to join us for coffee and she readily accepted. It seemed as though she had expected to be asked and we found her to be a very friendly soul and one ready for conversation. It was then that Mavis suddenly asked her if she had lived on the Island for long, to which she replied she had been born there and knew it very well. Eyes sparkling, Mavis said, 'What do you know about Appley House then?' She replied, 'Quite a lot! I used to deliver papers there years ago when I was just a girl.' We asked the lady if she would mind telling us what she knew and if we could take some notes. She readily agreed and here I relate her story, although for certain reasons I am not quoting her name nor many of those connected with the house. The good lady felt it would not be fair to any relatives who might still be living on the Island, though as quite a number of years had passed I doubted that anyone could be upset.

The lady remembered the house had been occupied by a 'Sir' and 'Lady' but was not sure if they had any other titles. The man was well known as a 'ladykiller' and the lady was tall, thin and regal-looking, who wore her hair piled up on the top of her head. In fact, exactly like the lady who followed us around the house. They had two sons, one of whom was known as Edworth. He was a down-at-heel type and had at some time been paralysed through a shooting accident and had to use a wheelchair. The other son was untidy and 'shaggy', in her words. Of medium height he gave the feeling of being unclean. He limped with his left leg, though she did not know for what reason. He was a drunkard and had made several attempts to take his own life. She seemed to remember there was something about him trying to jump off a tower. He did eventually commit suicide by cutting his throat in a bath, which was in one of the smaller houses on the estate. He did have a moustache and a sort of beard, and was a very unhappy man, as was Edworth, and both seemed to be dominated by their mother.

She remembered they were always having trouble with the staff and did not keep servants for long. She also said the butler was a strong personality in the household and seemed to hold a lot of sway. When our visitor said the lady of the house had a special room where she could watch the servants quarters and know all that was going on, I asked if there was any special relationship between the lady and the butler. Her reply was that rumour suggested there was but she would not like to say it was true. She remembered special things going on at Appley and that King Edward VII used to visit there, as well as lots of titled people. It used to be a grand place but had fallen into disrepute and decay. She did not think there was anyone to keep the house on for. As far as she knew, Edworth had been a bachelor and the other son, William, had married but left his wife, refusing to have anything more to do with women. Apparently there were quite a lot of funny happenings in the kitchen, but that never got talked about. She used to like to deliver papers there, not that anyone talked to her, but because it was such a grand place.

We sat listening in absolute silence and amazement as she had been allowed to go on without interruption. Those who had any doubts about our visit to Appley immediately apologised and Doris could hardly speak, realising it had not been a fairy tale at all. We had no idea this lady would call at such an opportune moment, nor that she would have known about the house. She was completely unknown to all of us except Doris and it was only through Mavis and her strong desire to find out more about this place that enabled us to get the lady's story. I would not have asked myself, having decided to forget the whole thing, probably because my dignity had been hurt. I hope that by retelling this story I will not hurt the dignity of the former occupants of the house. Perhaps the good wishes of those reading this story will help them to find peace, if they haven't done so already. As Mavis is now in the other world herself, maybe she has found out more, but if so she remains silent.

We never did find out why I heard the young girl singing. The lady did mention that the owner of Appley had his own yacht. He had a special pier built for it which was never used, as his wife did not like it. Perhaps it stirred up romantic thoughts in one of the servants and I caught the echo of a daydream, or homesickness. Perhaps someone in the house was happy then.

On one occasion Jim and I felt in need of a weekend away and thought we would like to go somewhere we had not been before. After much pondering over a map we both felt strongly it had to be the town of Frinton near Clacton on the east coast. It seemed almost like a compulsion, but at that point we felt anywhere would make a change and so we set forth ready to face any experience that might lie ahead.

We stepped off the train and immediately sensed a feeling of peace which suggested we might have chosen the right place. This feeling however was soon dispelled as, although Frinton was a very pretty place with well-kept houses and beautiful rose gardens whose perfumes pervaded the air, there soon arose an unfriendly atmosphere almost bordering on hostility. We soon discovered when seeking somewhere to stay that Frinton did not welcome visitors as there were no guesthouses and only one hotel, which was expensive and full anyway. After a long time of searching and even asking the locals if they could help, we realised that it was useless to try any longer. By then it was rather late and we realised we would not be able to get to another town, so we wondered just what we could do. As we stopped walking we found ourselves outside a newsagent's shop and Jim suggested we ask the owner if he could help us. I was reluctant at first but necessity forced me to agree even though I felt we would receive more hostility. How wrong I was, as the owner turned out to be a friendly man, who, when we explained our difficulty, said we had come to the wrong place as Frinton did not welcome strangers; he himself disapproved of this but it had always been like this and he doubted it would ever be different. He said how he wished he could offer us accommodation but he had nowhere to put us. Then he suddenly said he knew a lady customer who had recently lost her father and was now on her own and thought it might be worth asking her, but that we should not be surprised if the answer was no.

After he gave us the address and directions we found ourselves approaching what seemed to be a somewhat dingy house in an otherwise pleasant road. Well, beggars can't be choosers, we thought, so we knocked on the door. It was half opened by a very timid-looking lady who was obviously nervous at seeing two young men standing on the step. We explained that the newsagent had suggested we ask if she could put us up for two nights with breakfast only as we could not find anywhere else to stay and it was getting late and there was nowhere else we could go. At first she said she could not as she had never done such a thing before and was really not prepared for this. We put on our charm and said we would appreciate anything she could do and of course we would pay whatever she asked. Finally she relented, warning us we would have to take her as we found her, and asked us if we would go for a walk and come back in an hour when she would have things ready for us. By then we were famished and wondered if Frinton was prepared to feed strangers. After a while we discovered a restaurant and were able to satisfy our hunger and be prepared for whatever might come. One hour later found us back at the house where the lady said she had done her best and hoped we would find it comfortable. Being almost exhausted we were quite content if it meant somewhere to lay our sleepy heads.

Our hostess showed us upstairs to a room which was sparsely furnished and with just one double bed. This was something we did not care for and asked if she had another bed, but this was all she could offer, so Jim and I had to put up with sharing, which as it happened was perhaps meant to be. Jim fell fast asleep almost immediately but I could not. There seemed to be a very strange atmosphere in the room, which made me extremely restless and unsettled. After a while I saw an old man approaching the bed and waving a walking stick about. He was wearing a black coat, black pinstriped trousers and a black bowler hat. As he reached the bottom of the bed he suddenly lifted it up and started shaking it up and down which woke Jim up. He asked what was happening and when I told him about the old man he said he couldn't see him but he certainly felt the shaking. We told him to go away and leave us alone as we did not want to be disturbed and after some hesitation he disappeared and the shaking stopped so we could finally get the sleep we longed for. Neither of us was worried by the disturbance as we knew such things could happen, although we had hoped for a quiet break. I personally do not mind being haunted as long as it does not disturb my sleep or any other routine, but ghosts it seems do what they want to when they want to.

I awoke quite early to find Jim already up and looking around the room as though he was searching for something. I asked him what he was doing and told him not to be nosey but he carried on regardless. Suddenly he called me to come and look at something and I found him standing in front of a curtained recess in one corner of the room. Behind the curtain was a chair on which lay folded a black coat, a pair of black pinstriped trousers and a black bowler hat. In the corner was a walking stick and on the wall was a photo of several men, probably members of some sort of club or organisation to which the old man belonged. I say this because Jim pointed to one of the men and said he was the one who came in the night. He was exactly as I had described to him, even to the moustache, and I agreed. We immediately realised that this was the lady's father and it was his bed we were sleeping in. No wonder he had been so annoyed and angry but we knew then that this was why we had to come to Frinton. It was to help our hostess but also her father to adjust to a new life.

We went downstairs to breakfast where our hostess was running around trying to fix up something for us to eat. The whole house seemed to have an air of gloom but as we knew more or less what was happening it did not worry us and in fact she had prepared quite an adequate meal and best of all a good cup of tea. Gradually the lady began to talk and hoped we were satisfied with the bed and the food. She explained that she had never married and had always lived with her father in this house, and as they never had any visitors she was not used to entertaining. They were church people and she always had to go to church. She went there and everywhere else with her father. She had not travelled or had much social life and said her father was very strict and always followed a certain routine. There was a picture of him, she said, in our room, which of course we already knew. She said she missed her father very much and had no idea what she was going to do now but supposed she would get used to it. They had never had very much money but the house now belonged to her, though it would be too big and too much for her. When she had finished talking we left for a long walk by the sea, knowing that later that day we would have work to do. It was good to get out into the sunlight and away from the gloomy house, though this was what we now knew we had come for.

We returned later and once in bed waited for the old man to appear. At first it did not seem he would and we thought he might be nervous of us but after a while he appeared, preceded by the waving stick. I told him to be quiet and listen to what we would say to him. He shuffled around for a moment or two and then seemed ready to listen. We explained that he had died and was now in another dimension we call the spirit world and this was no longer his house. He must realise how unhappy and lonely his daughter now was and that he should try to help her to be happy and find friends and be able to do some of the things she always wanted to but which he had not allowed. He must be able to see how wrong he had been and, in order to find his own peace and happiness in this other world, he must let go of this world and do what is right. We also told him that, although it had been his bed that he was shaking, he had no need of it now. We gave him quite a talking to and finally he said he would do as we asked and not spoil things for his daughter any more. Then he shuffled off, turning just for a moment to smile and then disappeared.

When we went down to breakfast the next morning there had been a transformation as the whole house seemed to be bathed in light and everywhere looked bright and shining. Our hostess looked younger, was dressed differently and was singing as she went about her work. She talked about what she was going to do with her life and was very positive about her future. It felt as though she had been released from a prison, at least that was what it seemed to us, and we decided not to tell her what had happened, as my contention is that what you never know you never miss. It was only important for us to know that we had been guided to her in a sort of rescue mission and so the best thing to do was to leave her to her new-found happiness. She did not need any more complication in her life, but we were sure we would probably have to sort out things for many more people. It is something I have always been compelled to do..

Perhaps ghost *hunter* is the wrong word to use, as it would seem on reflection that the ghosts really come to me in a way, or I stumble on them by accident, as was the case in another of my experiences. I had got to know a lady named Eleanor Anderson who lived in Burlington, Connecticut, through my tape-recorded readings and after some time I got to meet her personally when I was invited to stay at her home. This was rather like a ranch-house, set as it was in a forest of trees covering many acres and consequently somewhat deserted, although it *was* extremely peaceful. Peter had also been invited but he could not arrive until the second day, which left me to make the plane trip alone. I was met by a friend of Eleanor's who drove me to her home, a three-hour drive which, after the long flight, left me quite exhausted and ready for bed and a long sleep.

This was not to be as, although it was midnight when I arrived, my hostess had prepared a full meal and was even dressed for dinner. I tried hard to go along with it but she began to make me feel very cross because she kept asking me when I was going to give her a reading. I told her it would and could only be when I had caught up on my sleep and recovered from the jet lag, but nothing seemed to deter her and she insisted I could do it the next day. I agreed to anything which would let me get to bed and I finally got into it at 3 a.m.! I was awoken four hours later by the sound of music and my hostess telling me that breakfast would be served at eight. Not in bed, mind you! I was expected to be up and dressed, which might have been all right for Eleanor but certainly not for me.

That day I was driven to the airport by her chauffeur to meet Peter. Another long journey but it was good to see Peter and on the way back I was able to tell him about my arrival. It was not that Eleanor wasn't a kind and very generous lady, because on the whole she was a good friend and gave us a pleasant stay; it was just irksome that she wanted a reading in order to contact her husband in the other world and who had not been very evidential on the tapes she had received. So after Peter had settled in she insisted I tried to contact him, which turned out to be negative as it seems he would not communicate and I thought it was maybe I was too tired. She then asked Peter to contact him as she had gathered he was not a professional medium but was psychic enough to have a try. Immediately her husband who was named Andy came through loud and clear, which made her tell me I wasn't any good because if Peter could do it then why couldn't I? I did try again on other days but still it seemed he would not cooperate. Came the day before we were due to leave and Eleanor suggested that in the evening we could have a swim in her heated pool. By then I was feeling very unwell and said I would go to bed as we had to get up early next morning to catch an onward flight. So she and Peter went off to have their swim while I climbed into bed hoping for a good sleep. It was a hot night and so I had just one sheet covering me and felt myself slipping into a deep slumber when I was rudely awoken.

Suddenly the room felt very cold and I was aware of creaking noises and footsteps in the hall outside. At first I thought it would be the swimmers returning from the pool but then realised that they would have been and gone a good while before. Still the footsteps continued and then there was a knocking on my door. I began to realise this was something out of the ordinary and immediately called out, 'Go away and leave me alone!' This made no difference because the noises got louder and louder and the eerie feeling grew even stronger. I was laying with my back to the door when suddenly it was as though someone lifted the sheet and blew down my spine. It was like a freezing-cold blast after which I could not get warm. The noises and footsteps were still going on and after some time, although I did not want to disturb Peter, I decided to call him on the internal telephone as he was only in the room next door. The phone would not work and after some deliberation I decided to awaken him by going to his room. I explained what was happening and said that no matter how I tried I could not convince whoever it was to leave me alone, and I assumed it must be Andy. Peter checked his phone and it rang through to mine without problem. By then all the noises had stopped but I asked Peter to come into my room and ask Andy to stop whatever he was trying to do. At first it seemed to work as everything remained quiet but shortly after Peter rang me to say it had all started in his room. In the end we had to just get what sleep we could.

The following morning we went into breakfast where Eleanor was sitting all bright and smiling. She asked if we'd had a good night, so we told her the whole story. As we did she burst into laughter and asked at what time it had happened. When I said it was at 1 a.m. she said that it must have been Andy, who was haunting the house or whatever we liked to call it. Apparently he had been in Eleanor's room opening drawers and moving things, something which he had been doing for some time. She had told him to go and haunt that man from England as he didn't believe Andy was doing these things to her and told him he was a louse for not communicating. She had told me of such occurrences on her taped letters to me in England, so she felt he ought to prove he was around that night and he did at exactly 1 a.m. as Eleanor also noticed the time. (I might add here that as I am writing this story, strange things keep happening with the computer, so perhaps Andy has still not forgotten me after all these years!)

By the time Peter and I left Eleanor's that morning we both felt wretchedly tired. We had to make our way to Grand Rapids where we would be staying with another friend, the wife of a clergyman. On the flight, we felt so drained that we decided we needed to have a drink or two to keep us going – the one and only time I've had alcohol for breakfast! By the time we met Mary and her husband, I confess we were a little worse for wear. Mary suggested I sit in the back of the car with her, and Peter in the front with Al, her husband. As we drove off, she whispered to me, 'Ronald, you're drunk and I want to know why!' When I told her the story

190

she laughed and asked me not to let Al know as he would not quite approve, although he was a very good man with quite a sense of humour. Luckily Peter did not look and feel quite as bad as me. By the time we reached Mary and Al's lovely home in Macatowa, Michigan we were both feeling a lot better and felt that we had well and truly left Andy behind, or at least hope we had! Somehow I don't think Andy meant any harm and perhaps in the other world they consider haunting to be just a bit of fun.

The whole idea of ghosts seems to make people act in quite absurd ways. Another time the Ghost Club of Great Britain asked me if I would accompany them on a ghost hunt in the National Maritime Museum in Greenwich. At the time I was still in my job at the town hall and so when they said it would be an all-night affair I said I could not do it. They begged me to reconsider and I asked exactly what they wanted me to do that would take all night. The museum, they told me, was supposed to be haunted and the idea was for members of the Club to hide behind the exhibits and as soon as I saw a ghost I was to point out where and they would all jump out from hiding and photograph it with infrared cameras. I could not help laughing and said, 'Don't you think it might frighten the ghost when you all jump out from your hiding places flashing your cameras? It would be enough to scare a human!' They took my point but said how disappointed they were as I was highly respected for my work and they so wanted me to lead their adventure. We parted good friends but I cannot even now believe that anyone could be so serious about such a plan and not see the funny side of it all.

On another occasion I was asked to find a ghost that was supposedly haunting a house in the East End of London. It was to be filmed by the Norwegian TV company and at first I accepted the task. However, I had to change my mind a few days later when I was given the instructions. The idea was for different pairs of psychics to go into the house on the hour all through the night, with me being paired with a fellow with whom I had never got along and who was known for his difficult personality. I told them the whole thing was a farce – why on earth would a ghost appear on the hour just to fit with in with such a madcap scheme? I heard later that they went ahead with the plan but nothing had happened, so perhaps the ghost did think it best to stay away from those crazy humans. A wise and sensible ghost, I should say!

16

Going My Own Way

One thing that has always been popular is the Ouija board. Of this I have enough experience to be able to advise anyone to leave it alone, as it causes a lot of frightening things which are claimed to be from the spirit world but which I think more than likely comes from the minds of those using it. My first experience was when I was in the army and some of the lads had been to a party where they played with the Ouija board and got some very frightening messages, which resulted in one lad being told he was going to die. He did not but it reduced him to a nervous wreck for some time after. I was once persuaded to join in and did so very reluctantly as I had seen what could happen. Certainly I felt something could happen for me but it was such a laborious affair having to spell out everything one letter at a time, and I think my presence stopped anything disastrous happening. It was the same with the glass and alphabet which many people have tried at sometime or the other.

A set of letters of the alphabet are arranged in a circle on a table and an upturned wineglass placed in the middle. Then everyone places a finger on the glass and usually a question is asked. Eventually the glass slides to various letters, which together form into a sentence with a message for someone in the group. It can be very disturbing but when I first tried this I felt a power in my finger and knew I was pushing, although I had to fight against other people also pushing. It was not deliberate but I then knew there was no purpose in it for me, as being psychic I could answer the questions anyway. Nonetheless it can be a dangerous thing to play around with, as it connects too strongly with the minds of those who play – and who knows what is hidden in the subconscious? No doubt there is a time when we all tend to play around with things which we realise may be dangerous, and maybe we need to have these experiences, but far better to listen to the voice of wisdom which is within us. I have experienced so many things in my life, good, bad and indifferent, but everything has made me realise I am richer for knowing. It helps me understand myself and other people and, although I often feel that my life has not been as I would have liked, I can accept it has been what was best for me. Some lessons are hard to learn but in the end we attain a higher pinnacle and find a greater strength

At one time I was involved with the Society of Psychical Research and did some experiments for them, which for me was quite a challenge as they were very sceptical people. Although they were seeking the truth about survival, they were not prepared to accept anything that was open to question. I was delighted when the then President described me as the only honest medium he had met. I had provided an interesting ending to a book which he and Guy Lyon Playfair were writing, called *The Enfield Poltergeist*, by doing a tape for Maurice Grosse and contacting his deceased daughter. It also introduced me to Playfair, whom I found to be an extremely interesting man (he wrote a number of well-researched books on different aspects of the psychic such as reincarnation and 'twin souls'). It was he who asked me to do a tape for the actress Hana Pravda, wife of the actor George Pravda, and which led to her having a great number of tapes over a long period. He has lectured on what he calls the Pravda Tapes and considers what I achieved for this courageous and brave lady to be outstanding work. The Pravda Tapes, however, are by no means the longest sequence of tape-recorded messages I have conducted. There are, for example, two different ladies in the United States for whom I have been providing tapes for well over thirty-six years. When you realise that each of these ladies has had at least one tape every month, it can be seen that this adds up to an extremely large number of tapes. There has never been a communication that was not successful and it has helped these ladies and their families to get through their grief. We will hear more of them later but I must add there are many other people who have had quite a number of tapes, too, but these two take the record.

Spiritualists tend to make a lot of rules as to what should and should not be done, or claim to know exactly how everything works. Unfortunately they call Spiritualism a religion and insist that it be followed in much the same way as in orthodox churches. When I first discovered my psychic ability I went along with it as it was, and indeed for quite some time. I soon realised, however, that, having broken away from conventional religion, I was being hypocritical. At that time the only way I could get to demonstrate my gifts was through the Spiritualist church, which really did not matter that much as I usually respect other religions and often take some of the ideas they have and use them in my search for the truth. Nonetheless, in my opinion the psychic and the search for proof of life after death is not a religion but it is something that can be combined with *any* orthodox religion. Regardless of race, colour or creed, we all come into this earthly world in exactly the same way, and we leave it also in the same way. So it is possible there is no religion as such in the other world but of that we can't be sure until we find out for ourselves. Gradually I began to do things my way, so to speak, and this did not make me popular with some people.

I can and will work only in a way I believe in and accept the responsibility if I am wrong. They say variety is the spice of life and I cannot bear to be stuck in a rut as it always seems to me there is no end to learning – just when you think you know it all you discover there is much more. I was called a rebel and accused of trying to destroy what had been built up by the pioneers of Spiritualism but I tried to explain that pioneers never finish their work as each step they take leads to another as there is always something new to discover. I must say I worked very hard and long during all the years but luckily I have been blessed with a great determination.

From a very early age I found I could write little poems and ditties which always amused other people. Somehow I had a natural talent for this and all sorts of things would flow from my pen. Usually I did these things for birthdays and weddings but later found myself able to express regret and sympathy with what always seemed to be the right words. People often asked me to compose letters for them, which always seemed to have the right effect, and it was something that made me feel very happy as I was able to help people. At no time did I ever consider writing a book as I felt my talents were not good enough for that and anyway I was too busy with my job and enjoying my leisure time, or at least trying to. It was not until a long time later and after I had started my tape recordings that I felt the need for a story to be written and sat down to try. I was amazed and delighted at how well it flowed and so my first book, called *The Little Dutch Boy: A Study in Psychic Communication*, was written and published. It came about after a Dutch lady wrote to ask if I could contact her son, and this eventually led to the production of a large number of tapes over a long period of time. From the very first one the young boy named Pat gave wonderful evidence of his survival and showed his parents and sister he was still around. He had passed from leukaemia and my book relates his family's – sadly unsuccessful – fight to save him and then his subsequent communications that showed he was still taking an interest in what was happening in his loved ones' lives. I was surprised at how well I was able to write the story and this encouraged me to write articles and a lot of other things (including the lyrics and book of a musical already mentioned earlier). It was a great feeling to know that, although I might have done these things earlier, I had a gift which would allow me to express the wonderful things I have discovered and what I feel so deeply within me.

My second book, which is a more recent one, is called *The Little Boy Who Listened: A Portrait of a Medium* and is in many respects even deeper than the first. It tells how many years ago I met a young man called Arthur Molinary with whom I became friendly and helped him to develop his extraordinary psychic gift. All mediums work in a different way but I dare to say none more unusually than Arthur. I love teaching and believe that a pupil should become better than his teacher or else they have failed. He was psychic at birth so I could not teach him how to be psychic but I could advise and help him with how to 'present' his gift and handle the many different situations that would occur. I presented him to the College of Psychic Studies where I had worked some time before and felt it was the right place for him to be, which proved to be the perfect choice as he has been there for many years and is in great demand. He is considered by many to be one of the finest mediums in the world, something which I also believe. My book shows this to be true and I am delighted to say it was a pleasure to write as it enabled me to develop my writing skills and the gift I have which still functions and is, I'm pleased to say, acclaimed. I have a lot of unusual ideas about which many Spiritualists scoff, but one must always be prepared to reach out and accept new challenges. With Arthur there is an honest and determined effort to do things his way, which means he is trustworthy as nothing ever goes beyond the room where he sees clients, unless it is something they are happy to share with the public.

Healing is one thing I have undertaken to some degree but there comes a time when one has to choose what is most important and decide what one can do best. Psychic healing is often called faith or spiritual healing but I prefer just to call it healing. At first I was told that the healing rays come through the guides and so with the laying on of hands they would determine what was best for the patient, and knowing no better at that time I went along with it. After long experience I am convinced that this healing power is generated from the solar plexus of the healer to wherever it is needed and is created through the sympathy of the medium or healer for the patient. It is hard for me to believe that people in this other world, which by any standards must be a huge place, can direct power to people in this perhaps even bigger earthly world we live in. One immediately thinks that communication with the other world happens regardless of conditions, so why shouldn't healing? I must confess that after so many years considering this subject I cannot be sure of what is the right explanation, but I subscribe to the idea that it doesn't really matter how it works as long as results are obtained. There certainly are many strange and wonderful things that happen and I personally cannot waste time trying to prove why and how as it is more important to get results that are of some benefit.

I was plunged into healing in a strange way. Previously I had never felt I wanted to be a healer, but the greater plan had obviously had it in mind at least for a time. It occurred not long after I started going to The Haven, where healing would be given after the service for those who cared to wait. On one occasion when I stayed behind to see if I could be of any help there was only one healer who had to deal with several waiting patients. This was John Blackwood, Nora's husband, and after a while he realised it was getting late and he needed help. He asked me to come and assist but I said I was not a healer and did not know how. He said I had been told often enough that I could be healer so here was the chance to find out. He made me take a chair and place it in the middle of the room and then called a lady to sit on it. I still maintained I was not a healer and did not know what to do. His reply was simply to put my hands on the lady's head and pray and then I would be guided what to do. I did not expect anything to happen and after a short time I could see in my mind's eye what looked like a silhouette of a Christmas tree and I felt as though I had to put my hands on the lady's spine and follow the pattern. After a few minutes of this I suddenly felt I had to stop and ask the lady if she felt anything but she said she did not but wanted to know how I knew it was her back that troubled her. In fact, she said she had been in terrible pain for a long time. It was disappointing but I said I would send out thoughts to her. I discovered she was in my class at the church and so I saw her four days later when she said she had something amazing to tell me. She had gone to bed on the night of the healing and had the usual troubled and painful sleep. The following morning she was awoken by her daughter with a cup of tea and a little later looked at the clock, which showed exactly 8 a.m. Suddenly the pain seemed to drain out of her and she felt marvellous (indeed she never suffered with the back pain again). I was able to tell her an interesting supplement to her story as that very morning I was making my bed before going to work when suddenly, as I bent down, I felt a terrible pain in my back which lasted a few seconds and then disappeared. I had to look at my clock and it was exactly 8 a.m.! It was this event that convinced me that I had a healing power and would use it if that was what was meant.

One of the most interesting healing stories does not involve the laying on of hands but concerns the power of thought, a power in which I very much believe. A few years ago a very dear friend of mine who is Australian but lived in the States telephoned me and asked for help. She had been diagnosed with cancer of the uterus and the doctors doubted if anything could be done. She had five days to decide if she would have an almost impossible operation or undergo a gruelling course of radiotherapy whose benefits might be small. Naturally she was in a very unhappy state and all I could say, because I was so upset by the news, was that she should leave it with me and I would telephone her the day before to advise her what would be best. As she strongly believed in the power of healing, I promised her that I, together with other friends I would tell, would concentrate on her so that she would have a lot of powerful help coming out to her. Norma was a fine opera singer and was told that, even if she survived, she would not be able to sing. I did all I possibly could and when I telephoned her I told her that she should have the operation as, if she did, everything would turn out all right. Later I heard that the next day the doctors asked for some more X-rays to be taken and were amazed to see that what had been a football-size tumour had shrunk to the size of a golf ball and they were able to remove it easily, which meant Norma could carry on as usual. What was more, against all expectation, she could still sing and indeed better than ever! There is no doubt that all the powerful healing thoughts sent out to her must have helped, if only to give her confidence. For me and so many others it was a wonderful occurrence and, no matter exactly how it was achieved, something momentous did happen!

Another interesting thing happened in quite a different but just as extraordinary a way. One evening after a service in The Haven, a lady came to me looking dreadfully ill and asked if I could help her as she had cancer. There was very little hope but they wanted her to go into hospital, which she could not do as she lived with and looked after her aged mother. I asked her if she would like to try healing and she agreed to come along to the church a few days later. Meanwhile I found three other healers, including my friend Jim, who said they would come along and help. At that time I was still doing so-called trance work and suggested a psychic operation, something which at the time was popular and which I thought might be worth a try. The lady was very nervous at first but all of us put her at her ease and I went into a trance. As I remember the others said it looked like I was performing an operation and the man who took me over said he was a doctor, though he gave a name that no one knew. When he had finished he told the lady what to expect and what to do regarding after-effects she might feel, what she should eat and what not to do. She went away perfectly happy and said that she had to go to the hospital a few days later and would let us know how she got on. Time went by and we heard nothing until one evening I was chairing a meeting at the church and I saw her come in and sit at the back. After it was over I stood at the door to say goodnight to everyone and as the lady came sailing through she just said goodnight and hurried on. I called her back and asked her if she had something to tell me as we had tried to help her and had not heard a word. She said she supposed I wanted her to buy some flowers for the church but said no more until I reminded her of the healing and the sad situation she was in. I asked her what had happened at the hospital and she replied that the doctors had taken some more X-rays and the cancer had miraculously disappeared! I was dumbfounded and said we did not want flowers for the church but simply to be told her good news and for her to acknowledge she had been helped. She hurried off without another word and when I saw her on a bus some time later she looked the picture of health, so different from how she had been when she had come to the church for the healing. She was so embarrassed and turned away from me and got off the bus as quickly as she could. We were able to check she had told the truth and the healing had worked, though it was hard to appreciate that anyone could be so ungrateful. Fortunately such ingratitude is a rare thing, but one wonders why anyone would act in this way – perhaps the very idea of being involved with Spiritualism and healing jars with many people's beliefs.

I always point out to everyone that I do not believe in miracles, although some things may seem to be miraculous, there is no reason why one should not keep an open mind on the subject. To me it always feels as if those who have passed to the other world, or at least some of them, are trying very hard to influence our lives and help in any way they can. They always tell us that they cannot work miracles but will go on trying, which to me is very heartening because in all of my experience I firmly believe we should never give up trying to do better at everything we do. I always endeavour to perform miracles in the hope that one day I might achieve such a thing. In many ways I feel my life has been blessed, but only through hard work and reaching for perfection can we hope to progress. Most of my life has been beset by illness of one kind or another but, however difficult it may have been, I have managed to carry on and do my work, not because I wanted to be a hero, but because I was mostly able to lose myself in keeping my mind occupied.

Doctors have often said they wish all patients could have the same attitude and try to forget their problems and see the funny side as well. They also recognise the fact that not everyone can do this but anything is worth a try. The thing that suffering has taught me is that I am able to understand what other people are going through and as a result of this am better qualified to help them. In some ways it is not much consolation but I always feel what Mother, from her store of many wise sayings, said about a little help being worth a great deal of pity is true. I believe that if people in this world need to be told such things they should appreciate what others may be going through. We believe this other world to be a better place than this one but for me it is hard to believe that suddenly, on passing to it, we lose all our problems and find what we might describe as paradise. If it exists, and I am sure it does in some form or other, then we still have a lot to learn and maybe need help. So communication with another world should be a two-way thing. I can only explain how I feel about what I have found so far with regard to the continuation of life and am sure that many will disagree with my findings. Unfortunately so many who become involved with the psychic tend to think they know all the answers, something which I try to avoid because it is a deep subject and still a largely unknown quantity. If in my mediumistic work giving messages I appear to be certain and definite about what I receive, it is because I feel some things so positively and can only communicate what I feel – if it should be wrong then I am prepared to accept that. As much as I would like to be 100 per cent correct in everything, I know I am not and realise we must try to learn by our mistakes. For those reading this who are not yet interested in the subject, I hope it might prove to be an interesting and helpful introduction to it. We will only take an interest in a subject when we are ready and need to, although for some that time may never come. I had to wait twenty-five years to discover my gift but it came at the right time, which confirms to me my firm belief that our lives are planned, whether we like it or not.

There is one more healing story which illustrates a very important point. I became quite friendly with a man named Ted who was in my class at The Haven. He asked me one day if I would give him healing in private as he had a back problem. He did not want to have the treatment in the church, so I agreed to see him at my home. On his first and only visit I worked on his back, finding that I concentrated on the lower area. While I was doing it I sensed his mother was around and, as he had never received a message from her, I said I would try to get one. She was obviously waiting for the opportunity to get through to Ted and there flowed a great deal of evidence about her which was quite remarkable except that he would not accept it. I knew it was right but he insisted that he could not believe it was her unless she mentioned one certain thing. I tried to get it but it seemed his mother would not say anything about it. Finally I asked Ted to tell me what it was and he said she had a wart on the end of her nose. I could not believe what he said as so many of the other things that came through were far more evidential than that. However, he had a fixed idea of what he wanted to hear, which is often a problem with some people. The only way to approach contact is with a completely open mind. Sad to say but Ted also disagreed with my healing work and insisted he had no trouble in the area I was treating. I felt I was right and told him he should check it with the doctor as I could not go to any other area than the one I did because I felt there was something very wrong there. He left my home in an unhappy state of mind and I did not see him for some time after that. He did not come to church or attend the class and I felt concerned because I knew he would be too proud to admit I was right. One evening as I was taking the chair for a service I saw Ted creep into the church and sit at the back, looking very sad. After it was over he waited for me and said he had been told he had bowel cancer and there was no hope for him. At once we resumed our friendship as I said I would help and stand by him in every way possible. For a time Jim and I visited Ted in hospital and helped him as much as we could to face the inevitable. He had a nasty operation and knew he would not recover. He was not too close to his wife, as they had gone through a bad patch, but when we realised his time was close we visited his wife and young daughter and told them he had a very short time to go and they should make the most of it. This they did and his wife thanked us because she spent every hour she could with him and they rediscovered their great love and so Ted passed on happily. There is a nice footnote to this story as one day a lady we called 'Auntie Kit', who was extremely psychic herself and had known about Ted from her niece Coral Polge, suddenly felt Ted around asking her to tell me that I had been right and he wrong but that he was happy now. Kit did not know what all this meant but of course I did and it was a great relief to say the least. Nonetheless I was sorry I could not save him but the story illustrates how one should keep an open mind about the subject whether it be healing or getting messages and that one should always put everything to the test.

Many years ago someone asked my guide about free will – whether we had any or not, and how we should accordingly behave. The reply was that before we come to this world we are shown a plan of the life we will have to live and then in effect sign a contract to undertake it. The trouble begins when we start to grow and think more for ourselves and realise we want to do something different, but are none the less bound by our contract. It is a good explanation in a way but most of us do not like to think we do not have free will to do as we choose, but as the guide said we are doing what we chose in the first place. I cannot vouch for anyone else but I have found during all of my life that the things I thought I wanted to do were not what I *had* to do. It has always felt like some strong force is making me do what I have to do, like it or not. Many times I tried to break away from the psychic, as I can honestly say I never wanted to be a medium full time, but in the end I had to accept this as my destiny because everything else inevitably got blocked off no matter how I tried. Even now I still try to use other gifts I have but always it comes back to the psychic. I can remember many years ago sitting in my home feeling utterly and completely frustrated and saying out loud to whomever in the other world might be listening, 'Well, you lot up there, if this is what I have to do then all I can say is that it had better be good!' It has been and still is, I hope, better than good, and for this I am truly thankful.

At one time I decided to join the Union of Spiritualist Mediums because it seemed to me a good idea to have some sort of backing in case any problems arose. The Union was set up with just that idea and in my enthusiasm I became a member of the social committee. I was sure it would be a good idea to arrange a social and dance for members and interested non-members and so put the idea forward to the main committee who more or less agreed but demanded I let them know about refreshments as they would have to agree to the sandwich fillings and various other things. As they already had a team of ladies who handled any refreshments beautifully, I felt it was an insult to them as well as me since it was a trivial matter by comparison and not one the high and mighty main committee should be bothered with. Despite this I made all the necessary arrangements. Unfortunately on the night chosen there was a terrific storm and only a brave few got to the hall. Nonetheless those present had a good time and also enjoyed the ladies' choice of refreshments. They asked if we could arrange more such occasions, which, of course, had to be put to main committee who said the whole thing was a failure and no more would be allowed. By then

I was so tired with all this petty red tape that I decided to resign and, unbeknown to me, the rest of the social committee also resigned. I was commanded by the main committee to appear before them. I was shown into a room and was not even offered a chair until I demanded one. The main officials immediately accused me of trying to ruin the Union and accused me of bullying my fellow committee members into resigning. At this I exploded and gave them a real piece of my mind. It was farcical and I felt like a prisoner being judged for some awful crime by a kangaroo court. I could not believe grown people could behave in such a juvenile manner and told them I had better things to do than play these games and walked out. For some time I was known as a rebel and as the man who tried to destroy the Union, but it did not worry me as I knew the truth and knew most people would not take any notice; if anything, it made me more popular. I realised how much the general run of people who were interested in Spiritualism were not too enamoured of committees and officialdom and had more respect for people like me and my gift.

When a group of younger people interested in the psychic decided to form a group called the Young Spiritualists I was encouraged to join them, being at that time reasonably young myself, and was asked to sit on their committee. At first it was refreshing to listen to their ideas and to be able to offer my own, and the enthusiasm within the group was seemingly very strong. However, it did not take long before the idea of committees made me despair, for when I worked in the town hall I had to deal with committees and found them to be nothing but a set of people sitting on their bottoms, pontificating and telling others what should be done but never doing anything themselves. It was just the same with the Young Spiritualists and if anything was ever done it was mainly by me, Jim (who had also joined) and Marjorie Osborn, a well-known medium and worker for the movement. The three of us all worked very hard, making and collecting things for bazaars, handing out leaflets and so on, and then doing all the preparations on the actual day. On one occasion we arrived early to set up the stalls, hoping then to go off for some lunch before the bazaar opened. However, no one from the rest of the committee turned up until it actually started, so we had to go hungry. Luckily the bazaar was a success as was the dance we had arranged for the evening, though by the end of the weekend we three were worn out physically and tired of being taken for granted. So once again I resigned from the committee along with Jim and Marjorie. We later attended a meeting to find that I was again being accused of trying to destroy the group. There were a fair number of ordinary members present, led by a very angry young man who said I had completely destroyed the Young Spiritualists, but I explained they had done it themselves and that I resigned for good reasons. I suggested *he* take it over as President and see if he could save the group. He did take over and sadly experienced the same apathy and lack of teamwork I had. He later telephoned me to apologise for his words and actions and said he was washing his hands of it all.

After that there was nothing else to join and I got on with my real work, which was to help anyone and everyone seeking my help through my psychic gift. It is not fair to be accused of trying to destroy something when I have only ever tried to build and promote things, but it taught me not to mind what others say and think as long as I know the truth. Truth is something one cannot hide or run away from because sooner or later the truth will out.

17

The Tape-recorded Readings

I think the proxy tape readings, of which I have sent thousands to all parts of the world, are the best part of my psychic ability. They have presented me with my great challenge and have provided a great deal of evidence of survival. I won't pretend that it is entirely easy to do as it can be frustrating when I cannot get any immediate confirmation. On the other hand, when doing personal face-to-face readings, it can be very off-putting to see people's expressions. So for me it is really best if I cannot see any reactions and just have to give what comes and wait for an answer after I have posted off each tape. Usually a tape will last for one hour, which represents a lot more work than if one was giving a face-to-face reading, and as I've said requires a great deal of energy, which has to be replenished 'naturally', not through the spirit guides as some like to claim. However, the results can be astonishing and people have drawn help from the tapes in all sorts of ways. For most, the taped messages have given them the will to live again after losing a loved one and helped them adapt and change their lives accordingly.

Out of the many successful taped readings I have done, it is hard to choose which ones to talk about. One I could not leave out concerns a young man in New Zealand who was killed in an motorcycle accident. At the time I was making tapes for a lady called Euleen in New Zealand who found them evidential and shared her good news with many other people. Her grandson Malcolm was very friendly with another lad named Ken Holland and when she heard through Malcolm that Ken had been killed on his motorcycle and that Ken's parents and sister were grieving badly, Euleen asked me if I would make a tape for the family (whom she did not know personally). I could not help but agree to do this as a gift; it was a big challenge but one I could not refuse. As soon as I could, I recorded the tape and sent it off, hoping it would be of some help. I never build up people's expectations, as I can never guarantee what the results will be and know that if nothing happens then presumably there would be a reason for it.

To say I was astounded when Euleen wrote to tell me that the tape had been completely evidential and had brought immediate relief to the family would be an understatement. Apparently Ken had collided with a taxi, the impact powerful enough to shoot him through the side window and out through the windscreen. He was on his way to his girlfriend's home and possibly he was distracted. Malcolm was absolutely distraught so the tape gave him some help as well. There were so many things on the tape that could hardly leave anyone in doubt that this was Ken communicating from another world, and so soon after his violent accident. The moment I started I heard a big sigh and I tried to copy it. This was accepted as accurate and exactly typical of Ken. I felt he was very shy and would always edge into a room rather than walk straight in, but that once he got to know a person he would have a lot to say. All of this was confirmed by the family. He had a strong sense of humour and a very wide smile which showed his teeth. The man I was in touch with kept pushing his hair back as if to show his protruding ears; Ken always arranged his hair to hide them. He was always doing something with his hands and forever fidgeting, which was also true. I then demonstrated a peculiar whistle which Ken used to make through his teeth. This was the way he used to call his dog. This was followed by Ken laughing about a joke concerning fishing. Apparently his elder brother bought professional fishing tackle while Ken used only an old line and hook, though his brother always caught nothing while Ken caught something every time. This was a standing family joke. His mother immediately recognised my allusion to Ken's bickering and said it was never anything nasty but done for sheer downright pleasure. Ken could not outwardly show love, which was true as, if he ever brought his mother flowers or chocolates, he always said he had found them in the gutter. He said he liked apples and cider, which was also true as he would have both of them whenever he had the chance.

He sent his regards to Malcolm, whom he called 'Sneezy' because of his hay fever, and reminded him of when they did funny drawings on the school blackboard. He then referred to a habit he had with his tongue, which, it was said, he poked out whenever he was concentrating on anything. He mentioned his dimples and his slimness as well as his big hooter. This was another family joke, as he called his nose a 'hooter'. I had to ask if he was always running out of socks. If he had a hole in one he would cover it with several layers of good socks in order to hide it. I felt he was often teasing his dog but only in a nice way as he would never do anything to hurt it. Ken then said he had slightly bowed legs and his left knee had a scar on it as a result of one of his close shaves. He also mentioned his liking for loud ties as whenever he had to wear one it was always very boldly coloured. His boots, which were in a disgraceful condition, were noticeable for their fancy studs. His brother had bought him a new pair to replace them. 'Ask Malc about the pens' was a question of Ken's. Malc said that Ken was selling pens for a club. He had bought one but had not paid for it before Ken passed. Moles and freckles on his shoulders were easily recognised. I felt Ken was a good swimmer but on one occasion he had nearly drowned. At his funeral his mother, who knew nothing of this, was told about it by his Scout leader. Ken said he wore a black onyx ring with his initial on it, which was true. He was a sceptic and had argued with Malc about survival. A moving message was to tell his 'old cobber' that he was quite right and that Ken was wrong.

One particular photograph I described was a direct hit. When Ken was young his father had given him some money for helping in the garden, which Ken blew on ice cream. His parents photographed him eating it and had written something across the corner of the photo, which was the word 'gutsy'. Ken relived the last moments of his passing and said the crash helmet was in a terrible mess. He knew his parents were puzzled about the amount of money found on him but explained he had just collected his holiday pay which had been more than he had been expecting.

Up till now it was a wonderfully correct description of Ken, but there was more to come. A peculiar toe on the left foot was recognised with the explanation he had once dropped a heavy object on his foot and one toe had been crushed. Ken teased his mother about pastry, which was almost correct as it was actually shortbread which sometimes came out wrong but Ken ate it regardless. Ken mentioned having trouble with his ears at one time, which seemed to refer to the fact that he had had abscesses in them. A crowning piece of evidence was when he said, 'Tell Mother one pillow was not enough.' This was quite significant as Ken always liked two pillows but there was only one in his coffin. He also saw the photo and flower which were placed in the coffin. He mentioned his love of skating and talked about his scarf which was apparently yards long but he would never go anywhere without it. Ken's reference to his funny navel or belly button raised a smile. He was born with a hernia which resulted in a protruding navel. His love of fairs and sideshows seemed very strong and he would go miles to attend anything like that. I was puzzled when Ken said he always seemed tired. He had always thought he would not live to a ripe old age and consequently lived his short life to the full. He put his energy into every minute of it, which must have made him tired. Euleen said to me that all of this was evidence which could not be ignored and how much it had done for his family. Coming so soon after his passing I would say all this was a wonderful illustration of communication which cannot leave any doubt that there must be another plane of existence.

This story had a most amazing sequel. Five years later Malcolm was also killed in a road accident, which meant he and his great friend Ken would presumably be together in this other world. When the famous medium Albert Best visited New Zealand, Euleen received a phone call one day from a friend who had attended one of his demonstrations in Christchurch. Apparently Best had asked if anyone in the church knew the name of Euleen Stritch or Stretch and said that Malcolm Isherwood was present and he was holding the hand of Ken Holland who was killed in an accident when he was seventeen years old. Euleen was speechless as Malcolm was her youngest grandson who was killed aged twenty-two. She felt their friendship was a positive thing and, knowing Ken and Malcolm were still the best of pals, she decided to ask me for another of my taped readings in the hope Malcolm would come through. She had received several tapes before with evidence of many people who had passed but could not resist another if it meant contact with Malcolm, of whom she was especially fond.

She was not surprised to receive a taped reading which contained no less than *sixty-nine* different points of evidence and said the number of correct references was staggering to say the least. One of the most unusual items mentioned was about his mother's ukulele, which Malcolm connected with his girlfriend, Penny. Once the girl had whacked him with it when he annoyed her and the instrument had cracked. Malcolm then showed me some items of clothing amongst which was a trench coat. This meant nothing to Euleen until Malcolm's sister-in-law remembered she had a photograph of him in an army coat. Something funny about trousers was mentioned. Malcolm had a habit of borrowing his brother's clothes. Once he took a brand-new pair of trousers and tore them badly in a motorbike accident. Talk of a long scarf was very true as he actually had two which were so long they went around his neck twice and still reached his knees. Wherever he went he always wore one of these scarves, which was surely a reminder of Ken as he had also had a long scarf. Relatives were able to place such things as a hammer – the boys lost their father's hammer by the sea – pennants and keys, which Malcolm collected, as well as a van. He and his friends had built the van themselves, which according to Euleen was the strangest-looking thing you have ever seen. They travelled hundreds of miles in it and had a lot of fun. Malcolm mentioned the things that had happened in the home, like his characteristic whistle through the teeth, shutting the front door and the sound of his footsteps walking across the hall. His bedroom door had inexplicably opened and closed and knocking on walls was heard. Malcolm's father had seen and spoken to his 'dead' son. These are but a few of the things mentioned on the tape but enough to make not only Euleen happy but all of his very close family, whom I met some time later when I visited New Zealand. It was interesting for me to see the scene and the people connected with the messages; if anything, it made any future taped communications easier to do. My happiest thought was in knowing that the two boys, Ken and Malcolm, were still close 'cobbers'.

For a long time I had hoped that perhaps someone would analyse my taped work since many people considered it to be 'sensational'. Several people told me I should analyse the tapes myself but I knew that such an analysis would be better done by an outsider, whose opinion would have a better chance of being unbiased. So it was not until later that this was in effect done for me by a lady named Pamela Mills from Sherbourne in Dorset who herself had had a series of tapes from me. She decided to write a book called *Belle of Two Worlds*, Belle being her mother's name and her principal communicator. I was truly touched to find she had dedicated it to both her mother and me. Half of it was about her mother's life in this world while the rest covered the first seven tapes I had sent her, including a full transcription and what was in effect an analysis. In the book, Pamela stated that, like many of those for whom I have given taped messages, she could not help but feel her loved one was watching on and seemed to be aware of all that had happened, was happening and would be. It is a book that needs to be read and, though it may not be sensational, it gives an in-depth insight into survival and the comfort that there is another plane of existence where we will all meet again. In my opinion it is little things that count when we make contact with this other dimension and our close relatives and friends. We do not want to discuss wars and politics but to hear the things which are personal and meaningful.

Pamela's tapes came about not by coincidence but by her noticing one day that a picture on a wall in her home looked as though it had been moved. She knew it had been straight as she was meticulous about such things, yet it was now definitely lopsided as she put it. A few days later the same thing happened, which led her to exclaim 'I know it must be you, Mum!' She was already interested in the psychic but, in living in a far-flung little place and being more or less confined to her home, she felt she could not get in touch with any mediums. This led her to make enquiries until she finally read an article in *The Two Worlds* magazine about my book *The Little Dutch Boy*, which led her to ask me for a taped message from me. When it came, her comment after listening was that she had never spent such an interesting hour. She heard amazingly accurate descriptions of her mother, as well as a great deal of evidence which showed Belle was watching on.

On the second tape Belle displayed a great sense of timing, for when Pamela was listening to the tape Belle said something about her doing something with flowers. I could see in my mind's eye lots of flowers which were very beautiful and it led me to ask her if she was doing something special with flowers and perhaps doing flower arranging. It certainly seemed as if something special was going on. As Pamela was listening to this on the tape, just at that moment she happened to look out through the window and was amazed to see a lot of people with beautiful flower arrangements on their way to the local village hall for a flower-arranging show. I also asked Pamela if she was writing a book but apparently she was not and had not thought about doing so just then.

The third tape was highly evidential and mentioned about a lot of things being moved, which was true. It was not until the fourth tape that, apart from more compelling evidence, Belle said that Pamela needed a kick in the pants. It was an expression Belle often used, and when later she mentioned it again, as well as saying, 'Come on, get to it. Get on with it, my girl!', Pamela realised Belle had mentioned earlier about writing a book and remembered that some time before she had bought a thick notepad and a sheaf of typing paper, but had not realised what it was for and why she bought it. So it helped make up her mind to write the book, which she accomplished with great success, helped along by another three tapes of excellent evidence from Belle. After the book she continued to have tapes and in the end there were a great number of them. Since I started this book Pamela has passed on and joined Belle and I feel sure they will now be working together to inspire others to great things.

To me it is gratifying to know that I have been able to reach people in remote places in all parts of the world as well as in England and to give evidence of survival along with comforting messages from those who have passed to this other plane of existence.

There are so many examples of the wonderful and often unusual evidence that people have received from my tape-recorded messages. It is strange to think that when I have made them it would be on a day and time which the recipient would not know, as I always have told anyone who asks that there will be an approximate waiting period; rarely do I make the tapes immediately. A lot depends on my schedule and I also work on the idea that what a person does not know about they cannot interfere with. It leaves me free to do what I have to do just when I feel it is right. It would not be unusual for me to make a tape in the very early morning, late at night, or when I am somewhere other than at my home. I have no set rules as, having experimented with the subject in many different ways, I know it will work when I am ready to apply my mind to it. I do not meditate before starting or at any other time; in fact I usually work better when I am running late and have no time to think or worry about what I am going to do. (This often happens when I give demonstrations of clairvoyance, too, as when travelling to different places one never knows how the traffic will be or whether there will be any other sort of hold-up. There have been occasions when I have only just got to the church in time, have taken off my coat, tidied my hair and then rushed straight onto the platform and into the demonstration. Strangely it works so much better for me!) One of the hardest things to do as a psychic is to set one's own mind aside (some would say it is impossible) but I am able to do this with an almost 100 per cent guarantee, though even now occasionally a little of my own mind creeps through. I freely admit this and try to correct it.

It is very interesting to offer some examples of unusual evidence, as sometimes I find things very hard to believe, though seeing and hearing is believing. I once made some tapes for a family in America. One of their sons had died somewhat mysteriously at an early age and the whole family were grief-stricken. I was able to help them by giving a description of the young man including his scars and various things which could be known only to the family. Over the course of time he was able to encourage and help them along and seemed to know exactly what was going to happen and when, such as his sister getting married and when she was expecting her first baby. The thing I most remember was when he asked his parents to plant a magnolia tree for him in their garden. They did this with pleasure, though they knew that it would take some time to grow and actually flower. It was not long before he said on one of the tapes that the magnolia tree had one flower on it. It astounded his parents as only the morning before the tape arrived they had been in the garden and looked at the tree but it was absolutely dead with no sign of life whatsoever and they had decided to pull it up, feeling it would disappoint their son. Then they thought they would leave it until another day and when they heard what the son said they immediately rushed out into the garden to find the tree green and very much alive with one flower in full bloom. This could not have happened normally so it seemed the son had exerted some sort of influence. Whatever the explanation, it was a phenomenon which made the parents feel the son must be around still.

The tree was again later the centre of another unusual happening. Some time after the first incident the son said on another tape that his father had lost or mislaid a twenty-dollar bill. His father had indeed spent a long time hunting for such a bill and had given up until the son said he should go into the garden and look under the magnolia tree. This he did and there under the tree was the bill neatly laid out just as though someone had placed it there and smoothed it out, which was also evidential as the father said the bill had been crumpled up in his pocket. It was simply amazing as there was no way this could have been put there by someone else. Both parents were sceptical enough not to have made up a story or played around with anything and it left no doubt in my mind that the son was really letting them know he was watching over them. Over a long period he gave many more pieces of evidence and brought comfort to his brothers and sisters as well.

A man in America who had received one of my tapes and found it to be highly evidential wrote to ask if he could have another one and if I could help him by telling where he could find water on his land. He had been dowsing but to no avail and, as he was running a holiday camp, he urgently needed a new water supply. So I agreed to try but felt it was rather a tall order as I had no map or anything to help me. However, I began his tape with a few items of evidence and then concentrated on his water problem. I immediately saw in my mind's eye a picture of a large piece of land and a ranch-house, which I described as best I could. The house was standing by a lot of trees and there was a fence running along from the left side of the house. This I mentally followed until I came to a point where it was broken, close to a group of three trees. I felt strongly this client should drill on that spot and there he would find water. I was not surprised when I got a very excited and pleased reply to say he had found a 'gusher' exactly where I said, which gave him far more water that he could possibly use, so he was going to open another camp. I was glad for him but I must admit I wished I could do things like that for myself. However, my psychic gift seems in the main only to work for other people!

18

Somewhere over the Rainbow

Since I was not a fan of his music I would not expect a legendary rock star, singer and composer like Marc Bolan to communicate through me, though, if the link is there, then there is no reason why he should not use it. I was giving a demonstration at Ventnor Spiritualist church on the Isle of Wight at which his road manager, Mick O'Halloran, was present with the healer Isobel Thompson, who had been instrumental in helping Mick overcome a disability. He had suffered a stroke and had two operations during which time Marc had been killed in a road accident. It was doubtful Mick would ever recover completely but with the help of healing he made good progress. His first message from Marc referred to a white swan, which, Mick said, was a hit record that the singer had made with that title. Later his son reminded Mick, too, that a record company had sent flowers in the shape of a white swan to Marc's funeral. He then said that Mick's wife would be going away but he was not to worry as good would come from the trip. His wife did go away somewhat unexpectedly to see her mother for a few days and while there a friend was instrumental in getting an old piano for Mick which he needed to help him exercise his hand and fingers which would not articulate properly after the stroke.

The greater evidence of Marc's survival came a while later when I was demonstrating in Ryde, again on the Island. I suddenly had to go to Mick and stand in a particular way which was most unusual. Mick said it was exactly the way Marc stood after finishing a recording session to listen to the playbacks. Only those present would have known how he stood, which convinced Mick it was Marc communicating. He said that if you took my head and put Marc's in its place you would have sworn it was Marc standing there. Marc had promised to help Mick and by then it seemed very much as though he was trying to keep his word. A few weeks later I felt compelled to send one of my taped communication tapes to Mick who found it to be evidential. It contained a full description of Marc's personality and told in detail of how Marc threw down his guitar and kept patting his bottom. Mick confirmed it was a very accurate description of the singer, who went on to remind him of a joke about a wig. Mick said that when they were in America he went to a store with Marc's wife who bought a huge brilliant-pink wig. She asked Mick to wear it back to the hotel where they were staying and when Marc saw it he fell about laughing. Marc recalled how he was nearly electrocuted on two occasions. This was true: in Japan his instrument had no earth wire and when he switched on it lit up like an electric fire; the other incident was in Canada when one of the lighting towers came down on him. Both accidents were nearly fatal. Finally on the tape he said Mick would be in touch with people connected with him.

A week or two after this, a Marc Bolan disco party was held at Newport on the Island. It was an enormous success and fans converged there from throughout Britain. One of Marc's greatest fans from Wales attended the meeting and Mick played her one of my communication tapes he had received. As far as she was concerned it was Marc to a tee and she was completely convinced he was communicating. The fan confirmed one item of evidence I had given Mick concerning a new song that Marc was writing. He did not know about this and had no way of checking but when the fan heard this she screamed with joy. She said that Marc's father told her that, at the time of his son's death, the police brought a little tape recorder round and when they played it they heard a new song Marc was writing. Marc also told Mick he still visits him and accurately described seeing Mick at work in his garage. He watched him when he thought 'I'll put that there then I will know where it is when I need it.' This was true. Marc also said that Mick would be doing something with a studio, which was correct as he was hoping to open one. Maybe some of these things are trivial but gathered together such details can provide a telling, not to say comforting, portrait of a loved one. In my opinion little things mean a lot and, if they bring anyone closer to someone they love and miss, then it is all that matters. Marc always sent his love to his fans and from all accounts was a kind and thoughtful man as well as an extremely talented one. He is still remembered and no doubt will never be forgotten. I often wonder if such people still use their gifts in the other world and if so one might easily envy those who attend such concerts free of charge and purely for the love of it! If one thinks of all the stars that have passed on, this other world must a wonderful place to be if they still practise their talents. It is also good to know that they can communicate with this world and provide us with reminders of the good things in life.

One of the greatest and possibly the best-loved and remembered stars is Judy Garland whose talents, if put to use in the other world, must be of immense pleasure to those who still wish to listen to her singing. I personally was not her greatest fan, although I did enjoy listening to her and watching her films. Many mediums have claimed to have had contact with her since her passing, something which gives the sceptics cause to suggest that it is easy to say one can communicate with someone like Judy who is famous when so much is known about her. I cannot refute what other mediums say but can honestly give account of what happened through my mediumship. This was perhaps because I believe that when we pass over we are all on the same level and therefore there is no reason why anyone of any rank or status could not communicate like any other person. I was instrumental in being able to link Judy to some of my friends and with evidence of details I could not have known about.

My friend Peter Ingold is considered as highly experienced in the psychic field and is convinced that Judy proved her survival at a series of seances. These were held in his home where I would go into a trance and my guide, Running Water, would relay the messages. Peter had only a tenuous link with Judy. The picture editor of *The Times* for whom he worked asked him to send any photos of the singer to a woman in the States who knew one of her daughters, superstar Liza Minelli. The woman often wrote requesting extra copies as Judy would call, take some of the pictures and say, 'Ask your friend Peter for another copy.' It was six years later when I gave Peter a taped message for Christmas which included a message from Judy Garland on which I felt her singing 'There's Gonna Be a Great Day' and giving me the impression that 14 January was going to be a special or significant day. She said, 'Watch out for Lorna and see how much she reminds you of me. She will sing one of my songs and remember "You Made Me Love You". Lorna will follow in my footsteps.'

In January 1974 Peter McAllister, who was working in the *Psychic News* bookshop at the time, told Peter Ingold that Judy's other daughter, Lorna Luft, was to follow in her mother's footsteps and star in a cabaret at London's famed Talk of the Town. He asked him to be a guest at his table when Lorna Luft opened on 14 January, a fact which was unknown when I made the tape. Against all the odds, Peter McAllister had a table at the star-studded premiere. Also against expectation she sang one of her mother's songs and was so like Judy Peter had to pinch himself to convince him he wasn't seeing things. She did not sing 'You Made Me love You' until 1976 when she followed in her mother's footsteps at the London Palladium, thereby fulfilling the predictions.

Three years later I started a series of seances for Peter Ingold and automatist Ann Naughton where sometimes Peter McAllister and the composer Betty Lawrence, whom Judy had met, would attend. Many friends and relatives communicated with them including Judy Garland. They had no idea that Ann knew Judy until the guide mentioned it and relayed a message from Judy to her. He greeted Ann on Judy's behalf and said she was reminding her of a meeting 'round the back somewhere'. This was correct as the pair had met at the back of a house. Judy recalled the garden and all the dogs. Ann explained they were in a neighbour's garden where there were four dogs. Two of them were yapping and running around. Judy asked Ann if she could remember what she was wearing but Ann could not. 'Are you sure?' asked the singer. 'You ought to! It looked like an old sack.' This jogged Ann's memory and she remembered the performer wearing a shapeless two-piece suit. Judy responded with the comment, 'It wasn't the only thing that hung on me like a bag, was it?' Ann diffidently said no but Judy urged her to give an honest reply. 'I looked a mess, didn't I?' Ann agreed this was so and said Judy had been very thin and had large bags under her eyes. Judy thanked Ann for being so kind to her kids, Lorna and Joe. She remembered a to-do by the swimming pool. Ann had invited the youngsters to use her swimming pool, but Judy insisted they went shopping with her. Children being children there was a big fuss.

Judy asked Ann if she could recall her silly shoes. Ann remembered the description Judy had given of a pair of shoes with high platforms and heels but no backs. She said: 'I couldn't walk straight! They were ridiculous things which might have been right for Carmen

Miranda but they certainly didn't do anything for me!' Ann confirmed all the details amidst gales of laughter. They reminisced in a most natural way as any two acquaintances might do when meeting after some years. Peter Ingold said of this that some might consider such references as trivial, but that these details could be very potent proof of the afterlife. He felt with someone as famous as Judy Garland the only details with any degree of credibility must be those only known to herself and the recipients, and trivialities can be crucial, as with a thread in murder trials.

Judy then reminded Peter McAllister of their meeting at her triumphant Talk of the Town opening when she had put her hands on his chest. This was correct as he was invited to the show by Judy's last husband. Backstage he made a very amusing remark at which Judy burst out laughing and put her hands on his chest. Judy sent love to musical director and composer Betty Lawrence and asked her to write a song dedicated to her, citing a composition Betty wrote as a tribute to Edith Piaf after she had passed. Betty responded with a lovely song called 'Remember Me', which Judy said she helped to inspire and that made her cry when Betty played it. At another seance Judy mentioned the comic-book cowboy Hopalong Cassidy, telling the sitters to remember it. Some days later my domestic help suddenly stopped in her tracks and said that same name, Hopalong Cassidy. The good lady said she had no idea what caused her to say it, especially as she had no idea what the words meant. Sadly, I couldn't tell her no one less than Judy Garland had made her say it; however, when I told the people who attended that seance they were quite thrilled to hear my story of how Judy put the words in a complete stranger's mind.

On one occasion Judy said she was accompanied by another star, Carmen Miranda. It delighted Peter Ingold who was a great fan of the latter. They said they had been around earlier and to prove it they described Peter's thoughts and actions in detail while he was shopping a few hours earlier. Judy told him, 'You turned the meat over and could not make up your mind... Worse than any woman! You looked in the frozen section, picked about a bit and changed your mind. You also turned your nose up at the cheese as you went by. Peter said everything was right and he did turn his nose up at the cheese. He had not mentioned these things to anybody before the seance. Carmen Miranda mentioned amusement about toilet rolls and sang a line from one of her songs, 'I yi yi, these toilet rolls cost very much', adding, 'I'm not a screwball, I know what I am talking about.' Peter had bought a packet of toilet rolls despite being shocked at the price. Due to an unusually heavy load he had to hold them out at an unusual angle and was mentally laughing at the ridiculous sight he must have presented to his fellow shoppers. The medium could not have possibly known about this.

Judy would often describe what Ann had been doing before the seances. She also told everyone there, 'You are going to hear about Liza. Oh, my God she exclaimed. But I suppose when I think about it the same thing happened to me.' Soon after her daughter Liza Minelli was taken ill while starring in *The Act* on Broadway. Judy said, 'Not to worry, it wasn't nearly as bad as the press made out. They always made the wrong things big.' Later Liza returned to the show. Judy said she had enjoyed her life and had had fun; it wasn't the tragedy the press tried to make it. 'It's the achievements that count; the failures are not so important as long as you do your best always. You should try to remember all the good things.'

Judy gave advance news about her films which would be shown on TV, which was quite uncanny as every time she mentioned a certain film it would be shown a little while later and the titles were always in the right order. This also happened with a Carmen Miranda film, and sure enough it was on as stated, though not many of these films were shown at this period. Between seances on one occasion Peter and I decided to take a holiday and stay with friends on the Isle of Wight. Before we left, Judy promised to make her presence known. While there we attended a meeting at Ventnor Spiritualist church, medium Ronald Harris told us he had seen a vivid rainbow between us all the evening. He said it must be significant in some way. It was of course one of Judy's most famous hit songs, 'Somewhere over the Rainbow'. We felt that perhaps at last after a stormy career she had found a pot of spiritual gold at the end of her personal rainbow. Judy told us many more things about the stars she had met in this other world, which one could well imagine, and overall she proved to be a superb and intelligent communicator, giving very evidential precognition. No doubt her millions of fans would be thrilled to know she is alive and well and living over the other side of the rainbow!

I have always felt that these seances, although I was in trance at the time, were somewhat special as they brought the afterlife down to earth, so to speak, more so than some of the more mystic and so-called higher teachings relayed by other mediums. I personally cannot see 'heaven' or the world beyond if it exists as anything but a similar place to this world. Here we can have fun and enjoy small talk, and so why not over there?

I was once asked by the *Sun* newspaper if I would record one of my taped experiments for them, the idea being that they would give me numbers representing certain celebrities and I would record messages for each one without having any other details. As one might expect from the press it was all wanted in a hurry and on the day I was meant to do it I had a very bad cold and consequently very little voice. I was persuaded to 'croak' the messages and then to wait for a courier to collect the tape. Later an assistant editor told me the messages were for various show-business personalities including Joe Loss, Vince Hill, Hilda Baker, Cat Stevens, Malcolm Vaughan and Dickie Henderson and on the whole the results were quite good, although some of the celebrities had denied a few things. I told him it was possible that some of the things could have rolled over from one subject to another, but that in any case I had not been at my best at the time. He told me that the chief editor himself had listened to the tape, had declared me to be an honest man and ordered the article to be printed. I was given a whole-page splash with pictures, together with a fair and credible account of my efforts, which made me feel that overall they were pleased with the results. For a week before the article appeared, the *Sun* ran a television advertisement with a blindfolded man resembling me and the caption 'Can this man read your mind?' The *Sun* also published a two-page spread on my ghost hunting stories on the following day and all this did a great deal to boost my confidence as I was the first medium to receive a favourable report in that paper.

Just after the *Sun* publication I received a call from a television company asking me to appear on the programme *Pebble Mill at One*. After reading about me they felt they would like to give me a half-hour spot to talk about my work as a medium, which I gladly accepted. I had to travel to the studios in Birmingham and arrived an hour early. I was met by a producer who was very charming and gave me the news that my spot had been reduced to just ten minutes. I was also expected to talk about ghosts only, which did not please me so I said I was going home and would not appear at all. The producer begged me to stay and apologised for what had happened and said he knew I could handle it and would make it an excellent ten minutes. When I calmed down he said that as there was some time before the programme was due to start, perhaps it would help if I met the interviewer and talk things over? So I sat down with a personable young man, who began by telling me that he did not believe in either ghosts or Spiritualism. My hackles rose somewhat and I told him that it did not matter one bit what he believed as his job was to interview me without bias about what *I* believed. He was somewhat shaken but asked me to tell him a bit about myself, which I did and my story seemed to impress him. He then said that during the programme I would be shown a clip of a man named Canon Pearce Higgins doing an exorcism and he would like to take me to see the clip. He was not supposed to but felt he owed it to me as an apology for his earlier behaviour. I did not feel this was necessary but went along with it to please him.

He had said to me earlier that he would be posing some potentially difficult questions on the programme and I had replied that he would not catch me out as I was known as a master of the smart answer. Then just before the programme started I was told I would be sitting on a couch with one of the other guests, only to be informed just as everything was starting that this very well-known lady would not sit with me as she did not like what I did. Actually I was relieved, as I didn't much care for what she did either or what she stood for. As it happened, my spot went extremely well and those who saw it said I put more into that ten minutes than some do into much, much longer. The interviewer behaved perfectly and was amused when the clip on exorcism was shown and I was asked for a comment. I said that it would all depend on if one was religious or not, as if I were a non-religious ghost I would probably laugh at the silliness of a man all dressed up and swinging incense about, and take no notice. The whole interview went well but did not make the headlines – not that I expected it to. I did learn, however, that in dealing with television and other media-related things, one has to be prepared for anything because for those who work in such fields it is very often just show business.

19

Strange Phenomena

One of the many things I have tried during the course of my psychic career was automatic writing – a venerable branch of psychic mediumship. The idea is that you hold a pen or pencil over a sheet of paper, then concentrate and let your hand be guided where it will. I found myself writing a lot of things but all in my own handwriting and things which were already in my mind. It seemed a laborious way to get messages, at least for someone like me who could get them by more direct means. I felt the same about the Ouija board. I admit I am impatient in some ways but to me it was pure common sense to use the gift I had in a direct and upfront way as possible. I did read one or two books on automatic writing by well-known automatists and found them very interesting, but although the honesty of the writers was never in question it still made me feel that by writing everything down it gave the automatist more time to think about what was happening. Perhaps I am too critical and my previous Intelligence training has always made me dig deeper into any subject in the hopes of finding something which leaves no doubt about its validity.

Only once did I have an experience which made me feel that perhaps I was wrong. I was sitting in my office at the town hall one day many years ago and was enjoying the peace and quiet that pervaded the place while all the other staff were out at lunch. At the time I was concerned as to what to do with my life as I felt it had become somewhat stale. I wanted to leave the job and do something more interesting but could not see a way out. I had the habit of doodling, drawing little pictures and designs on my blotter and any spare bit of paper I could find. My boss used to tell me off about it and said if the big chief saw it I would really be in trouble. Strangely enough, he did see it as he happened to pass my desk one day but all he said was: 'My goodness, that *is* a bobby dazzler. You must have an artistic gift!'

So sitting alone with a sheet of paper in front of me I was wondering how to begin a doodle when the pen started to write and not in my style. It said: 'I know you are worried about your life but if you get your hair cut it will make a big difference.' It was signed 'Joe'. Whether it was his handwriting I did not know but he was a friend of mine who gave me a lot of fatherly advice when he was in this world. Even though I was not completely sure this had not come from my mind, I decided I must do something about it. I usually like to put things to the test and so I went to see Jim who worked in another office and we decided to take the afternoon off. Before we had some fun, I decided to find a barber and see if anything could be done with my hair. It was a good head of hair which I had always worn in the same style and it took a lot of courage to get into the barber's chair and ask for a different one. He took a look and said there is only one different style I could give you and showed me roughly how it would look when he finished. So it happened and I emerged from the shop feeling strangely different and wondering if I had done the right thing. Jim thought it was really good and made me look younger and more 'with it', but I felt the real test would be when I went to the office the next day. I was in for a big surprise as everybody who saw me said how good I looked, even the juniors who all said it was fabulous and made me look very different. Then I knew Joe had been right because I felt different and from then on knew I could and would live my life in the best way possible. That's not to say the new hairstyle itself opened doors but that it did certainly help to boost my confidence and give me the incentive to kick those doors open! This story may seem trivial but is an example of how things can be helped along by strange phenomena that *may* be some odd trick of the mind but which could just as well be the influence of someone in another world.

Strange things have often happened to me and luckily there has always been a witness around to verify the event. The story I like most concerns an organ. I love organ music and at the same time like to see inside churches. I was staying in the little village of Schwangau in Bavaria. One day I decided to go for a walk with a friend across the idyllic meadows full of wild flowers and go to a little church we could just about see in the distance. As we drew closer, suddenly an organ started to play and it was so wonderful to hear I could not wait to get inside the church and be right there in close proximity. My friend was not interested so as we reached this tiny church he decided he would not come in with me. As I went inside I realised the music had suddenly stopped and there appeared to be no one in the place. I searched everywhere, even up in the organ loft, and as there was no back door whoever it was could not have left without my knowledge. I asked my friend, who told me he had seen no one coming out and he agreed to come in and search again with me, all to no avail. There was only one explanation: it must have been a psychic happening. My friend thought it was strange but I knew some greater force must have been at work.

I had several inexplicable happenings to do with organ music and one was witnessed by three other people. We were in Wales and were on a visit to St David's Cathedral in Pembrokeshire. As we approached from a distance we could hear the organ playing and the music continued even when we reached there. The trouble was we could not get into the church as it was all locked up and in total darkness. In desperation we tried to look through the windows but, although it was possible to see in a little, there was no sign of there being anyone inside. As we went to leave, the organ suddenly stopped and, although we waited a while, it did not start again. It seemed as though we had heard the organ playing for us but there was nobody in this world playing it. Something similar happened on several occasions. I was grateful for the experiences but always wished there had been some corroborative evidence which could make me more certain it was all due to some sort of psychic occurrence.

On another occasion I was staying with Jim in a little village called Westendorf in Austria. Our hotel was directly opposite a large church and if one leaned out of the window one could almost touch it. We were often woken up early in the morning as mass was held at six, seven and eight, not to mention hearing the bell clanging rather than ringing. Because of all this we were reluctant to look inside the church. One day we decided to go for a long walk and had not gone far when the thunderclouds appeared and we had to turn back before the heavy rain fell. I was rather glad as, although I had not told Jim, I was not feeling at all well. I had a sort of fever and felt ill and out of sorts. All I wanted to do was to lie down, which I did while Jim sat on a seat by the window of our room reading a book. After some time, just as I thought I might have to find a doctor, I suddenly saw a figure of a nun standing by the door and beckoning to me to follow her. Although he could not see this, Jim realised something was happening and when I told him he said we should follow her. Even before I could drag myself up, he was already halfway out of the room.

We followed her along the corridor of the hotel, across the road and into the church. At the door she disappeared and all we could see was the interior of this beautifully ornate church. What was more important was the feeling of utter peace and quiet within those walls. Jim asked what we were supposed to do, but I had no idea until I felt I must follow a route which led up to the altar and then around to a left-hand aisle that ran alongside a wall. Suddenly I stopped in my tracks and found myself facing a painting of the very nun who had led us there. Apparently she was known as St Theresa of the Flowers amongst other names, though that was only what we found out later. Jim, once again, asked what we were supposed to do next but all I could feel was that we had to leave. As we went out through the main door the sun was shining and I suddenly realised I felt completely better and we were able to go for a very long walk. It was a strange but wonderful experience and must have been a form of healing. I did acquire a picture of the nun some time later though that did not seem to have any powers.

Psychometry is something that is often misused. Most people feel it is about holding an object which enables them to make contact with the other world and give messages accordingly. The true art of psychometry is to hold an object and in effect to tell its history, which in itself can prove to be a very interesting and remarkable thing. It is one of several psychic things that I have been able to do successfully, though it is not of any great use except perhaps to give one some idea of past connection. It is especially useful, I have found, in uncovering missing links in the past which can be used to solve present mysteries. I would have loved to be able to work more in this area, but no one seemed to be much interested.

A good example of what I call real psychometry occurred when I was visiting some friends in Southsea. One of them asked me to close my eyes and hold out my hand. She then placed something in it and closed my fingers around it so that, if I opened my eyes, I could not see what I was holding. She then asked me to say what I felt about the item. Almost immediately I felt hot and could see in my mind's eye huge stretches of sand, as though I was in a desert. Then I got the feeling of ancient Egypt as I could see pyramids but nothing else. When I could get no more I was allowed to open my eyes and see what I was holding. It looked like an ordinary piece of stone one might pick up almost anywhere, but apparently it was a piece broken off a pyramid. It was encouraging and made me enthusiastic to try more things, which I did and always with success. Despite the efforts of a producer–writer friend to get TV people interested in doing a programme in which I would try to fill in some of the missing links in history, his idea was not taken up as nobody seemed especially interested. Not being one to get upset, I was not too worried as there are always many other avenues to explore.

As I wrote much earlier, on a number of occasions in my career I had the honour of working with the famous psychic artist Coral Polge, whose unusual method involved drawing portraits of people who had passed on while another medium working in tandem gave messages that would help to identify them. Mostly it seemed that as Coral drew, the medium tended to give messages that were very little to do with the person she was drawing but nevertheless they got identified because Coral herself was able to give some pieces of evidence as well. Whenever I worked with her I did not tell her what I would be doing but I decided that, as well as concentrating on what she was doing, I would try in some way to get control of the situation so that there would be no one but the subject of her picture sending messages. It usually worked wonderfully well and we produced some excellent results. She would usually do six or eight drawings in one evening and I cannot remember any occasion when the drawings were not recognised along with all the evidential details I was able to supply. Sometimes a recipient would have to take their picture home to check with their family and find photos to compare but they were always able to identify the connection. To say the least, the drawings were mostly a perfect likeness and all were eventually identified.

One of the best collaborations between Coral and me took place at Richmond Spiritualist church, where the results were quite amazing as every picture she drew was immediately recognised and extremely accurate, backed up by the messages I was able to give as each portrait was drawn. The high spot was when, as Coral drew a very elderly lady, the subject of the portrait sang an old song to me, with the apt title 'Ain't It Grand to Be Blooming Well Dead?' It captured the mood of the whole demonstration. Coral did not see clairvoyantly but worked by feelings and impressions which she then transferred onto large sheets of paper in full view of the audience. Coral remarked of the lady she was drawing that she enjoyed being the centre of attraction because she was old and when I quickly picked out the old lady's grandson from the audience he agreed that was true. I told him the lady's name was Eliza and that she was saying his mother had a saying for everything to which he agreed, and when his grandmother asked him if there was anything wrong with his back, and he said yes, she said that what he needed was the good old-fashioned remedies. I felt she hated interference, just like her grandson, and she said about her funeral, 'Well, what a to-do!' The young man squirmed and said, 'Yes, one of my aunts got drunk.' His grandmother then said, 'You thought I wasn't there I suppose; I had my beady eyes on you.' Then two names were called which were the grandmother's daughter and her sister. The young man said to me, 'My mother won't believe this, you know,' to which his grandmother replied, 'She will ruddy well have to lump it!' She was none too complimentary about her grandson's use of teabags, demanding to know what was wrong with the old-fashioned method of making tea. This delightfully blunt old lady must have thought she was the star of the evening as everything I relayed, and the picture that Coral drew, left no doubt in anyone's mind that she had survived and was enjoying her new life in her own inimitable way.

All the other pictures that evening showed the sitters looking younger than they were when they passed. It seemed that a lady named Nell introduced herself as someone outrageous who did not care what she did. She showed herself to me while lifting her skirts and dancing around and she had a wonderful sense of humour as well as a gap in the middle of her teeth. The recipient of the message admitted this was true and was able to recognise the portrait Coral had drawn. Next a grandfather, whose name was Charlie and who, indeed, *was* a right Charlie, was soon claimed and the recipient of the message confirmed all the things he said were correct. He understood his grandfather when he wondered whether it was right for him to be there that evening because he was not smartly dressed and was someone who said what he thought without meaning to be offensive. I felt him saying to me 'Go on, say it – I'm common.' His grandson admitted he didn't know his grandfather very well but could accept him as having country links. He also agreed when grandfather said he used to fiddle about with wood and thought this was very evidential. The last message said, 'Don't fiddle about but get on with it!' and, when the recipient wondered which of his many enterprises was meant, the reply was 'All of them!' The evening held one note of sadness which came from a communicator named Caroline. Coral felt that people would have said that she was far too good for this world. There was a sadness about Caroline as she gave her an almost resigned feeling and it was as though she was lost in a grey fog. The young girl was accepted by a woman in the audience who knew she had been in a mental hospital but did not know if she had passed on. I felt she had played the piano and saw marigolds and ballet shoes, which were accepted as being evidential. I then saw Caroline holding a little watering can with a broken spout, which the recipient said referred to her liking for gardening and she did indeed have a little watering can with a broken spout. I concluded that all this was showing that Caroline was very much alive and well – she had shown herself in this morose state because it enabled her to be speedily recognised. I can say that this whole demonstration was a great success as all of the portraits were recognised, though one or two needed extra confirmation, which was eventually found and the messages fitted the people portrayed.

Sadly Coral is now in that other world herself but she left behind something of immense value in which I am grateful to have played a small part. I have never felt that sharing a gift is a bad thing as it often produces superior results. There is an old saying that two heads are better than one, and if those two heads are in harmony the results can be amazing!

A good example of cooperation between two mediums whose gifts complemented had occurred many years earlier. I had fallen out with Nora Blackwood (you may remember this medium played a formative role in my early career) over some trifling affair that I will not mention as it was soon forgotten. I eventually found myself booked to give an address at a church where Nora would be demonstrating clairvoyance on the same platform. I felt somewhat uncertain but decided it was time we forgot our differences and hoped she might feel the same. When we met there was an air of uncertainty but I greeted her and said I hoped we could forget the past and work well together. She was tremendously relieved and said she had hoped we could get together and work as a team and I heartily agreed. She was a brilliant clairvoyant and I had become known as an excellent speaker, and before we went onto the platform in the packed church Nora said, 'Come on, Ron, let's sock it to them!' It was a fantastic evening and the atmosphere was electrifying and we both delivered something that will, I am sure, not be easily forgotten. Although we never met again after that night, and Nora has since passed on, our collaboration left a powerful and positive feeling within me.

To end this chapter on 'strange phenomena', I am afraid I must sound a darker note. Probably during my life I have undergone and endured a lot of things which could be considered 'evil'. I do not like to use that word and think that 'misguided' might be better. My worst experience, perhaps, was of black magic, in which many do not believe but in which I certainly do since I have had to suffer at least two nasty experiences.

The first of these occurred when for some time I had been feeling unwell and sensed someone or something was getting at me. I had a depression and everything seemed very dark. After staying the weekend at Peter's home on one occasion, I returned home early on the Monday morning intending to deal with some correspondence. As I entered the room and sat down at my writing desk, it seemed as though there was a heavy mist in the room, not to mention a very eerie feeling. Suddenly I felt a hand was gripping my shoulder and trying to force me out of my chair. It was frightening to say the least, so I did no more than pack my bag and return to Peter's. We could not figure out what it was all about except that someone must be wishing me harm. We concentrated thoughts for whoever or whatever it was to stop, but although things calmed down a little the problem was still there. Strangely enough, a few days later I had a letter from a lady in the States to say she had caught her husband practising black magic on me by tying knots in some string from a package I had sent and doing some weird chant. She said she did not know how to stop him but I assured her that I did and she was to tell me if and when anything happened to make him stop. I then used an exercise someone had told me about where one sits quietly and alone in a room and follows a certain procedure which entailed concentrating on self-protection and returning all wrong and evil thoughts to the sender and, while wishing them no harm, made them responsible for whatever was happening. In this case, I could name the person. Some while later I heard from his wife that he had fallen off a ladder but had not been not badly injured and that several other things had occurred which made him say to his wife that he realised that I was on to him and he was paying for what he had done and would stop immediately. It was a case of jealousy really, though I could not see why. We are not always aware of what goes on in a person's mind but happenings like these can be very dangerous.

The second experience was similar in a way and again a case of jealousy. I had spent many enjoyable short breaks with a friend in her home. Then one day I met one of her cousins, who, I realised after some time, was jealous of me because he thought she and I were lovers. He wanted to marry the lady but she did not feel the same, although she was very fond of him. After some time I began to feel extremely unwell with fierce headaches and all sorts of bodily pains, plus a really bad depression. It was like everything I tried to do was blocked off and I knew someone was sending out wrong or negative thoughts. When I told my friend what was happening she wrote back to me and said her cousin had told her he was practising black magic on me as she discovered him holding a letter I had sent her and chanting some strange words. So I put the same exercise into action as before and a while later it all stopped. The cousin said he was aware I was working on him and that he could not win. Some time later he developed cancer and passed on.

Before he went he asked my friend to tell me he was sorry and told her that he believed his illness was his own fault and that he deserved it. I do not personally share that belief and think that his latent cancer was more likely the *cause* of his actions rather than their result. Nonetheless there is no doubt that he resorted to black magic and caused me to suffer, and that was a terrible thing to do. There have been other lesser demonstrations of this evil art, as it is called, but luckily I have always been able to counteract it.

20

Moving On

For the first forty years or so of my life I lived at home with my parents, brother and sister. During that time my brother left home and got married, then sadly my mother passed on, so that for the last ten years my sister and I were left with Father, which was a very difficult time. He was lost without Mother and his normally difficult nature was not easy for us to bear. He could not understand that we were all lost without Mother, who had been the mainstay of the family despite the fact that for the last six years of her life she had suffered a stroke which left her unable to do anything. Our home was more like a hospital in a way and we lived with the daily problem of keeping her going. There was not one of us who would not have done anything we could to help her, but Father took over and I have to admit he was wonderful in caring for her day and night. He would often take her out in a bath chair and wheel her for miles so she could enjoy the outdoors and sometimes get to see people she knew. She had always been very popular in the district and, as I said earlier, was always known as 'the lady with the white hair'.

I did receive some wonderful evidential messages of her survival and one in particular about her white hair. I had been giving a demonstration of my work in a Spiritualist church and the chair for the meeting was taken by a lady I had never seen or heard of before. After it was over this lady told me that although she was not very clairvoyant, all the evening she had seen a lady standing with me who had the most beautiful white hair. What was more she was wearing a white coat such as doctors use and she was cradling a tiny white poodle in her arms. It is hard to explain how I felt at that moment but tears were welling up in my eyes because it meant so much to me to hear this. During her last illness she had begged us to let her have a little white poodle, but, as she was bedridden and we lived in a flat, it was not something we could do, although she never gave up on asking. Her wearing the white coat was also very good as often Father would tell her that she cared more for animals than humans, to which she would reply by saying that she would love to work in kennels looking after animals. It was a wonderful piece of evidence that I very much needed at the time, and to know she had found something that would make her so happy was indeed a great comfort to me. Nobody else knew about all this except her immediate family, which helped to reassure us all that this happening was Mother's way of finally achieving something she was unable to do while on earth.

Mother had already given evidence some time after her funeral when she showed a medium a particular red rose of the kind she loved and who said she saw it laying right in the middle of a cross as though it had been carefully placed there. I had thrown one rose of the kind she loved into her grave and it landed exactly in the middle of a cross which was etched on the coffin and did look as though it had been carefully placed. She also gave evidence of the fact that I had thought some of the lettering on her gravestone had fallen out, until I realised a bird had dropped something which obliterated one of the letters and cleaned it off by using one finger of my gloved hand. All this came eleven months or so after she had passed, which tended to show she was perhaps waiting until she could do the job well.

I loved my mother dearly as she had always been my friend. She never really understood my psychic work but was very proud of me and thought I knew what I was doing in everything I undertook. In some ways, despite the fact that she loved Father, she was afraid to be left completely alone with him and consequently made me promise never to leave her, which I never did. I felt that this was not only my duty as a son but as a caring person, knowing that she would not survive so very long anyway. I did miss out on a few years where I could have done other things for her and I did miss good opportunities, but I have no regret as I can only measure love and devotion as something I can afford to give.

Mother's passing was to change my life not only because it freed me of any dutiful obligation, but also because she had made me promise to leave Father when anything happened to her. Something which was easier said than done as I was close to my sister Winnie and I felt I could not leave her. She did not want me to leave her there alone. She was not married or likely to be as far as I could see, so I tried to find a flat or some other accommodation which we could share. It was at a time when housing was almost impossible to find but I did try very hard, while inwardly knowing that sharing would not work even if we could find somewhere. It was getting to the end of the 'ten years with Father' when I realised I must be on my own; it would be better for Winnie, too, though she did not like it when I told her. However, things turned out well in the end as I had a word with Father and by then he was happy about my going; in fact he had found himself a new lady friend and I felt he did not want me in the way.

I had already helped my friend Peter, who was living in Wandsworth, to find a house and this had proved to have an interesting psychic connection. We had tramped around looking for a place, first on the Isle of Wight and then keeping it to the Wandsworth area, close to the common. After searching around one morning I strongly felt he would find a place in something to do with Seagrave, which we felt must be the name of a road somewhere. Scouring a map of the surrounding areas, we found the only road of that name to be in Fulham, a place Peter did not want to go to. So we continued the search after dismissing the name of Seagrave. As it neared lunchtime, we began to despair until suddenly we turned into a road where there was quite a pleasant-looking house for sale. Peter stopped to look at it but I continued to the end of the road, turned left into what seemed to be more like a main road and suddenly spotted another 'for sale' sign. Feeling this was perhaps what he as looking for I called him over to look. Immediately he was very taken with it from the outside and I liked it too. He knocked at the door and asked the lady of the house if it would be possible to view it without an appointment. She said she was sorry but she had to take her children to school but if he could come back a little later she would be delighted to show him round. We went to Peter's home where his mother had prepared a meal for us and he could scarcely contain his excitement as he was sure it was the house for him. So we returned at the appointed time and were shown around: the moment we stepped over the threshold we knew it was right and had all he could wish for. It was only when we went back to tell his mother that it dawned on me that there was a cemetery right opposite the house where one could 'see graves', and so we had been led to the right spot after all.

About three months later, and after I had started to look for a flat for myself, Peter's mother, who was a very kind lady, told me about one she had seen advertised in an evening paper and thought it might suit me. It was now the Friday evening and I felt the flat would have gone before I could get there and anyway I had an appointment which I could not cancel. Nevertheless I decided I would ring first thing Monday morning, even though I was sure it would be gone, and to be honest at that time Clapham was the last place I wanted to live anyway. On the Saturday evening we held one of our seances at Jim's home and during this time Peter said he could see my mother and she was sitting with a shotgun on her lap in front of a building. He felt she was guarding the flat for me and I would get it. This did not surprise me in a way as, although Mother had never met Peter, I knew he was the sort of person she would like. She had communicated through him before and gave some wonderful evidence of her being around. On one occasion when I was feeling rather depressed she showed Peter a picture of a lemon which appeared to be crying. This referred to an incident when I was young when Mother and I had been on a bus and had seen an advert for fruit squash, featuring a lemon crying and the caption 'Who made the lemon squash? Idris of course.' It made us both laugh but afterwards whenever I was unhappy Mother would screw up her face and say 'Who made the lemon squash?', which immediately cheered me up. Another time when I was feeling very angry about something and threatening to do all sorts of things there was something she always used to say which Peter heard and pictured very clearly. First he saw a big red handkerchief in which something was tied. This was then hooked on to a walking stick and offered to me. This was exactly right as Mother would say to me at such moments 'Are you going to leave home then?' and when I said I would, she said 'Wait a minute, I will make you some sandwiches and wrap them in a red handkerchief and tie it to a walking stick. You can sling it over your shoulder and off you go!' These were wonderful memories of a mother who cared and knew I would not run away. She would only entrust these stories to Peter, knowing we had been meant to meet and would have a long-lasting friendship.

When I rang the estate agent and asked if the flat was still available his reply was in the affirmative. I asked him why it had been so slow in selling and he said he couldn't understand it because so many people had been to view it over the weekend but it did not seem to suit anyone. He thought it was too small for two people perhaps but it was ideal for one. Later in the day Peter came with me to see the flat, which was surprisingly pleasant and in a private road which was a landmark in Clapham Common. It was called Crescent Grove and had Edwardian houses and a beautifully kept green in the centre, not to mention the Common itself, which was just over the road and created a very pleasant atmosphere. Apparently the flats had been built on the site of some beautiful ornamental gardens and had originally been meant for single women, which maybe explained why Mother had been guarding one for me, as she had been a Suffragette. It comprised two large rooms, a kitchen and a bathroom and was adequate for me and my work. Also it was quite close to Peter's home where I spent a lot of my leisure time. Suddenly Clapham did not seem such a bad prospect after all, although it had a very different atmosphere to my first home.

Once I moved in and settled down I felt quite at home, especially as I now had a place to work in and where I could relax and do what I liked. Also it was good to be reasonably close to Peter's home as it was where I would spend a lot of time with many happy memories. My sister was left with Father for a time but when my brother Bill and his wife moved to Braintree in Essex it gave her some new interest as we would often go to visit them. Sadly Bill's wife passed not long after and he was very much on his own and eventually asked Father to go and live down there. Surprisingly he agreed and, although Winnie was left on her own, it was a relief as Father was still not the easiest person to live with. It was not long before Father decided he would return to London. It seemed that he and Bill could not get along together so Winnie had another spell of Father, though fortunately this time things seemed to go better. By then Father had formed a very close relationship with a lady who lived locally and that was indeed a great help, but Winnie still needed to get away and live her own life.

That, however, was not meant to happen until after Father passed. I was in Sweden at the time doing my psychic work when Winnie phoned to tell me that Father was in hospital with bronchial trouble but he did not want me to come back, although he knew it was serious. A few days later she phoned again to say that Father had passed and she and Bill would arrange the funeral for when I got back. This happened the day after I returned. The floral tribute Bill had ordered on my behalf was very poor and not what I would have chosen. However, all went well and I did not suppose that Father would care about it that much.

About two years before Father passed I went to visit him at his home one day when I was surprised to find him listening to the morning service on the radio. I asked him why he was doing this as he had never been religious and disliked the church anyway. His reply was that 'When you get older you turn to the comfort it brings, and I always listen to it now as I feel it brings Mother close.' I sat down and we talked like we had never talked before. A lot of things got sorted out and we became much closer, which had never happened before. He had such a lot of good points and I can honestly say that, despite his being out of work when we children were young, we were always fed and clothed. If he ever had any spare money he would take us to the cinema or the music hall or some other little treat. The only trouble was that everything had to be done as he wanted and he had a bad temper which did not help. On the other hand, he had quite a sense of humour and often recited little ditties, which always raised a few smiles. Strangely I must inherit this trait from him as I do the same, except that I usually write them down. Father did not drink much and we always felt lucky that he was not a man who 'boozed' his money away. He was also a gardener to some degree. We only had a very small garden but he made it look good. He had acquired a job in the local parks which was where he learned the art and from where he obtained some lovely plants.

A few days after the funeral I was walking down the road with Peter in the neighbourhood where he lived and at the bottom of the road was a barrow with a lot of flowering plants. I suddenly felt I must buy some to make up for the miserable floral tribute Bill had ordered for me, but the question was: where would I plant them? I went back to Peter and asked him if he would mind if I planted them in his garden. He was pleased as he had a large garden and it needed something done with it; he also knew my father, who was known as Fred to everyone. Fred liked Peter and they often laughed together. So we returned to his home and I planted everything, which seemed as if it was all being directed. There were carnations and pinks, petunias, lavateras and delphiniums, along with some other colourful plants. When I had finished I looked at the array and said out loud, 'Well, Fred, you knew it all, so see what you can do with that lot!' If one ever said to Fred that he couldn't do it, he would say he most certainly could. That's another thing I have inherited from him, as if anyone tells me I can't do anything, I always say, 'Oh yes I can!' Just like Fred!

A few days later Peter and I were going away for a break and, before we left, we went out to look at the garden and in particular what I had planted for Fred. We were appalled to find all the plants had drooped and looked as if they were dead or dying. I felt so mad and said, 'Well, Fred, if *that*'s the best you can do with that, then I don't think much of it.' I can't say I heard Fred reply 'I'll show you!' but when we returned and looked at the garden again I can well imagine he had. It was a magical sight as all the plants during our ten days' absence had found new life and were not only very much alive but had grown to great proportions and were a sight to behold. The petunias were fantastic and already full of flowers. Eventually they grew so tall and had as many as a hundred and fifty blooms on one plant. Luckily Peter witnessed all this as otherwise no one would believe it. The delphiniums had grown very tall and one in particular later reached eight feet high, not to mention the flowers which were enormous and of an unusually deep colour. Just about everything had grown unusually big and made a most amazing show. There were two exceptions as the carnations and pinks were only about average though quite pleasant. I mentally said to Fred 'Well, you couldn't do it all!' but I somehow felt he would not be beaten. It was not until the next year that the carnations and the pinks flourished a mass of blooms, with so many flowers on each plant it was almost impossible to count them. We also noticed that even some of the other plants, those we had not put in for him, were doing strangely well. It happened for many years after that something unusual would happen in the garden and it was good to feel Fred was around. It was especially good for me to have happy memories and reminders from him.

After Fred had gone there was the problem of finding Winnie somewhere to live, as our original home was owned by the local council and was now needed for a family. They offered her other places, and I was able to help and guide her as some of the homes they offered were not right for a woman on her own. Eventually she opted for a flat in Wembley which was truly right for her. Peter and I helped her to move and I was worried that she might not like being on her own as she was inclined to be very nervous about such things. Right from the start she was happy and said it was as though she had always lived there. This was a worry off my mind and I often visited her there and helped in any way I could. We were always close and remained so. She was fond of Peter and often spent weekends in his home where she too liked gardening and was a great help in making his garden what it now is – a beautiful and peaceful place.

Brother Bill was the next to pass on and it was a sad occasion when he departed. He had been troubled by illness for some time and felt very much alone since his wife passed. We kept in touch with him and went down to Braintree as often as we could, and we also telephoned regularly, but he just seemed to let go and he was found in bed having had a massive heart attack. I was very fond of my brother but he was always difficult to get close to. It may have been the age difference as there were seven years between us, but I know he was fond of me in his own way. He was a very good-looking man and extremely talented where his work as a chromium plater was concerned. He was quite popular and had a good sense of humour, although I doubt if he found his life very funny. He tended to be very moody and difficult at times, but he, like Winnie, always looked up to me and trusted me. I found it amusing in a way that I was the youngest but the one who was the leader and was able to advise and help. That seems to have been my role in life, as much as I sometimes feel I would like the position to be reversed!

My half-sister Marjorie, about whom I have not said much, also passed on and in many ways I felt sad that things for her had not been as she had hoped, but unfortunately there was not much I could have done. Although I did have contact with her at times, there was not the closeness I would have liked. Although I knew Marjorie had been born out of wedlock and was adopted by my father's parents, I never actually knew she was my half-sister until I was twenty-one. For some strange reason, although she was known before she married as Marjorie Yeo, it had never occurred to me or my brother and sister that she was in fact related to us. In those days when Mother gave birth to her, it was considered to be very wrong and had to be hushed up as people were less tolerant than they are in the present day. I always felt sorry for Mother, as it seemed to me that she had been very unlucky, but I also felt sorry for Marjorie. There was nothing I could do and as in many families the whole thing seemed to engender a lot of wrong feeling. Marjorie was a very kind lady and in many ways I could see a lot of Mother in her. She had a good sense of humour but was outspoken, especially when she felt left out of things. Our paths did not cross very often but I can honestly say that I cared about Marjorie and loved her as a sister, even though circumstances created a somewhat difficult situation. Marjorie married Don Hamlet, who was a chef, as was Marjorie herself, so it seems like good cooking ran in the family! She had the same generosity with food as Mother did and one always left the Hamlet home more than just well fed. It was a happy marriage for them and they had two children, Joan and Paul, who both married and have children of their own. I have rarely seen my niece and nephew but, even if things had been any different with Marjorie, I doubt it would have made much difference to that. My abiding memory of Marjorie is a very happy one as to me she was a warm, caring lady and one who maybe deserved better than she got.

Winnie was the last to pass with a stroke. I always felt I would go first but it was not to be as I believe I still have something to fulfil. It was a blow when this happened as I had done so much to help her and there was hardly ever a time when we did not see each other. She was so much like her mother in looks and ways but latterly seemed to be more like Father. She never married, although she could have done, but fortunately she seemed happy to be independent. She was very popular and had that gift of speaking to strangers and becoming quite friendly with them. She was very talented with knitting and needlework and a good cook. She was very hospitable with a great sense of humour, although rather inclined to worry too much and be uncertain about the future. Considering her circumstances she made a little go a long way and kept a very comfortable home in which she made everyone welcome. It was a sad loss when she went, not only for me but for many people, but being the last of my close family, it left me feeling very much alone and knowing that this would change my life yet again.

I was now free of all responsibility and obligation and could do exactly as I liked, at least where family was concerned. I do have some cousins, as well as a nephew and niece, but as I hardly ever see or have contact with them I am in effect on my own. Of course I have a few good friends but it is not really the same as having a family. My family life was not all I would have liked, of course, but we can choose our friends but not our family, and when I look back over my life this far, although it has been a struggle with illness and trying to find my real way in life, I have few regrets. For a long time I have seen life as a great challenge where if we are wise and able we should always keep trying. There have been times when I have been prepared to give up but then I remember the words of an old song 'Pick yourself up, dust yourself down and start all over again.' Simple but good advice.

I have had many happy experiences both in my career as a psychic and in my 'everyday' life and no doubt in some way they all balance out. My greatest pleasure has always been in giving (although, of course, it is nice to receive sometimes!). My mother was exactly the same as she would often give things she could not afford in order to help others. There is still a part of me that wants to contribute something worthwhile to mankind and I hope that I already have done so to some degree or other. And even though I am entitled to rest and take it easy at my age, I doubt if I will ever be able to sit and do nothing. I have so many ideas racing around in my brain but it is hard to make people listen. Perhaps it is because people feel I am too old or because we seem to be living in a more selfish age where everyone is out for themselves. Whatever the answer, I will go on trying to get through to as many people as possible.

Something happened to me recently which has given me more impetus and possibly more hope for the future. It has every connection with the psychic and tells a fascinating story. It has helped me to discover more about myself and in some ways to change my mind about a number of things, but most of all I now know who I really am and it has made me even prouder to be an Englishman. I am proud to be *British* but England is and always will be my home, one of the most beautiful places in the world. Wherever I have been – and I have seen many beautiful places – it all comes down to the fact 'there is no place like home' and home, of course, is where the heart is.

21

A Yeoman of England

After my family had all passed on I felt very lonely and alone for quite some time, and perhaps even now I do to some extent. I wish I could have shared with them what I discovered, although if they are in this other world and still watching on I am sure they must know about it; in fact they probably know even more than I do! When in this world Mother sometimes talked about her father, she often remarked how like him I was, not only in looks but also in personality. He had passed before I was born, as did his wife, my grandmother, and even on Father's side of the family his father died young. I only knew father's mother and I felt it was so unfair in a way because I would have so much liked to have known the others. It was the same with my father as with Mother insofar as when I asked questions about them I could not understand why they never told me much at all.

There was so much I didn't know about my parents and forebears that eventually I decided I would like to try to find out more by tracing my family tree. Today there is the possibility of tracing one's family history on the Internet, or with a 'do it yourself kit', but both those ways, I realised, would take a long time, especially for someone like me who's not that good with computers. The only answer, then, was to find someone who could do it for me. I was talking with some friends one day about family trees when one of them said she knew a lady genealogist named Beryl Padgham who was highly qualified, undertook some part-time work and who she was sure would help me. At that time someone had just sent me a generous gift which was to be spent on something important and worthwhile, so I made up my mind to start the search. I contacted the good lady and asked her if she could help me and received a pleasant reply in the affirmative. She asked me to send any certificates of births, deaths and marriages that I had, and any useful information to help her get started. I had such a good feeling about her and knew she would come up with something worthwhile. I bless the day I found her, as it not only cleared up a longstanding family mystery but led to something so extraordinary that, if it wasn't for the fact it was there in black and white, nobody would believe it.

First I asked my genealogist if she could concentrate on my mother's family line as I did not remember anyone beyond Mother and was particularly anxious to know about my grandfather, Henry Yeo, whom as you may remember had been a schoolteacher in Devon and later became a subeditor on the *Manchester Guardian*. I thought it might be good, too, to know about my grandmother, Mary Yeo, who was only thirty-three when she passed on. I have a picture of her and could also see a likeness to me when I was in my late teens. I always felt maybe she was somebody quite special. In fact, I felt her whole line might be, perhaps because her maiden name was Buckingham, Actually when Beryl traced Mary's line it proved really quite ordinary, and in the end we thought it best to concentrate on the Yeos.

The surname Yeo is very popular in Devon and Cornwall and there are many different lines but Beryl managed to find the right one without too much difficulty. At one time records were not kept as well as they are now and one has to rely on Census findings which are quite often vague or even inaccurate. Henry Yeo was described as a journalist, a newspaper manager, and one or two other odd descriptions, but it left no doubt that he had been connected with newspapers and journalism. Incidentally Mary was described as a journalist, too, but there had never been any mention of this as far as I remember. There was no evidence of Henry having been a schoolteacher, though I do have two photos of him outside a school in Landkey in Devon. He is standing with what must have been the other teachers, though he is very young. It could have been that he did teach but not for very long, although Mother had always stressed the fact he was a teacher and, when I wanted to become one, she felt I had inherited his ability to teach. Perhaps it is more the ability to write that I have inherited from him, but, however as that may be, I have always felt drawn to this man whom I never knew.

There were one or two things which had always seemed rather mysterious to me that Beryl was more or less able to clear up.

The first of these concerned Mary Yeo and why she had seemingly been buried under her maiden name in that little churchyard in Landkey. What Beryl actually discovered was that she was never buried in Landkey at all but was actually buried in the North near to where she and Henry had lived. I even found a photo amongst my collection of a gravestone covered with flowers and with the inscription 'Mary, beloved wife of Henry Yeo.' What is more, I now have a copy of her death certificate, which is the definitive proof that she was not buried in Landkey, even though in the parish records there is the entry: 'I baptised Mary Yeo, I married her and I buried her.' So a certain mystery remains.

The other thing I found very strange was that Mother had said her father had married again (that matron from St Thomas') and had one son. Beryl, however, could find no marriage certificate and could find nothing about a son. Some time later she wrote to me and said she had discovered something that might shock me. On Henry Yeo's death certificate, it states that he died from a serious heart condition in an asylum. This did make me feel something was wrong as I could not believe that such an intelligent and clever man, for that he certainly was, would have gone mad. Apparently in those days it was not unusual for asylums to be used for ordinary patients as well, which must have been the case in this instance, but the certificate also says he was put there by Edith Lawson, the lady he was supposed to have married. It still left a mystery as to why Mother thought her father had actually married again but this was something that, in the end, I did not think was worth taking any further.

The story I liked most about my grandfather was one that in a way linked with my current career as a psychic and one-time ghost hunter. From all accounts Henry was a very brave and fearless man who was prepared to accept a challenge. One night he was drinking with some pals when the subject of ghosts came up and they bet him that he would not walk from one end of Manchester cemetery to the other at midnight. He accepted the challenge and at the appointed time strode fearlessly through this huge cemetery carrying his cane with a silver knob. When he reached the exit gate he was – surprise, surprise – confronted by a group of his pals who had covered themselves in white sheets. They jumped out from behind some gravestones making all sorts of noises that they supposed ghosts would make, but it did not scare Henry, who lifted his cane and banged one of them on the head. Fortunately the man was only a little bruised but obviously wished he had not taken part in this escapade which had only been meant as a joke. I'm sure Henry saw the funny side of it all but clearly he was not going to take any chances.

I can recognise something of Henry's overhasty doughtiness in my own character. Once I was woken from a deep sleep. The bedroom seemed to be full of light and as I turned in my bed I saw a huge man standing before me. He was possibly Persian, as he had long hair and was wearing a turban. I jumped out of bed and attempted to punch him, only to find my fist went right through him. At that moment I also observed he was naked to just below the waist, although the rest of him was missing. Then suddenly it was as though he melted through the floor. I sat on my bed and felt angry with myself in having reacted that way but of course he had taken me by surprise. I sent out thoughts asking him to come again as I thought he might have had something to say, and when a light began to shine in one corner of the room I thought it would happen but nothing more occurred.

I think Henry must have had a romantic side to his nature although from his photos he tends to look quite serious. Mother once told me that every morning on his way to work he always bought a buttonhole from a flower seller outside Manchester station. Mostly it would be violets, which he liked and would set off his smart appearance, as he was very particular about that. He was also the sort of person who would always arrive far too early if he had to catch a train or had any kind of appointment. He often said apparently, 'It is far better to be too early than even one minute too late.' This is again something I have inherited on all accounts, as I am very particular about dress and appearance, and am a stickler for punctuality. The only thing I do not do is to wear buttonholes unless it is absolutely necessary as, for example, at weddings and certain social functions. Even then I tend to discard it as soon as I can. All in all I began to feel that perhaps I did know Henry as when I learned about him it was often as though I was looking in a mirror. I am especially glad to have inherited two things in particular from him: teaching and writing. The latter, especially, is something I really love to do and often I mentally send out thoughts to Henry to ask him to help and inspire me. If it is in the greater plan I hope to write a lot more and make him proud of me, not only because he is my grandfather but because we both come from a very interesting line of people.

After she had found all she could on Henry Yeo, Beryl asked me if I would like to continue following the Yeo line and I readily agreed, being hungry to learn as much as I could about some of my forebears. Mother had told me that her father came from farming people and that *his* father, William Yeo, was what was then described as a 'gentleman farmer'. She could not give me a lot of information about him but did remember him as being very proud and every inch a gentleman. A photo I have seems to corroborate this. He was apparently very kind to animals and used to drive a pony and trap. If he was carrying passengers, each time he reached a hill he would ask them to get out and walk up it as it would be too hard on the pony. He was a popular man and greatly respected in the community, but more than this mother could not tell me. I liked what I felt from his photo and the little Mother could tell me.

William was born in West Buckland, not far from Swimbridge, which is perhaps the most significant location of my family connections. Mother often talked of Swimbridge and I did visit there on one occasion to try to locate graves of my family but everything was overgrown so I could not see anything. Beryl went to the record office in Barnstaple and was able to uncover some useful information, but the farther back one goes the harder it usually becomes, as old records are often not reliable or accurate as to the exact occupation and situation of the individual. For instance, the words 'gentleman farmer' were not always used and there are instances of my forebears being described as 'farm labourers', which in one sense is true but incorrect in another.

After William the line goes back to James Yeo who was born and lived in Swimbridge, and again to another William who was born in West Buckland. The latter would be my great, great, great-grandfather and all followed the same occupation of gentleman farmer. The last William Yeo Beryl was able to trace married a lady called Ann Courtier in 1776, but at that point Beryl told me that she could not take the line back any further. Before that time records did not exist and the only way to find out anything more would be to travel around to churches and any places that might yield further information. This would be very expensive and time-consuming and she was sure I could not afford to do this. Naturally I was disappointed but agreed it would not be possible.

Very shortly after this, however, I had an extraordinary stroke of luck. A friend who was interested in what I was doing wrote to tell me she knew of a lady in Australia who had traced her husband's family tree much farther back than mine. It so happened he was a Yeo who shared much of the same line as me except it branched off at a certain point. She suggested I write to this lady and ask if she would share what she had found. This I did and a while later received a very short note to say that my great, great, great-grandfather, William Yeo, was a direct descendant of William the Conqueror, which of course meant that I was too. She offered to send more details if I wished and I eagerly agreed, not knowing quite what else to expect. When she sent me a full family line from the Conqueror down to my grandfather Henry Yeo I was completely bowled over. In fact, it was a shock!

There had never been any suggestion of royal connections in my family and I am sure that not even my mother would have believed such a thing had she still been here. We considered ourselves to be a working-class family and even on father's side there were no connections hinting at anything like royalty. Yet here it was in black and white, a record of a line which had all been verified. Even now I still find it hard to believe but it is something I cannot argue with as it is all factual and can in no way be challenged. I have never been very interested in history, although as a subject in school I received an acceptable pass in my exams. Like most people I have enjoyed historical films and the pageantry that has been associated with royalty in more recent times, but I would not call myself an ardent royalist. This in no way reflects a working-class attitude but I am mostly a realist – I do have my dreams and yet always try to keep two feet on the ground. I prefer to know the truth, whether I like it or not, and my feelings at this discovery were that if it were true then I had to accept it is a part of me. In fact, the idea became more than interesting as I decided to see if I could relate to my ancestry in any way. Several people have in the past said I was born with a silver spoon in my mouth and thought I lived in a big house with servants and all the trimmings. It was hard to convince them it was not so and that I belonged to a working-class family. However, there must have been something in my bearing, though I was never conscious of it. Had I pretended to be posh my father would have knocked it out of me, but at that time I lived as circumstances dictated. It was not until later in my life when I owned my own flat that I felt able to have a few of the nicer things in life. Even then one could not associate it with anything upper class as I was just enjoying something I had worked very hard for.

Through most of my life so far I have always managed somehow to give people the impression of being important. For example Jim often referred to me as 'my Lord', my photographer George Burns always called me 'Baron Hearn' and even addressed his letters to me as that, and countless people have called me 'Sir', especially assistants in shops where it is noticeable they do not address other men so. Then, of course, there is my title Colonel, which I have already mentioned, but people at one time often addressed letters to me by that title, and I have even had some call me 'the Honourable' and even 'The Reverend'. I took it all as good fun but on reflection I think maybe they were sensing something I did not know about myself. Whatever one may think, it is an interesting point as we do not see ourselves as others do.

The list I received from Australia was quite staggering. From William the Conqueror the line descended through Henry I, Henry II, King John (his brother, Richard the Lionheart, would have been a great-uncle many times removed!), Henry III and Edward I. After that Elizabeth Plantagenet, the daughter of Edward I, married Humphrey de Bohun, 4th Earl of Hertford, whose descendants eventually married into the Yeo line when Ellen Grenville married Edmund Yeo who was born around 1458 and continued directly down to my mother, Winifred Yeo, and on to me. That alone was amazing but when my friend Peter saw the chart he could see that the line would go further back as William the Conqueror was married to Matilda of Flanders who was descended from Alfred the Great who came from a line of kings going back to Cerdic, the first king of Wessex who conquered the area, including the Isle of Wight, in around AD 519.

Peter and I uncovered a lot of connections through history books and the Internet. Surprisingly he found a Scottish connection going back to Kenneth MacAlpin who is regarded as the founder of the Scottish monarchy and a line of kings including Duncan I who was killed by Macbeth (a very distant great-uncle of mine) as in the famous play by Shakespeare. This Scottish line conjoined with the English monarchy when Edith (Matilda), daughter of King Malcolm III, married Henry I, making it an even more impressive direct line of descent. So it seems that I have a mixture of royal blood in my veins as apart from the kings there are the many of foreign princesses they married. Finding out about these links has made me realise it is a possible reason why I always feel at home in most foreign countries and often seem to get mistaken for one of the inhabitants.

After receiving the letter from Australia another person told me I should contact a lady called Sheila Yeo who lived in Devon. She belonged to the Yeo Society and might be able to give me more details about my family tree. This I did and she had records of all the different Yeo families, including mine. She knew about the line going back to William the Conqueror but didn't appear to know much further back, or perhaps she was not concerned with that. What she had was enough for me and I received a large number of pages listing the various families on my line, plus details of births, deaths and marriages, also of their wills and possessions. It was fascinating to read but too long and perhaps too tedious to relate here. I can only say that for me it was all helpful in building up a detailed picture of what is an extraordinary direct line of descent. Beryl told me that it is rare for anyone to trace a direct line back so far and I am content to know as much as I do. However, what is perhaps more startling is the fact that this discovery also threw new light on some of my psychic experiences in the past.

When I first became interested in the psychic and was attending The Haven I witnessed many different mediums at their work, which was in itself a valuable experience. I received many 'star-studded messages', as I called them, most of which seemed to be far-fetched and fanciful. It was very common, then, to be told about one's guides in the other world and I freely admit that for quite a long time I went along with the idea, knowing I did not have enough experience to say I didn't believe it. On one occasion I attended a psychometry session during which one places something personal on a tray and the medium picks up each one in turn and passes on messages from loved ones. The medium on that occasion was a little lady who seemed sincere in giving what she sensed. I had placed my mother's ring on the tray and what she told me did not make any sense. In fact, when she said that whoever the ring belonged to was a descendant of French royalty, I almost burst out laughing but managed to control myself. I just thanked her for what she told me and took the ring back to Mother, who asked me what had happened. When it got to the French royalty part she laughed and said she had never heard anything about this in her family and it made no sense at all.

Over the years other mediums gave me messages which seemed to be just as extraordinary and outlandish and I was convinced they were getting carried away. I was told by more than one that they saw a royal purple cloak around me. Others saw an archbishop's ring on my finger and a crown over my head. I was told two or three times that Richard the Lionheart was with me and one medium insisted he was my guide. At the time the idea quite thrilled me as I had always been very interested in this man and in a way felt very drawn to him, but all the time my own common sense was telling me it was all a lot of nonsense. Nonetheless I had to ask myself why it was that so many different mediums got on to the same theme. One evening when I was sitting in class I had quite an amazing experience as I drifted off into what might have been a trance. I suddenly felt I was in a golden coach, something like the Queen's coronation coach, and it was trundling along and rocking from side to side. It was far from comfortable and I was glad when it stopped at the foot of some stone steps. I got out of the coach and walked up them and entered a church, though it was one I did not recognise. It appeared to be completely empty but a wonderful air of peace pervaded the atmosphere. I found myself walking up the central aisle towards the grand altar and it was then I saw what must have been an archbishop with his back turned to me. He was wearing the most magnificent gold-embroidered robes with a mitre to match. As I got near to him I suddenly felt myself saying, 'Now I will know who you are!' but as he turned around there was no face under the mitre. After that I came to in my chair and felt none the wiser for my experience. In fact, it seemed quite crazy, but I did not know then it was perhaps leading up to something else.

It was quite some time after that I visited Canterbury Cathedral with Peter, Jim and another friend. We entered by the back door for some reason and walked down an aisle which ran alongside the high altar. As we reached a certain point we all froze on the spot. It was a strange sensation but all of us being psychic it was not surprising when we discovered on a nearby wall a plaque telling us it was the very spot where Archbishop Thomas Becket had been murdered; had we entered by the front door we would have read the notice before reaching the spot. When we all had shaken off this strange feeling I realised Jim had disappeared and felt I must go to find him. He was actually at the back of the high altar looking at a semicircle of statues of all the former Archbishops of Canterbury. I asked him what he was doing and before he could answer I suddenly went to one of the statues and said, 'That's the one!' When Jim asked who it was, I said, 'I don't know but that's the one.' I then realised our other friends would be waiting and wondering where we were and, as we had to be home by a certain time, we had to hurry away. The other two were sorry they had missed seeing the statues but I felt I would have to go back another time and sort it out.

Quite a long time after that Peter and I had a visitor from America who was staying with my sister. We thought it would be a good idea to show her Canterbury Cathedral and she was delighted to have the opportunity. No more than I was because I had never forgotten the archbishops' statues and I would get to have another look. Once there I quickly left my sister, our visitor and Peter to look around while I hurried away to look behind the high altar. I was puzzled to find there weren't any statues there and the semicircle where they should have been standing was empty. I thought they must have been moved and searched all over the cathedral in vain but there was not a single one to be seen. In a state of frustration I asked a verger if he could tell me where the statues were or what had happened to them. He said there had never been any statues and he had been with the cathedral for many years and knew every part of it and all its history and I must have got mixed up with somewhere else. I suggested that maybe they could have been moved to another church and his reply was 'Why would statues of the Archbishops of Canterbury be put anywhere else but here?' Of course, he was right, but I told him that a friend was with me when I saw them and nothing would convince me we didn't. I think he thought I must have been 'seeing things', which in a way I was, but it was no use telling him I was psychic.

Once we got back home I felt I had to telephone Jim and ask his reaction to this. All I asked him was if he remembered the visit to Canterbury Cathedral with our two friends. Immediately he recalled everything but especially the statues and repeated all we experienced exactly as it happened. When I told him that these statues had never existed and certainly were not behind the high altar, he did not believe me, but as I had witness to the fact they were not there we could only come to the conclusion we had both had a psychic experience at the same time, which to my knowledge is a very rare thing. So the mystery was not solved, although later it seemed to tie in with something else that happened.

There is a very interesting story with regard to Richard the Lionheart whom I never accepted as being my guide but who might nonetheless be interested in me in some way. On one occasion Jim and I were out on a long walk. I cannot remember where we started from but eventually we found ourselves in a thickly wooded area and as we felt tired we welcomed the sight of a bench to sit on for a while. After a time I became aware of someone standing in front of me who said he was Richard the Lionheart and would prove it. He said that, if we followed a pathway to the left and then turned right and went on, we would come to a tree that was split right down the middle, which he called a forked tree. True enough, as we followed the route exactly as he described, there was the tree. It was quite extraordinary as it looked as if someone had cut it into exact halves, straight down the middle. Having followed his instructions we waited, expecting to receive more but came there none. So we continued our walk and nearby discovered a plaque which said the area was connected with Richard the Lionheart, which by this time did not surprise us!

Another time the psychic artist Coral Polge drew some pencil sketches for me of people who had passed on. There was one among them that looked like a knight of old and whom she thought could be Richard. She had no idea of how he looked and neither did I, so I obtained a book from the library and found a picture of him which compared very favourably with hers. I can guarantee that Coral had never seen this picture and neither had I. If anyone then had asked me if I knew what Richard looked like, I most certainly would have had no idea. There was yet another incident that connected me to the Crusader King. When I was visiting Stratford-on-Avon with Peter and my sister we happened to go into a shop where they sold all sorts of souvenirs relating to Shakespeare. My sister chose to buy a statue of a knight in armour. I rather wanted one too, but as it was the only one left I let her have it. So I chose a small bronze bust of Richard the Lionheart, not knowing at that time it would be so meaningful to me. I did not especially have any feeling for it then but of course, now knowing that he was a distant great-uncle of mine, it has since become quite a treasured possession. It has pride of place in my flat and I often greet it with a 'Hello, Uncle Dick!' It also stands near to the knight my sister had bought, which came into my possession after she died and which I treasure for her sake. I often wonder if Winifred has met our uncle and what they might say to each other but no doubt one day I will find all the answers.

Before I knew about my ancestry I had seen the film called *The Lion in Winter* three times. I was most fascinated by the story of Henry II and his queen, Eleanor of Aquitaine, and while watching I felt very much at home with it. Mostly I had a strong sympathy for Eleanor as, although from all accounts she had done some bad things such as poisoning a lot of people, I felt I could understand her motivation. Naturally with such fine actors as Peter O'Toole and Katherine Hepburn it was easy to get drawn into the story, but I also felt a strong sympathy for Richard, who also featured, though I felt he was not portrayed as the man he really was. I felt like I was part of the family but being so interested in the theatre and acting I more or less put it all down to the quality of the players who had to bring the characters to life. At that time I did not know that Henry and Eleanor were my great-grandparents many times removed.

I recall a time when a medium told me that I had a guide who was a Crusader and that I was one myself. She even dared to say it was Richard and, although I could not think of him as a guide exactly, I was quite impressed to think that if it was really the Lionheart who was in contact then I was indeed honoured. I had been drawn to him during my schooldays and looked upon him as a kind of hero, although he was severely criticised for leaving his country to fight in the Crusades. From all accounts he was a very brave man who believed in what he was doing and stood by his principals. This is where I feel I may have inherited some of those same qualities and, although I do not pretend to be especially brave, I always try to do the right thing. I endeavour to be a man of strong principles and to be prepared to fight for what I believe in. My mother certainly inherited those qualities attributed to Richard.

Another film called *Becket*, which was about the relationship between Henry II and Archbishop Thomas Becket, also came to have a great meaning for me. I had seen it many years before I knew about my ancestry but when I learned about Henry being on my line of descent I felt it would be interesting to see the film again. It was well acted by Peter O'Toole and Richard Burton and brought out a lot of emotion within me that had not been there all those years ago. To relate the actual story is not important as there was one thing I needed to see that would tie in with a previous experience. In the scene just before Becket is murdered he is shown being dressed in his robes for a service. What should I see but the most beautiful gold-embroidered robes and mitre, exactly like those I had seen when I was in class. I can't say the church was the same but that did not matter. I was amazed to see the robes and yet I cannot say that those shown in the film were authentic copies but it was nonetheless very interesting. All this might answer the question of whom I had seen in my trance-like state and the identity of the 'psychic statue' in Canterbury Cathedral. Although Becket is in no way related to me, his friend Henry II certainly is, and so perhaps all these experiences relate to those momentous events. Another discovery suggested yet another interpretation, however.

Sometime later when trying to find out more about my ancestral line I found some details about another of my forebears, Hugh de Courtenay, the son of Humphrey de Bohun. He apparently had thirteen children, one of whom was William Courtenay, Archbishop of Canterbury. William was a great-grandson of Edward I and from all accounts was a very good man who fought for reforms and was unafraid to oppose those who he felt were doing wrong, even at the cost of incurring the displeasure of the King. Perhaps it was *his* face that could have been the one missing in my psychic experience, and it made me proud to know that my distant Great-uncle William was a man of principle and a determined fighter. There is no doubt in any case that in my ancestry archbishops play an important part.

A medium told me on one occasion that a man called Alfred was with me, and when I said I could not think of anyone of that name in the other world, she said, 'You know, the one who burnt the cakes!' This referred to King Alfred the Great whom I found many years later to be one of my very distant great-grandfathers, though I had no knowledge of it at that time. I thought it must be some kind of joke, as I was doing a lot of cooking at the time, though I had never burnt any cakes! Looking back, now, this too could well have been another one in my line trying to make a link with me. I think maybe we need someone like Alfred around today as he was considered to be a good monarch who united England under one king. He was also fair and just and had the required strength and might needed in his time. Our present-day monarch is a great queen who has to deal with far different situations and would probably welcome any such helpful influence as Alfred and others might be able to give.

In studying my forebears I find there are many foreign connections but there seem to be very strong French ones. Strange though it may seem when I was much younger I tended to dislike the French, although I had never been to France, except for a few hours in Biarritz and when I travelled home on leave from the army from Austria. At one time I did see some French films which I enjoyed but I did not like French people, and as for their language, I could never get my tongue round it then and never have since. As the years passed, and being a great music lover, I discovered a deep feeling for and enjoyment of their music; in fact, I now think their composers produced some of the world's finest music. The thing that most drew me to the French was their art. I had never been very interested in the subject, although I am artistic in certain ways. I began to collect prints and various pictures and bought many books on all the great masters. I confess that I have read very little of them but the books have glorious colour plates of all the great paintings, and I felt myself drawn very much to the work of the French school. I am also an ardent ballet lover as I consider it to be the perfect physical expression of music and found myself collecting DVDs of many ballets and especially those performed by the French Paris Opera Ballet Company. I like all types of ballet and go to watch them in the theatre when I can, but one of my dreams would be to go to Paris and see my favourite company, although I doubt now if that will ever be possible. The French ladies are so beautiful and dance superbly, as do their handsome partners. I must add that having seen films and photos of the French countryside, which is very beautiful, I would love to go there and I think I would now find it more interesting. Why I had to wait so long to have my mind changed I do not know, but seeing so many French past connections in my ancestry it certainly seems as if this was meant to happen and I am glad it did. As the medium stated long ago, my mother was indeed descended from French royalty and the more I think about her the more I can see she always had a sort of queenly bearing. I sometimes wonder how it might have been if Mother had known all these things when she was in this world, but I somehow think it would not have gone down too well with my father!

Many people are descended from William the Conqueror of course, but I find, if one mentions the fact, a lot of people immediately react by saying he was a bad lot and it is nothing to be proud of. I possibly thought that at one time but when learning of my ancestry I made it my business to find out more about this man. He was a great fighter who apparently would not ask his men to do anything he wouldn't and he cared for them. He called his archers 'yeomen' and it is believed that is where the name Yeo originated, although some think the name is derived from the yew tree. I like to think it was owing to William as it would mean that my ancestors' name would be associated with strong fighters nobly battling for the causes they uphold. I have a deep admiration for William and find I can identify with him in a lot of ways. I think genes can be carried down through every generation but not necessarily to everyone in the same family, as genetic hereditary appears to be quite arbitrary. I can see a lot of inherited characteristics of our ancestors in my parents, brother and sister but not the same in every one of us.

While on the subject of French connections I now feel certain that the lady my great, great, great-grandfather William Yeo married in 1776 could well have been of French origin as her surname was Courtier. It might be possible to find out for sure but it would take far too long and may in the end be a fruitless search. I am happy enough to think it may be so but even if it is an English name it does not alter anything as far as the ancestral line is concerned. What I have noticed is that the Yeo line is quite a long one and only changes in 1481 when the name of Grenville comes into the line, and later De Courtenay and Bohun, too, which begins to take it into the more aristocratic period. Hugh de Courtenay was the second son of the Earl of Devon. He was created a Knight of the Garter and is buried in Exeter Cathedral where his tomb can still be seen. Humphrey de Bohun was the 4th Earl of Hertford and Essex and was killed at the Battle of Borough Bridge. He married Elizabeth Woodstock, the youngest surviving daughter of

King Edward I and Eleanor of Castile, in Westminster Abbey, so here we find a strong link with my royal ancestors.

There are so many things to be considered and I have looked for anything that in a manner of speaking may ring a bell. I can see some characteristics in different ancestors which may have passed down to me but it is the connections with various places that interests me more. I have always loved the Isle of Wight and have been a regular visitor for many years; in fact I had a little holiday home, which I had to give up very reluctantly, in Wroxall, which is one of the loveliest spots on the Island. It was the most peaceful place I have ever been to and which gave me a strong feeling of belonging. Not that the rest of the island did not do much the same but we all have our favourites and with my little bungalow it was like being in another world at times. Of course I had no idea then of the past connections but now I often smile and think of how one of my ancestors, Cerdic, conquered the Island long ago. I have several friends there and remember many happy times when we shared a compelling interest in psychic matters and everyone of those friends felt it was a very special place. I often demonstrated my psychic gifts there and somehow felt the atmosphere to be most conducive to the subject.

I also eventually decided to ask Beryl to trace my father's line, which I knew would not hold the same surprises as Mother's did, but there was something I needed to know. I had always heard that the family name of Hearn had been changed by deed poll from Hitchcock because a great-grandmother did not like it. I knew that my grandfather had been found drowned after recuperating from an illness at the age of fifty-two and I felt so sorry that I had not known him, as from his photos he looked every inch a gentleman. Beryl managed to find a few facts fairly easily but it eventually became very difficult and puzzling. There was definitely no change of name by deed poll but what she did discover was that there were two families in the same area with the names of Hearn and Hitchcock who had intermarried, which left my grandfather as being described on his birth certificate as Herbert Edward Hitchcock-Hearn. He must have decided to drop Hitchcock when he married and the mystery for me had been solved. I could not see anything outstanding about either the Hitchcocks or Hearns, as they all seemed to be ordinary working-class people. It surprised me in a way as, although my father could be difficult and not always easy to get along with, there were times when he had an air of being quite the 'gentleman' himself. He could never remember much about his family anyway and moreover he did not seem to care. He simply said they were a mixed bunch of 'all sorts'. Nevertheless, Beryl uncovered what I could only describe as a big surprise when she told me that my great, great, great-grandfather, Moses Hearn, had connections with the Church of the Latter-day Saints, which made me think he must have been a Mormon, although on checking with the Mormons, who have all the records, it seems he wasn't. I remember Father saying there were some family in the States, probably in Buffalo. It does not follow they were Mormons, as he thought might be the case, but they could be as that is where the religion seems to have started. If my father is now in another world as I believe him to be, then I wonder what he thinks about this as when he was here he was not religious and would have laughed about the Mormons, although I seem to remember him saying something about liking the idea of having several wives!

I did start to explore my father's maternal line but did not manage to find out much of any consequence but possibly may find more later. What I do know was that my paternal grandmother's father was a chimneysweep, quite a respectable job in those days, and I already knew that one of her sisters and her husband were mediums. Apparently they used to go around Spiritualist churches and demonstrate their gifts, but I have never heard of them. Also one of my great-uncles apparently caused a stir when at a great age he married a young beauty queen. It was reported in the newspapers and was quite a scandal at the time. There is nothing I inherit from him as far as I know, but my father thought it was very funny and said he wouldn't mind being in the same position. Somehow I do not think I inherit much at all from Father's side but I am sure I do from Mother's, as sometimes I have felt almost like a stranger in the family – no one else seemed to like and do the things I did. I loved my family but felt that if one could improve on anything one should and I developed tastes for what some might call the finer things in life.

I recently discovered that one of my clients, Catherine Petty from Baton Rouge, for whom I have recorded many taped sittings, is distantly related to me. When I told her of my own discoveries she wrote to remind me that she had sent her family tree to me some years ago and we were very distant cousins. It seems we are both directly descended from Cerdic via Alfred the Great, William the Conqueror and Edward I, after which our family trees branched off to the present day. I met Catherine with her husband and son, Lee, when they visited London some years ago before we knew anything about our family trees. By then I had already recorded some tapes for them, including two for Lee, which he found helpful. I had hoped to talk with him as I felt there was something special about this 'shy' young man. It caused me to feel very sad when I heard not long after he had been killed in a car accident. This caused his mother to request more tapes in the hope Lee would communicate. He most certainly did and still is after so many, many years.

Lee is an excellent communicator and I always found it easy to be in touch with him; he felt like a real friend and was loving and seemingly happy to make his contacts through me. As time went on, his closeness became stronger and even quite affectionate. One time I felt him hug me and on another occasion I felt him kiss my cheek. It felt as though he was trying to tell me something, like we were connected in some way, but I tended to dismiss this, although it was always a pleasure to communicate with him. Once I discovered we were very distantly connected, I realised Lee had been trying to indicate a family closeness of which I had not previously been aware. I doubt if much happens by accident and it is indeed very rare for two people with direct lines of descent to link up in this way, but it is interesting to discover the possible reason why the communications with Lee have gone on for so many years and have been so good. Since our discovery, Catherine and I always refer to each other as 'cousins', even though our relationship is very distant.

For a lot of my life I frequently dreamed about living in a nice house with a servant or two and afternoon tea served on a silver tray, but as Shakespeare wrote, 'we are such stuff as dreams are made of.' But I have always realised I did not really want that, probably because I know it could not happen unless I came into a large fortune and I doubt that would happen anyway. It is understandable but strange one should find oneself on the poor end of such a great lineage but common sense tells us that all things change with each succeeding generation. Nevertheless some things do not change and I can honestly say I am indeed a Yeoman of

England and very proud of it. In knowing my mother came from a Devonshire line of the great Yeo family, I have often been tempted to change my surname, although it would, in a way, seem disrespectful to my father. I feel deeply, however, that the Yeo line with all its colourful ancestry is the stronger part of me. The song I quoted at the beginning of this book was always a great favourite of mine and when the song asks 'Where are the Yeomen of England?' I can truly, truly answer that 'One of them is here.'